Sir Thomas Beecham

Sir Thomas Beecham was the greatest British orchestral conductor this century, with a legacy of invaluable recordings to demonstrate the fact. Dynamic, many-sided, witty and oracular, he stamped his own personality on a wide range of music — on Sibelius, on Mozart, on Berlioz, and on many French composers of the lighter sort. He was also a keen planner of opera seasons and founder of orchestras.

Born in Lancashire in 1879, Beecham partook of the wealth his family derived from chemical products, such as the famous therapeutic pills and powders. After composition studies in London and Paris, he taught himself to conduct; the first major event in his career was the founding, in 1909, of the Beecham Symphony Orchestra, which was composed of young players, given to adventurous programmes and playing for opera and ballet.

Opera was to dominate the decade starting in 1910, with the introduction of new works by Richard Strauss and by the composer Beecham staunchly championed throughout his life, Frederick Delius. Beecham was also responsible for the first London appearances of the Diaghilev Ballets Russes. Such ventures were a steady drain on Beecham's private fortune — these were the days before public subsidy — and he had to withdraw from musical life for a time to put his affairs in order.

The most distinguished, and long-lasting, orchestra founded by Beecham was the London Philharmonic, which he brought swiftly to the front rank in the 1930s. He had unusually strong gifts of communication and believed in firm rhythm, singing melody and shapely phrasing — and he conducted mostly from memory, sometimes without a stick. As the composer Ethel Smyth said of him: 'Beecham worked out his own destiny on lines of his own.'

Although his tastes in music were eclectic, Beecham was not drawn to Bach, to modern composers after Stravinsky, nor to the sterner side of Beethoven. His mercurial temperament, his teasing of both players and audiences, his railing against musical institutions — these have all resulted in a body of anecdote and wit, both abundantly displayed in *A Mingled Chime*, the only autobiographical work he completed.

The Lively Arts

General Editor: Robert Ottaway

A MINGLED CHIME

Leaves from an Autobiography

*

SIR THOMAS BEECHAM

FOREWORD BY
SHIRLEY, LADY BEECHAM

COLUMBUS BOOKS
LONDON

This trade paperback edition
published in Great Britain in 1987 by
Columbus Books Limited
19-23 Ludgate Hill
London, EC4M 7PD

First published in 1944 by Hutchinson and Company Limited
Reprinted under a licence granted by Shirley, Lady Beecham

British Library Cataloguing in Publication Data
Beecham, Sir Thomas, 1879–1961
A mingled chime: leaves from an
autobiography.—(The Lively arts).
1. Beecham, Sir Thomas, 1879–1961
2. Conductors (Music)—Biography
I. Title II. Series
785'.092'4   ML422.B33

ISBN 0–86287–376–2

Printed and bound by The Guernsey Press
Guernsey, CI

To Betty

CONTENTS

CONTENTS

FOREWORD

Sir Thomas Beecham died on 8 March 1961 and since that time at least three books have come into print based on his life. Sadly none of them can compare with *A Mingled Chime*, the acknowledged masterpiece of the first part of his autobiography written in the 1940s and covering his life during the period from 1879 to 1923. Although he made sketches for the second volume these were never published.

Today Sir Thomas is considered a 'legend' in the annals of British music, but in his lifetime he also enjoyed a very special and unique position in British musical and social life. Both he and his father, Sir Joseph, spent a fortune of their own money and persuaded other people to do likewise, producing operas and giving concerts at which the British public were able to hear for the first time works never previously performed in this country, some of which are now in the standard repertoire.

Sir Thomas championed the music of many British composers such as Granville Bantock, Dame Ethel Smyth and Joseph Holbrooke, to name but a few. He was a pioneer in early recording techniques. In the summer of 1910, whilst engaged in giving an opera season at His Majesty's Theatre, the then Mr Thomas Beecham made his first acoustic recordings at the Gramophone Company Studios. In the early 1930s he conducted the Mozart Jupiter Symphony in one of the earliest experimental stereo recordings. It was by sheer chance that in 1936 he took part in the first recording on magnetic tape of a live concert, during a tour of Germany with the London Philharmonic Orchestra. He was also no stranger to film music; probably the best known and widely viewed film with which he was associated is *The Tales of Hoffman*, produced by Michael Powell and Emeric Pressburger for British Lion Films in 1950. Earlier, at the age of only thirty-two, he had been responsible for bringing to Britain the Russian Ballet, an event which in his own words 'took London by storm'.

Sir Thomas not only enjoyed the respect of the musicians who played under his baton, but could number among his personal friends leading figures throughout the world whose names now form part of history. His generosity was well-known, particularly towards those who might be described as 'up and coming young performers', whose tuition fees he often paid. His tremendous wit and his knowledge of classical literature made his lectures highlights for those fortunate enough to hear them. The famous Beecham stories are legendary, but with the passage of time stories are now attributed to him falsely. He shared the same birthday with Sir Malcolm Sargent, although of course there was some difference in their ages. A friendship existed between the two men, and Sir Thomas revelled in telling orchestras harmless tales about Sir Malcolm which Malcolm took pleasure in repeating. Sir Thomas had no malice in his nature; a lot of the anger which he could on occasion display was often to get something moving more quickly.

From 1907, when he first met Frederick Delius, he championed the works of this composer and with his unique editing of Delius's scores was able to bring his music to a much wider audience. I had the privilege of working with Sir Thomas on the manuscript of his last book, *Frederick Delius*. Even in the twilight of his life, Sir Thomas had tremendous energy for work which would have left a man half his age exhausted.

My own first encounter with Sir Thomas was in 1947 when, as a very young girl, I heard him conduct at a most unlikely venue – Haringey Arena as part of the London Music Festival arranged by Jack Hylton. Three years later I found myself working as part of the small team who managed Sir Thomas's affairs and those of the Royal Philharmonic Orchestra. In the next eleven years I was present at most of the concerts he gave and travelled with him on tours in Britain and abroad. His performances were unique occasions. He indulged in few rehearsals, particularly in later life. Before a concert he would spend several hours studying the scores, although sometimes he may have played the same works hundreds and hundreds of times; during a concert he was able somehow to will the players into giving a performance sometimes far in excess even of their expectations. He appeared at festivals throughout the world and for a number of years made an annual tour of the United States, where he was always assured of enthusiastic audiences. His 'lollipops' at the end of concerts were looked forward to by all his audiences as much as the arranged programme. Sometimes he made a speech, which would be listened to by enraptured music-lovers, loath to see him leave the platform. Such was the genius and magic of the man.

Shirley, Lady Beecham
May 1987

I

INFANCY (1879–84)

IN PLANNING THIS BOOK I MADE THE PROPER RESOLUTION TO SET DOWN nothing that I had not seen or heard for myself. I therefore left the opening chapter until the end, hoping that the shadowy impressions of my earliest days might by that time have taken a more tangible shape. But, to my dismay, that far-off period continued to be as vague as ever, and it was clear that if I were to give any account of it all, I should have to seek the aid of others who were then on the scene. There was the alternative of leaving it out entirely and beginning my tale at a point of date where my remembrance of the past was less uncertain. But if we are to believe with Wordsworth that the child is father to the man, it would be only natural that even "in the silken sail of infancy" I gave forth some sign, no matter how insignificant, of the way I was later to go, which ought to be faithfully recorded here.

Among my distinguished contemporaries there is hardly one who cannot trace back the origin of his talent to an unbelievably early age; and although I knew well that such phenomenal accomplishment had never been mine, I must surely have shown some bent for, or anyway taken some interest in the art which was to be the main preoccupation of my life. But the trouble about gathering knowledge from other persons is the comparative unreliability of their testimony. This anyone will endorse who has observed the distracted efforts of half a dozen different witnesses in a law action to describe the same event; and certainly no magistrate of experience would dissent from the opinion of Pilate in the first century, and Pirandello in the twentieth, that final truth is beyond human discovery. Yet in rare cases the elusive goddess has been known to disclose, if not the whole, at least a small part of her mysterious countenance. And so might it be in mine if I approached the shrine in humble mood and with honest intent.

A survey of likely sources of information led to the unwelcome discovery that the only person available for my purpose was an aged relative, whose society I had hardly been sedulous in cultivating for twenty years past and whose reception of me might be far from gracious. But no other choice offered itself, and bracing myself for the ordeal I set out to drop my pitcher of enquiry into the forbidding well of family judgment. Should any man desire to know, I will not say the truth, but the next worse thing about himself, let him hasten to his nearest of kin. There he will look into a mirror which diminishes the reflection of his personality as effectively as the wrong end of an opera glass lessens the size of objects upon the stage, and he will see himself just as the disillusioned Hoffmann saw all around him after the loss of his magic spectacles.

Without question there are times when silence is the wiser portion of narrative, and none ever understood this better than the author of *Tristram Shandy* in his discreet handling of Uncle Toby's romantic adventure with the Widow Wadman. For when that gallant old fellow went a-wooing, two of the chapters given up to this immortal affair, which with a less tactful author might have been as overflowing with impertinent detail as a cinema love scene, are left wholly to the chaste imagination of the reader. In like manner I might have advantageously dropped the curtain here for a few blank moments and, raising it again at a more satis-factory stage of my story, spared myself the chagrin of a confession truly humiliating, had I not consecrated myself to the upright spirit of candid avowal. For whether it be in one of those capacious tomes of a thousand and one pages, some slenderer volume, or even an illustrated article for a popular magazine, we are always invited to believe that the hero of the tale performed fabulous feats while hardly out of the cradle. In one instance we may read how the mighty atom of virtuosity committed to memory the entire well-tempered clavichord of Bach before mastering his alphabet. In another there is a beautiful account of an oratorio for double chorus and orchestra, all composed at the age of five and informed with the deepest religious feeling. Not all of our prodigies scale such heights as these; but there is never wanting in the least remarkable of them some touch of that divinity which separates him from the common or garden little boy and betrays from the very beginning the presence of Apollo and his sacred Nine.

None of this god-like dispensation was my lot, and nothing could shake the tenacious recollection of the revered relic of my clan that I as a small child had not the slightest taste or aptitude for the arts. Indeed I was the most ordinary and, in some ways, the most satisfactory kind of youngster any parents could wish to have. I disliked noise of any sort, never indulged in it myself, was a model of taciturnity and gentle melancholy, and altogether an embryonic hero for a Bulwer-Lytton novel. My mother, feeling now and then some uneasiness on my account, would talk rashly of calling in expert opinion to solve the problem. But my father, who had a larger share of this world's prudence, was profoundly grateful for the unexpected blessing that had come his way and, fearful lest something might suddenly happen to bring it to an end, always managed to restrain her from doing anything of the kind.

But did I think of nothing or fail to find an interest in something all those months and years I sat in my corner and silently looked out on the world? Indeed, I thought long and earnestly, but never for a moment about music, poetry or pictures. The whole world of beauty and romance was summed-up for me in clothes, and never did I weary of regarding them and reflecting on their wonder and meaning. And the longer I think about it, the more I question if there can be any more fitting subject for the growing mind to exercise itself upon, and whether it has ever been studied by any writer, ancient or modern, with the high seriousness it deserves. Otherwise we should have been told long ago what Helen of Troy wore when she went off with Paris, what Venus herself tried on when she first emerged from her island water, how Romulus came by his famous red boots and why he fancied this particular colour. Things like these, were they known, would throw more real light on the culture of the antique world than three-quarters of the repetitious narration found in the bulk of its chronicles; and although I have now and then conjectured if the lost books of Livy contained something to enlighten us, the chances are against it if we take into account the indifference of the average historian to most subjects in which posterity is genuinely interested. The great task remains unattempted, and I commend it to some of our present day scribes who are groping about for fresh material, with much the same success as rewarded Diogenes' search for an honest man.

My impressions of the fashions of that day would fill a dozen ladies' journals, but one or two specimens only of the taste of the last quarter of the nineteenth century will be noted here, as, despite the doctrine of the Eternal Return, we may not see them again in our time. My father took pride in some special articles of apparel for the ceremony of smoking, then a luxury enjoyed in moderation at appointed times only, but now a necessity practised universally and on every possible occasion in and out of season. Even the sanctity of the dinner-hour has been profaned by its more abandoned addicts, to the misery of that dwindling minority which still retains an appreciation of good food and fine wine. In our establishment it was sternly disallowed in most rooms and barely tolerated in any; and for the due fulfilment of the rite my father had to ascend to a remote den on the top floor, sometimes with a few congenial devotees but more frequently alone. There he would put on a cap of Turkish design crowned with a long flowing tassel, and a richly coloured jacket decorated with gold-braided stripes and silver buttons. On the rare occasions I was admitted to this holy of holies I would gaze upon this gorgeous spectacle with rapture while my sire puffed away in placid and silent content, absorbed in reflections which I felt sure were of world-shaking import.

Less impressive but equally exotic were my grandfather's trousers, which then might be seen only on octogenarian farmers in distant parts of the land. Voluminous in build, of rough and thick material, and variegated in hue, they perpetuated a design that was probably of vast antiquity. We know that as far back as the epoch of the Flavian emperors, Britons wore trousers of a staggering amplitude that provoked high hilarity among the wits of Rome; and there is no reason why, in a conservative country like England, this particular model should not have survived throughout eighteen hundred years in undiminished integrity. Hitched well up to the chest and minus that disfiguring line of division in the façade, which only an inartistic age could tolerate for a moment even on the grounds of utility, there was no visible means of entrance or exit. And as I never had the courage to ask, I daily worried my young brains near to distraction over the way he both got into and out of them.

I shall refrain from describing how my curiosity was aroused by the wardrobe of the distaff side of the family, as I should not like it to be thought that I am wanting in domestic piety: indeed, I am as full of it as was the great Aeneas himself. But there was one specimen in it which I cannot pass over, for the reason that it effected a powerful revolution in my entire mental equipment and was responsible for the cast it has taken on ever since. This was my grandmother's bustle. The ordinary contraption of the kind is designed confessedly to disclose or hide, add or subtract, according to the needs of the case. But the bustle must be in a class by itself, for no one has ever been able to explain to me its precise purpose; and it would seem more akin to one of those inexplicable ornaments we see on Gothic churches, which have little or no apparent connection with the main design. But whatever it was, or howsoever it arose, it was the first potent revolutionary influence in my life and the source of my earliest disenchantment. For I lived long under the agreeable delusion that it was no garment at all, but a portion of my venerable relative's own person; and it is hard to imagine and impossible to describe the shock to my youthful senses the day she arrived without it, bustles just about then beginning to go out of fashion.   That same hour I became a philosopher, filled with a lively appreciation of the mutability of all earthly things; a fully fledged disciple of Heraclitus to whom had been vouchsafed a revelation as miraculous as it was complete.*

My own habiliments were mainly of that picturesque species which certain doting mothers inflict upon their helpless offspring, thereby exposing them to the derision of those luckier infants who can roll in the mud and split their pants to their hearts' content without drawing wailings and reproaches from solicitous nannies.   And as my discontent was increased by the possession, long after it was due for removal, of a luxuriant crop of curls which excited the malevolent attention of every other boy or girl who came anywhere near it, life on the whole was a grim and bitter business for me.   My pleasantest moments were our annual visits during the summer months to the seaside, where the whole family renewed its amphibious nature after the immemorial fashion of every inhabitant of the British Isles.   There I was permitted to shed my detested finery, and it was during one of these excursions, I am happy to relate, that I lapsed temporarily from that lofty level of moral perfection which was both the pride and perturbation of my circle.†

It was at Southport, that most untypical of watering-places, where the sea goes out daily about three-quarters of a mile, leaving broad stretches of dry hard sand that reach nearly to the next town.   On these ran wooden ships built upon wheels and propelled by sails, each holding twenty or thirty passengers and travelling at a really formidable speed over a surface as smooth as a billiard-table.   Into one of them I crept like a stowaway when no one was looking, attached myself to a kindly-looking female, and was off and away hundreds of yards before my absence was discovered and a small army of persons set to roam the beach in search of me.   Fortunately my father was not on the spot or I should have been made to realize the enormity of my crime, according to the method approved by the wisest of Israel's rulers.   But my mother and nurse, with that blessed disposition of all good women, were so overjoyed at my safe return that I was not only fully forgiven but awarded an extra helping at my tea of the principal delicacies of South Lancashire—fresh potted shrimps and Eccles cakes, ecstatic joys in those days and still very appetising trifles to a palate that has grown, like Iago, nothing if not critical.

---

* I never look back upon that landmark in my earthly experiences without repeating to myself the words of the sublime Seneca, who has written more eloquently on such matters than anyone else before or since.

Omnia tempus edax depascitus, omni carpit,
Omnia sede movet.. . . .

† The opinion I have expressed about the value of corroborative testimony is amply confirmed by an incident which occurred after the completion of this chapter.   During the summer of 1942 while in Los Angeles I renewed acquaintance with my second nurse, who took charge of me when I was about six.   This clear-minded and vigorous old lady, so far from supporting the legend of my moral impeccability, declared roundly that I was a more than ordinarily mischievous urchin, to whom she delighted (as often as her conscience permitted) to administer corporal chastisement.   She lamented, however, that her good intentions were not always appreciated by some of the family, and on one occasion my grandfather, resenting what he thought to be an ill-timed effort of disciplinary zeal, threatened retaliation upon her with an umbrella of Magog-like dimensions unless she at once desisted.

2

EARLY CHILDHOOD (1885–88)

THUS MY EXISTENCE MOVED ONWARD IN SILENCE AND CONTEMPLATION until my sixth year, when I was taken to my first concert.   It was a piano recital, and a series of new pieces by Grieg gave the programme a distinction we find none too frequently in events of this kind nowadays.   Long after I had been put to bed that evening I lay awake thinking hard about my novel experience, and the music revolved distractingly in my head over and over again like a blatant merry-go-round at a country fair. Suddenly a daring idea came to me: I got out of bed, went downstairs to the drawing-room, where I heard voices, opened the door and walked in. There I found several of the family as well as my nurse, to whom my mother was giving some orders, and amid profound and astonished silence I advanced to the middle of the floor and said: "Please may I learn the piano?"

The spectacles fell from my grandfather's nose as if removed by magic; the book he was reading dropped just as precipitately from my father's hands to the floor; my mother tried to scream, but surprise had deprived her of voice; and my old nurse, nicknamed Tiny, who was of immense physique and suffered from heart trouble, burst into tears and nearly fainted away.   I was hurried quickly out of the room and submitted to an exhaustive examination, as if I had been a complicated piece of machinery run down in some vital part; but as nothing untoward was revealed I was returned to bed, and the little party went below again to determine what was to be done next.   The debate was long and animated, but once the shock of bewilderment had worn off, it began to be glimpsed that the crisis was less physiological than spiritual.

The following day the Don Basilio of our establishment, the local organist, was called in, and I was made to undergo another rigorous but this time aesthetical inspection.   This excellent man, who derived most of his income from teaching the piano and the rudiments of music to the children of half the families in the district, pronounced emphatically that I was suffering from a long suppression of the artistic instinct and should be given relief without delay.   I must have had some innate, if unconscious, acquaintance with the great Carthusian principle—"Now or When", for to his evident satisfaction I decided to have my first lesson there and then.   I was promptly placed before the keyboard, and for a few minutes several pairs of eyes watched, as breathlessly as if Liszt or Rubinstein were upon the stool, my attempts to penetrate the mysteries of five consecutive notes.   In this modest and not unromantic fashion was I introduced to the divine art.

I found the lessons wholly to my liking.   There was sometimes a little practice and always a great deal of conversation, or rather monologue, on the part of my master.   He was a single-minded enthusiast, with Mozart as the object of his worship, and any criticism or depreciation of his idol, however guardedly expressed, never failed to arouse in him a storm of agitation and disgust.   Some of this adoration, I fear, proceeded more from faith than learning, for one of his favourite compositions was the notorious "Twelfth Mass", much of it obviously the product of another hand.   But a small Lancashire town of the 'eighties was hardly the place where nicety of taste or scholarship was likely to be found *in excelsis*, and I am not ashamed to confess that for many years I shared his guilty attachment for this pleasant example of musical forgery.

Discovering that what I loved best to hear were the stories of the operas, he would relate to me at almost every visit those of *Figaro, Don Giovanni*, and *Die Zauberflöte*, punctuating the narrative with excerpts from the better-known vocal and instrumental numbers.   And so it came about that, almost before I had struggled through my scales, the joyous shapes of Susanna, Zerlina, Cherubino, and Papageno were nearly as living to me as the real people I saw daily in my home.   It was an agreeable system of instruction, if possibly not the soundest on which to found a method of pianoforte-playing; for though I worked along conscientiously enough to acquire an early knowledge of the gentle flights of Dussek and Clementi, the glamour of the stage, even if seen from afar, gradually dissipated much of that other and earlier spell laid upon me in the concert room.   A longing for a nearer view of my enchanted world began to take possession of me, but this was not easy to gratify, as my age was considered far too tender for the profane contact of the theatre.

The mechanical genius of the present age has decreed that if Mahomet cannot go to the mountain, then the mountain must go to Mahomet; or, in other words, if man does not want to go forth in search of music, he can stay comfortably at home and have it brought to him there.   But even in those unenlightened days we had our makeshifts for the genuine article. My father nourished a passion for musical-boxes of every description, and the house almost overflowed with them.   Some were cunningly designed as bits of ordinary domestic furniture or objects of common use, and the visitor who hung up his hat on a certain peg of the hall rack, or who absent-mindedly abstracted the wrong umbrella from the stand, would be startled at having provoked into life the cheerful strains of *William Tell* or *Fra Diavolo*.   But others were serious and solid affairs, elaborate of build, full of strange devices and bringing forth sounds of elfin delight. That delicate tintinnabulating tone, those laughing cascades of crystalline notes, that extravagance of ornament truly rococo, the comic battery of drums and other tiny clattering things, how I loved them then, and how I lament their absence now!   For they would seem to have vanished utterly from the earth like a part of some submerged civilization, and though I have wandered over most of the land of their origin in search of surviving specimens, a generation has grown up to which they are almost as unfamiliar as the velocipede or spinning-wheel.   And yet to have them back again I would cheerfully throw into the sea or on to the dust-heap most of those triumphs of modern invention which claim to be trust-worthier instruments of reproduction.

I am often asked if it is not all to the good that music should be conveyed, no matter how, to tens of thousands who knew nothing of it before.   It is an artful question, not to be answered after the style of a witness in the box by a plain yea or nay; and I reply by countering with another from my side.   Can some of these whirrings and whizzings, these metallic dronings and lugubrious whinings be said to be music at all? But if I don't like the sound, surely I must admit that some of the spirit of the great masters is there.   Yes, I do, and just about as much as there is of the real thunder of Jupiter in the little box that Calchas the Sooth-sayer carries about with him in Offenbach's *La Belle Hélène*.   I am begin-ning to think that a certain supersensory percentage of the human tribe of today must be evolving in a way that enables it to absorb music through some other medium than their ears alone.   Not otherwise can I account for the growing disregard, even among musicians, of what is after all an important element in music, sound.   What largely distinguishes good music from bad is the beautiful sound of the one as compared with the ugly sound of the other, and the nice question arises to which I have yet to receive a plain answer.   Does music which is beautiful when played exactly in accordance with its composer's intentions, and which is made to sound ugly by being played under totally different conditions, remain good or turn bad?   But my musical-boxes, what of them?   Although toys, and none pretended they were anything better, they were lovely toys and harmless to offend the most fastidious ear.   Hearing them render anything grave or monumental suggested tiny copies of Michel-angelo or John of Bologna done in Dresden or Chelsea porcelain, and if one could not help laughing, at all events the laughter was kindly and affectionate.

It was the custom during the greater part of the nineteenth century, while they were building up their businesses, for Lancashire merchants and manufacturers to live on or very near the premises where their ware-houses or factories were located, and work started at six in the morning. But in the 'eighties there came a relaxation of this Spartan régime, em-ployers and employees alike were allowed to remain a little longer abed, and the increase of branch railway lines gave easier access to the adjacent country, enabling those who could to move out of town.   In was in my seventh year that we left St. Helens for Huyton, a village six miles south-ward and half-way on the road to Liverpool.   Our new home was a moderate-sized but commodious mansion, and my father, whose chief hobby after music was building, lost no time in adding a large wing of which the ground floor was a single room of small concert-hall dimensions. The front of the house had a clear view over several miles of meadows to a rising slope which was the limit of our horizon, and beyond it was a gradual descent through fields to other villages and the river Mersey.   On the edge of the ascent was a picturesque group of fourteenth-century buildings which had formerly been a monastic establishment.   Of these only the Abbey Church remained ecclesiastical property, the rest having been divided into two parts and converted into an imposing castellated house and a delightful country inn.   The latter, with its terraces and sunken bowling-green, was a favourite spot of ours for drives and picnics, and in later years when I was in the neighbourhood for concert or opera perform-ances I often went out to stay a day or two there in preference to the huge modern hotel in Liverpool.

There was a private school about a hundred yards beyond the bottom of our garden, and to it I was sent to pick up those elements of instruction which have harassed the soul of every small child for the past two thousand years, and which no one ever seems to question must be the basis of all human knowledge.   But I have to confess that during my first year or two I was a thoroughly idle and indifferent pupil and much preferred to be at home, especially in the music-room, where had now been installed a pipe organ, an American organ, a concert grand piano; and musical-boxes of every kind. My mother disdained the services of a housekeeper 'and ruled her little domain very much as my father did his business, giving personal attention to every side of it. She enrolled me in her service whenever she thought I had not enough to do to keep me out of mischief, more especially on Sundays, when I was sent into the kitchen to assist in the preparation of the midday meal. Invariably an ample loin of beef 'was roasted on a spit before an immense fire, and, like the young Tournebroche, my function was to keep it in motion, pouring and repouring over the meat the juice which flowed from it.* While this, the major part of the ceremony, was going on, there would be cooking of Yorkshire pudding, pies, and pastries in the back kitchen, and during the final stage my mother would appear arrayed in a beautiful silk dress with sleeves rolled up, to appraise our labours and give the finishing touches to everything with her own hands.

In spite of my disinclination for regular scholastic work, I was not wanting in industry where my real interest was excited. I had learned to read at a very early age, and as we had an excellent library I dipped into everything I could understand, from boys' tales of adventure to Shakespearean plays. It was in my eighth year that it was discovered I had an unusually retentive memory. Seeing me one day with a copy of *Macbeth*, my father suggested that I learn a portion of it (one of the witches' scenes) for recitation before a party of friends. When at the end of my performance one of the guests asked if I knew any more, I replied by giving him the rest of the act and, encouraged by the praises I received, had the entire play on the tip of my tongue in a few days' time. But the recollection of verse, although not of prose, was always a natural and unlaboured process of mind with me, particularly if it had the rhythmic and musical quality which to my way of thinking the Elizabethans possessed in larger measure than our later poets.

Meanwhile, my piano lessons continued with regularity, my preceptor coming out from St. Helens once or twice a week. It was impossible for me not to sense that he was almost desperately anxious that I should be something of a success, and I gleaned later on that almost at the beginning of my studies he had declared that I had a musical talent which might go far, if I could be induced to practise with greater regularity. As I was not without some real affection for him, which the frequent gift of Everton Toffee and Edinburgh Rock did nothing to decrease, I did work as hard as I could, but without much enthusiasm for the sort of piece he placed before me. With his passion for eighteenth-century piano music he was incapable of understanding that I could have progressed three times more speedily had he fed me on a wholly different musical diet. I would listen with joy to anyone playing Chopin, Schumann, or some of the later writers for the instrument such as Grieg. But the pre-Beethoven classical

---

* "*J'avais six ans, quand, un jour, rajustant son tablier, ce qui était en lui signe de résolution l me parla de la sorte:*
"*. . . Miraut, notre bon chien, a tourné ma broche pendant quatorze ans. . . . Mais il se fait vieux. . . . Jacquot, c'est a toi, mon fils, de prendre sa place. . . .' À compter de ce jour, assis du matin au soir, au coin de la cheminée, je tournai la broche, ma Croix de Dieu ouverte sur mes genoux . . . .*"—Chapter I, *La Rôtisserie de la Reine Pédauque*, Anatole France.

masters did not hold a very high place in my esteem; I had never heard them rendered by a great artist, was unaware how much more difficult they were to make grateful to the ear than their successors, and of their symphonic work I knew nothing, as the sound of an orchestra was as yet unknown to me. The youthful mind has no creative imagination of its own, and to awaken its interest in certain kinds of music it is necessary that they be given with all or most of the effect intended by the composer. Even in maturity we are surprised and delighted by some penetrating stroke of interpretation which throws fresh light on a piece with which we have been familiar for years. But in childhood we start from nowhere and are apt to wander about blindly as in a fog, unless we have the luck to find the rare kind of pedagogue who has a clairvoyant insight into the needs of our nascent personalities.

The consequence of this was that most of the time I spent at the piano was given up to hammering out all the opera scores I could read. Observing that in these the points of orchestration were frequently indicated, I endeavoured to reproduce as many of them as I could on the organ. As my feet did not reach the pedals, my father would sometimes collaborate by adding the missing part, but usually more to my embarrassment than gratification. Even at that age I listened to his efforts on that none too tractable instrument with mixed feelings of respect and bewilderment, for it seemed quite outside his power ever to bring about a synchronism of manuals and pedals, and the bass part always had a lower octave played in perpetually disturbing syncopation. But as no one had the heart to draw his attention to this little foible, he would dream away at the keyboard for hours at a time without the slightest suspicion that he was not the soul of accuracy. And these, it may be, were his happiest moments.

3

LATER CHILDHOOD (1888–91)

IT WAS NOT UNTIL A YEAR OR TWO LATER THAT THE EVENT OCCURRED which threw all the previous excitements of my life well into the shade. This was the arrival in my home of a gigantic object, as big as the side of a cottage, which reproduced not too inaccurately the sound and effect of an orchestra of forty or forty-five players. This super musical-box performed symphonies of Mozart and Beethoven, preludes and selections from the operas of Verdi, Rossini, and Wagner, and miscellaneous pieces of a dozen other composers great and small. As the young Walt Whitman learned the meaning of song from the birds of the South that sang to him, a child on that lonely beach of Long Island, their carols of joy and despair, so I, listening every day to the magical sounds that rolled about my ears, began to comprehend something of the grandeur and pathos, of the fire and tenderness, that dwelt in the souls of those masters dead and gone. I had each piece played again and again until I would strum or whistle it by heart, and consumed with the desire to hear these glorious outpourings in their integrity, I importuned my parents with tenacity until I had gained my point. To my going to concerts there was no really serious opposition, although, as they were nearly all given at night, it meant late hours and a carriage drive of seven miles each way between our home and Liverpool. But the opera house was a very different matter, and many were the family consultations before it was conceded that I was old enough for such a high adventure. For in those days there were sharply divided opinions about the stage in our part of the kingdom, and if anyone had then prophesied that within half a lifetime it would come to be regarded as the most moral and respectable of British institutions he would certainly have run the risk of being locked up as an outrageous lunatic.

When I pay my visits, all too rare, to the blameless entertainment provided by our lyric and comedy theatres, when I hear that ultra-refinement of speech, and view that decorous restraint of action, both of which have become models for the young people of our best families, I find it hard to believe that all this was once an offence and stumbling-block to millions of my countrymen. In a play I saw some years back, the heroine puzzled me by her cautious interpretation of a part which was crying out for a strong infusion of what our American cousins elegantly call "pep"; and as I knew she was not without talent I expressed a little surprise to the lady sitting next to me. She agreed, but considered that there was good and sufficient reason for it, as the subject of my criticism was shortly to be joined in matrimony with the scion of a noble house owning decided views about the demeanour in public of its female members. As this thrilling piece of information was imparted to me with an obvious touch of compassion for my ignorance of such important matters, I did my best to be suitably impressed, although I could not help adding that the intimate link connecting the two hitherto independent (but not mutually excluding) entities, propriety and the peerage, was something wholly new to me. But what was obscure in my case seemed clear enough to everyone else. For on the evening following the publication of the happy news, the dear chocolate-munching, paper-bag-rustling, and teaspoon-dropping creatures of the pit greeted the fortunate young lady on her entrance with a thundering ovation. The enthusiasm spread to the stalls and boxes; old gentlemen entirely unacquainted with one another rose solemnly and shook hands, and even the orchestra betrayed an emotion which had been conspicuously wanting in its rendering of the incidental music. It was one of those occasions that reflect credit on us as a people of sentiment and character, and several minutes elapsed before the piece could resume its ordinary course. Some of us, dating from a rougher and ruder generation, may have a nervous feeling that this continued process of keying down is being carried a fraction too far, and that there appears to be looming in the near distance the pale spectre of an universal anaemic gentility. But we are probably wrong, and anyway what are such trumpery losses when set off against the immense gain in purification and uplift? It is pretty certain that we English are the only nation which is one hundred per cent sound about this sort of thing, and it must be a comfort to many that, although in the years preceding 1939 we seemed to have lost the desire to impose the way of peace upon a distracted world, we were resolute that the pretensions of Art must yield place to those of Society.*

Hae tibi erunt artes, pacisque imponere morem.—Virgil, *Aeneid*, Book 6.

But in those earlier days of which I am writing I knew dozens of nice sensible persons who had never been inside a theatre, and whom no material inducement could ever have enticed there. Concerts possibly, especially if an oratorio was in the programme, but the play never. Some ancient prejudices expire as slowly and painfully as the Pickwickian frog, as I discovered a generation later when conducting the Choral Society of a large town in the neighbourhood of Manchester. At the close of the concert I received a deputation from the ladies of the choir who wished to ask a favour of me. Would I write to the secretary of the Society that in my opinion a number of attendances at my annual opera season, which was then running in Manchester, was indispensable to the completion of their musical education? Inquiring the object of all this, I was told that none of them had yet been allowed to see a performance, as the right sort among their people never went to the theatre. But there was the birth of an idea that opera might be less baneful in its influence than other forms of dramatic entertainment, and this promising revolution in public opinion could be expedited by a word or two from me. I have a very particular esteem for this enterprising town and its amiable chapel-going citizens, for out of the hundreds, it may be thousands, of letters I have written publicly and privately in support of some musical cause or other, this is one of the few which ever obtained a tangible result. Shortly afterwards a great battle was fought and won, and the fruits of victory included a special train, provided by the railway company, to transport a numerous band of operatic pilgrims to the shrine of their devotions and the innocent enjoyment of that chaste masterpiece, *La Traviata*.

As nearly all those who fall heavily in love profess to find their faculties stimulated in every direction, and to discover a fresh colour and meaning in all they see or hear, even so had the revelation of the beauty and eloquence of great music a like effect on me. I became attentive to my lessons in school, worked a bit on my own at home, developed sensibilities and sensitivities which troubled now and then my elders, and ceased to draw pleasure from the books which most boys of my age at that time would be found reading. An uncle, my father's younger brother, was living in our village, and it was his custom every Sunday afternoon to retire to his library, where he remained absorbed in some book or other until dinner-time. He frequently visited our house to play billiards, and, discovering there a kindred spirit, took to inviting me to lunch and a reading séance with him afterwards. These occasions became an institution with me, continuing over several years until he left to settle in London, and the number of books I got through must have been prodigious. There was hardly a novelist, big or little, British or foreign, of the nineteenth century that I did not dive into and digest, although my access to the latter was determined by their fitness to be placed in my hands. My decided preference was for the more vivid and picturesque style of the French masters like Victor Hugo, and it was over his *Quatre-Vingt-Treize*, my especial favourite, that I fell into temporary disgrace with my sympathetic relative. In spite of a gentlemen's agreement between us, I surreptitiously abstracted the work from its shelf, intending to return it before he should discover its disappearance. But alas, I left it in our garden, where I had been re-reading it for the fifth or sixth time; that day it rained hard, the unfortunate volume, which was elegantly bound and one of a set, was completely ruined, and several weeks passed before I was restored to favour.

He was an odd personality, this uncle of mine, and something of an enigma not only to me but to everyone else who came in touch with him. While yet a very young man, he had been sent by my grandfather on a year's trip round the world, spending several months in Far-Eastern lands, particularly Japan, then a mediaeval country with habits and customs unchanged for five hundred years, and an army equipped (shades of Dugald Dalgetty!) with bows and arrows. He had returned from the Land of the Rising Sun with an unhealthy admiration for its art, which infected both my father and mother to the extent of lumbering our house with hundreds of those utterly useless and unattractive ivory figures, screens, and other preposterous knick-knacks which even then I regarded with dismay and aversion. His manner and behaviour, I think, were laboriously modelled upon some character he had read about either in history or fiction, his speech was almost tiresomely precise, his dress was immaculate, and he wore a top hat on every possible occasion. He took an intelligent interest in conversation but was never known to commit himself to a definite view or to betray bias on any subject under the sun. Towards humour or jest he took up an attitude unfailingly discouraging to the unhappy joker of the occasion, appraising and analysing every word uttered with the cool curiosity of a scientist examining a new-found germ under a powerful microscope.

He had one indubitable virtue : he was an admirable host with as fine an appreciation of wine as I have known in any man. Dining with him was a privilege, for one was certain to find not only that the Bordeaux or Burgundy was of the best, but that the temperature of either, an almost forgotten refinement, had been perfectly calculated before appearance on the table.

My father about this time began to make more frequent trips to the United States, where some ten years earlier he had established a branch of his business, and each time he returned he brought with him some product of Yankee invention to be used in his factory or home. Thus we had a system of central heating when such a thing was almost unknown among us, and, I believe, the first private electric lighting plant to be installed in the country. My bedroom walls were covered with pictures of the Yosemite Valley, the Bridal Veil Falls, the Grand Cañon, and the Big Trees, and as I had as yet seen no part of the world other than our corner of South Lancashire, as unexciting a spot as any to be found in the kingdom, I longed for the day when I too would have the chance of gazing on these wonderful sights. I asked him for American books, of which we had none in the library except *Uncle Tom's Cabin* and a volume of Longfellow, and he obtained for me all the works of Poe, Bret Harte, and Mark Twain, the first of whom shared my poetical idolatry for years to come with Shakespeare and Byron.

My mother was a slightly built creature who preserved an admirable figure until the end of a long life, in spite of numerous children and an intermittent nervous malady, which first manifested itself when I was between ten and eleven, and which obliged her as time went on to relinquish more and more the care of her house and go southward to some place on the sea like Eastbourne or Bournemouth, where she could be looked after until well again. As these absences became more frequent and, coupled with those of my father, made a large house half tenanted hardly the cheeriest place for children, I was sometimes sent off during school holidays to friends or relations. It was through a closer contact with persons whom I had known only casually that I made what was to me a startling discovery—namely, the absence of similarity between the private and public behaviour towards one another of most married people. Husbands who were loquacious and confident when encouraged and protected by the presence of half a dozen others relapsed into submissive and silent humility when alone with the partners of their joys, and *vice versa*. This phenomenon, together with an aphorism I had recently read in a French philosopher, that while there were heaps of satisfactory marriages, there were no charming ones,* inspired me with distrust of a convention which I had regarded some years earlier with unqualified favour. The number of my romantic attachments to little girls between six and ten had been a source of constant entertainment to the rest of my family, although I was never teased about them at the time. Very clear in my memory is the flattering gravity of attention which was given to my announcement of formal engagement to at least four of my fancies on the same day.

I had endured, as I have related, one overwhelming revelation of the truth that "so may the outward shows be least themselves", and here was another to deepen the questioning vein in my growing mind. Already I had noted in all the romances I was reading that while their authors devoted hundreds of pages to the trials and sorrows of two young people sighing and panting to be united in holy wedlock, to the unending intrigues and struggles set going to bring them to the foot of the altar, as well as to the divisions created in happy families and between devoted friends during the accomplishment of this sublime purpose, very little was ever said about its aftermath. A long observation of my fellow creatures has led me well on the road to a belief that the world is about equally divided between those who are dying to rush into hymeneal bondage and those who with an equal ardour are dying to rush out of it. But this is a thorny and delicate question, the eventual determination of which I am quite willing to leave to those who spend their lives in drawing up on paper one scheme after another for the reformation, alteration, and amelioration of everything on earth, the planet itself included. In the baffling world of humanity there was, however, one unchanging element, the super-musical box, for which every few months there arrived from Switzerland a consignment of newly perforated rolls to give forth some great strain of melody that I had not heard before. Here was a world at once real and ideal, diminishing care, augmenting pleasure, and shutting the door on the community outside with its eternal load of problems which no one seemed able to solve.

I had by now been taken to a number of orchestral concerts and opera performances, but not so many of the latter, as any stage piece had an exciting and sometimes disturbing effect which did not wear off for days afterwards. The three works which made the greatest impression on me were the *Romeo and Juliet* of Gounod (which I much preferred to *Faust*), *Figaro*, and, most of all, *Aida*, which for long I considered all that an opera

---

* *Il y a de bons mariages, mais il n'y en a point de délicieux.*—La Rochefoucauld.

should be. There were, perhaps, passages in the earlier Wagner works (the later had not yet reached us) which made a greater musical appeal to me, and the stories I found enthralling; but the Venusberg scene, the "Tournament of Song" in *Tannhäuser*, and most of the second act of *Lohengrin*, jogged along far too deliberately for my juvenile taste. After the sounds and sights of the lyric drama, simple plays seemed dull and shoddy. Unaided or palliated by the influence of music, I found them almost unbearably unconvincing, and the grotesque noises produced by a foolish little band of five or six playing incidental music only increased my contempt for this feeble sort of show. As I suffered from a wholly misplaced sense of humour my responses to it were often inexcusable, and on one occasion so deplorable that I was not again taken to a play for at least a year afterwards. It was during that good old national melodrama *East Lynne*, which has reduced to copious floods of tears as many millions of my countrymen as that perennial rib-tickler *Charley's Aunt* has to hilarity. The appearance of the ill-fated heroine was always heralded by a performance on the solo violin of the air "When Other Lips" from *The Bohemian Girl*, and after a few repetitions of this languishing trifle I was suddenly taken with a fit of the giggles which neither the threats of my father nor the entreaties of my mother, who were sitting on either side of me, were effective to control. As our little party was in the front row of the stalls, we became the unwelcome object of attention from both stage and house, and I had to be taken out and left in charge of the bar attendant until the conclusion of the piece. This fatal tendency to uncontrollable mirth in the presence of sob-stuff is something I have never been able to conquer. Twenty years or more later, having been induced to see another full-blooded specimen of the same class of entertainment, *The Worst Woman in London*, I was so moved, in exactly the opposite way the authors of the piece had intended, that I was requested to retire upon the plea that I was seriously interfering with the enjoyment of the rest of the audience.

4

MUSIC IN LANCASHIRE

SO FAR AS I KNOW, A HISTORY OF THE PART PLAYED BY ENGLISH MUSICIANS in the development of their art during the nineteenth century in Lancashire has yet to be written. But he who one day attempts the task will find it easily the shortest on record, and if there were another Tacitus among us he would dispose of the whole period in a single word—Germany. For there was scarcely a town of any size with the slightest musical culture (outside choral singing) that did not owe every ounce of it to some enterprising son of the Fatherland, amateur or professional, who had settled there. Orchestras, opera companies, or string quartets, it would be hard to find anything that was not their handiwork; spiritually we were as a conquered, or at the least an occupied, territory, and over it all reigned in unchallenged sovereignty the genial figure of Charles Hallé.

Of Hallé's gifts as pianist and conductor there were opposing divisions, even schools, of opinion. Formerly there were no more than two sorts of virtuosi, the exceptions being so rare as to count hardly at all. The first relegated emotion to a back seat from which there was no danger of its interfering with the calculated operations of technique; and the second gave it free rein to go dashing ahead as contemptuous of its harassed satellite as the North Wind of the obstacles it sweeps from its course. Hallé definitely belonged to the former class, although Berlioz, who, had he been an executive artist, would assuredly have been included in the latter, writes of him somewhere as *"ce pianiste sans peur et sans reproche"*. This is magnificent, but hardly criticism. I know scores of performers who are obviously *sans peur*, but I should hesitate to apply the rest of the phrase to them; and as for the few who may be deserving of the *sans reproche*, I usually feel when I hear them that their perfection hangs upon a discretion far too wary to have kindled the enthusiasm of the lively Hector. But whatever may have been his actual accomplishment as an artist, there can be no question of one thing: this energetic Teuton did more for music in the North of England than all the men who came before and after him put together.

No one can honestly maintain that the lives of musicians taken as a whole make exciting reading. They create too often the melancholy impression that their subjects have been victims rather than rulers or priests of destiny. It is a relief therefore to note some stirring and fortunate enterprise such as Hallé's invasion and conquest of Manchester, an achievement worthy almost to rank with the stories of Arthur or Roland. Possibly it was something more like this or a prevision of it that Berlioz had in mind when he penned the splendid compliment borrowed from the annals of chivalry. Otherwise, to a true Frenchman, the exchange of his own exhilarating capital for a sombre provincial town in a land where music was supposed popularly to be as scarce as the sunshine must have seemed outside rational explanation; and certainly no man could have exiled himself from the Paris of the eighteen-forties or -fifties with a light heart. A full generation had yet to pass before the favourite city of Julian* was to be gladdened with the sight of the Eiffel Tower and the Trocadero, those architectural glories of the Third Republic; nor had the Tuileries yet succumbed to the rage of the Commune or the Place Vendôme to the boon of foreign commerce. And what good company abounded there, especially for an artist who happened to be both likable and sociable! The list of resident musicians, in addition to Berlioz, included Chopin, Rossini, Auber, Gounod, and Meyerbeer, and as for painters, sculptors, and men of letters, there were geniuses of varying rank in nearly every other street. On such a circle and environment young Hallé

---

* Few things in history are stranger than this preference of the great apostate. It might have been expected that the most lettered of the Emperors since Marcus Aurelius would have favoured one of the famous centres of learning in Gaul like Toulouse or Bordeaux. But he who had passed his youth beneath the venerable shade of the Athenian myrtles and in the splendid schools of Constantine's new metropolis spent the happiest years of his life in a remote little town virtually untouched by Roman culture. The certificate of good conduct he gives the place and its inhabitants may have an interest for those who associate the modern Lutetia with a different outlook upon earthly delights. "They worship Venus," he writes, "as the goddess of holy wedlock, and make use of Bacchus' gifts only because that deity is the father of honest pleasure. Dancing of all kinds they shun as licentious and the theatre they avoid like the plague." I once showed this historical extract to a distinguished French ecclesiastic whose erudition it had escaped. His comment was, "I am hardly surprised, for it has often been alleged that we were slower to accept the blessings of Christianity than most other parts of the Empire."

turned his back, and for ever; and if I have spoken of his descent on Manchester as an adventure both spirited and romantic, I can compare the subsequent forty-odd years of his life there only with the sustained fortitude of St. Simeon Stylites on his Thebaid column. Peace has its heroes as well as war, and, while it is impossible to compute, it is easy to imagine the dozens of battles, skirmishes and other minor encounters fought and won in the name of art, and the hundreds of strongholds of prejudice and indifference attacked and carried by storm or strategy. For the land was barren, and the soil he had marked out for working was frequently hard and intractable. But by slow degrees the desert underwent an impressive transformation, and the good tidings were carried to every corner of that region of cotton, clogs, and chimneys, until Hallé and his orchestra became household words where the mere names of the great composers had once been unknown.

The metamorphosis of Manchester into an oasis of civilization reacted nowhere more healthily than upon the great rival city on the banks of the Mersey. Liverpool, proud in the possession of an older musical culture as well as the most beautiful concert hall in the kingdom, had declined upon that state of ease without dignity generally begotten of an absence of competition. Dethroned without reasonable hope of reinstatement from its position as chief centre of orchestral music in the county, it flung itself for the consolation of its injured self-esteem into the siren arms of grand opera. The leading impresario of the day, Carl Rosa, was encouraged to make his headquarters there and was given a support so solid and sustained that after a while he purchased the principal theatre in the town as a permanent home for his company.

Its annual season, which lasted from Christmas to spring, was the important social event of the year. Not to be a subscriber or to be seen there often was to confess oneself, if not unmusical, at least unfashionable, and the representations were crowded except when some complete novelty was brought forward. Then the general public, just as it does today, would mark its disapproval by staying away until the offending work had gone round the rest of the world at least half a dozen times. By and by certain persons would begin to demand in the Press why they were being persistently denied the hearing of a masterpiece that was growing almost stale everywhere else, and the periodical complaints stimulated a flood of general indignation, which was permitted to rise to boiling-pitch before a crafty management appeased it with a production. Then we turned up in our thousands, indulging in an immense amount of self-congratulation at having vindicated the good name of the town in artistic affairs, and thoroughly happy in the belief that we were backing the right horse. But, being a well-balanced community which rarely remained for long in a condition of mental exaltation, our ecstasies speedily subsided. We soon returned to our normal outlook, very much after the fashion of an injudicious reveller who faces the cold morning that follows a hectic night, and proceeded to deal with the next new work in precisely the same way.

There were many who found admirable this steady refusal of the British public to traffic seriously with art or artists until either had been sealed seventy times seven with the blessing of every other nation. Why, they asked, waste time, money, and, what is far more prodigal, brainwork on discovering merit for ourselves, when others appear only too willing to relieve us of the trouble and responsibility? Surely a people which has secured such predominance in the world has the right to insist that all things which are presented for its approval should first pass through the testing furnace of foreign opinion. Our youthful geniuses, however, so far from acquiescing patiently in this perfect scheme of things, clamoured loudly to know what part in it had been reserved for them. I regret to admit that, with our habitual tendency to compromise and our kindly desire to hurt nobody's feelings, we shrank from telling them that it was infinitesimally small. But this pretty game of evasion could not avoid playing itself out sooner or later, with disillusionment on the one side, embarrassment on the other, and on both a realization that the epigram of the greatest American of the last century on the subject of hoodwinking the masses remains for ever the one unassailable maxim of sociopolitical science.

But there is always a minority, odd folk generally, that pines for newness, and such existed among us as it did everywhere else. I have often wondered why the sibyl who rules over the shadowy realm of prophecy declines to take the faintest interest in art. Certainly there is no instance known to me of an accurate forecast in one generation of the state of music in the next. Perhaps this is well, for with a clairvoyant vision before our eyes of the surprises of 1920–1940 we might have been less complacent about the achievement of our own day. Of course we had nothing like the wonderful fellows of recent times, all of them busily staking out claims in a brand-new Jerusalem of music; and while it may be that few have yet penetrated the inner courts of their temple, it is a comfort to learn that the privilege of entry can be ours through submission to a novitiate which seems to be hardly less arduous than that of the lovers in *Die Zauberflöte*. There is a cross-grained and cantankerous clique that strives to refute the necessity of what it denounces as a purgatory of probation, and asks why, if there be anything in this recondite message of real beauty, it should not be surrendered less reluctantly. Otherwise, by the time it is freely and fully vouchsafed there will be another fashion let loose on the world and a fresh set of demands to test its endurance. Should that happen, it is conceivable that a true comprehension of today's music never will be obtained and that all its soaring inspiration is destined to an immortality of misconception.*

I turn from the contemplation of this melancholy contingency back to the times when man was of cruder fibre and Art was shallow enough to be fathomed in a week or even in a day. We were innocently happy in the steady stream which flowed from the pens of men like Brahms, Grieg, and Dvořák, and hardly a month would go by without bringing us a volume of songs, a piano sonata, a quartet, or some minor orchestral piece. Now and then, usually about twice a year, a bigger gun would be fired off in the way of a symphony such as the Fifth of Tchaikovsky, or an opera like the *Manon* of Massenet and the *Otello* of Verdi. Nor can it be forgotten that Wagner's later works, although completed twenty years earlier, were only then beginning to filter through and were just as new to us as anything written in the previous week. Many are the thrills which I have

---

* Upon this perpetually recurring delusion of humanity Pope has said the last word:
"We think our fathers fools, so wise we grow,
Our wiser sons, no doubt, will think us so."

enjoyed from the sound of melody fresh to my ear, but none keener than those excited by the first hearings of *Tristan* and *Die Meistersinger* in the full flush of their modernity.

It is only of professional musicians and organizations of the period that I so far have written, and there remains for brief consideration the amateur, by no means the least important element in any artistic community; for without a certain degree of culture in the audience, a virtuoso reproduces the subtler and finer sides of his art in vain. It must be allowed too that amateurs have an honourable place in the history of music and that we owe to them more than one reform or innovation, not the least being the invention of Grand Opera; although I have often wondered whether its creator would not have paused after the first experimental effort if he could have foreseen the incredible amount of trouble he was bringing into the world. Furthermore, that which goes on within the walls of the house, the sort of book that is read or class of music that is studied and practised, mirrors the intellectual life of a people even more faithfully than the public careers of prominent individuals.

If the opera season was the most fashionable institution in Liverpool, the most interesting and esteemed was its orchestral society. The founder and conductor was a cotton merchant of German origin who had gradually increased the number of his players to one hundred, of which only a small percentage was professional. Rodewald's policy was progressive, and by giving works that were either unknown or off the beaten track he and his colleagues acquired a good deal more than merely local prestige. It became the ambition of every young musician who could scrape or blow a few notes to become a member, and this stimulated the study of instruments which are not usually the hobby of amateurs or that make for the greater tranquillity of the home. Anyone who walked through my village on a winter evening might have heard in every fourth or fifth house the pathetic wailings of flutes and clarinets, the solemn chortling of bassoons and horns, or the more majestic complaints of trombones and tubas. There was for several years quite a minor rage for this harmless species of indoor entertainment, with here and there a few out-of-the-way manifestations of it. I wish that some inquiring spirit would write a little work on the elective affinities between players and instruments; the mystical promptings that fire a man's soul with a life-long passion for the bassoon or triangle; why large men so often find their joy in the piccolo, and small in the contra-bass; and, more cryptic than anything else, the preference in a certain community for one instrument over another. In ours it was the "soft complaining flute" that became the chosen object of its fancy, and the practical impossibility of using more than a limited number in all the organizations of the district was powerless to check the unbridled pursuit of it. Four of its devotees, unable to find opportunity for individual display in either an orchestra or a chamber-music combination, sought consolation in playing together. As the quartet consisted of a wealthy landowner, a doctor, a greengrocer, and a gasworks man, we were privileged to behold a demonstration of social equality that alarmed the county families as much as it cheered the lesser fry. They met regularly for practice about twice a week after working hours in a room on the ground floor of one of their houses, and as they never troubled to pull down the blinds, they provided a free peepshow that was an unfailing delight to all in the vicinity.

5

PUBLIC SCHOOL LIFE (1892-97)

AS I APPROACHED MY FOURTEENTH YEAR THERE CAME UPON ME THAT vague but familiar dissatisfaction with everything in the scheme of existence which the mind at that age is powerless to analyse. Little more than the organic need for new outlets and fresh surroundings, it is none the less a dangerous moment at whatever stage of life it appears; for men do not go in search of adventure, even the ultimate adventure, for most of the reasons that poets, politicians or coroners' juries would have us believe, but simply for change, without which they would perish slowly or quickly according to the demands of their different natures. As there was little to dislike and much to love in my home, I often strove to silence the voice of discontent within me, but the fullest parental indulgence could not have appeased the unsleeping desire to be up and about something else. At length the hour struck for the fulfilment of my indefinable longings, and I was duly despatched to a public school.

Nemesis descended upon me swiftly, and for the best part of my first year I was the most desolate and woeful of small objects on this earth. In Mr. Shaw's play *Caesar and Cleopatra* there is a passage where the great Julius excuses the insular prejudices of his henchman Britannus by saying: "He thinks that the customs of his tribe and island are the laws of nature." Even so had I childishly imagined that the conditions of my own home life must have their counterpart everywhere else, and I was lost pathetically in an environment which touched at hardly any point the little world I had hitherto known. No opera, no concerts, not even a string quartet; and perhaps worst of all no super musical box to turn on some familiar master strain at a moment's notice. Here I was transported to a sphere alien to mine in habit and mentality, and I began to realize the full meaning and value of that which I had lost, from the day when I had no longer the unlimited chance of enjoying it. In classroom or chapel fragments of *Aïda* or *Tannhäuser* haunted my brain, and scenes from a dozen other operas passed before my eyes. I thought and dreamt of little but music, and even the mild exertion of construing Cornelius Nepos and the Gallic Wars was a painful effort of concentration. It is true that we were not wholly without entertainment of a kind, but those who ruled us had decreed that what was fit for our aesthetic health was an occasional party of glee-singers or comic recitalists.

As I sat in the great hall with three or four hundred others listening to these artless diversions, I fancied myself once more in short frocks playing with toys in the nursery, and the shock of joy was almost too much for me when, in a miscellaneous concert made up chiefly of Scotch ballads and imitation negro songs, a foreign violinist appeared to play an arrangement of the "Preislied" from *Die Meistersinger*. The beautiful melody sounded doubly alluring to my starved ear, and I sat in a state of half trance with my hands tightly clasped together, from which I was rudely aroused by a sturdy kick from the boy sitting behind me and a scornful reminder that it was not a prayer meeting that was going on. Carried away with fury and careless of the consequences, I seized the disturber of my halcyon dream tightly by the hair, and a lively scrap followed, which resulted in both of us being ejected from the building. The combat, which was renewed with vigour outside, was decided in favour of my assailant, who was somewhat bigger and stronger than I; but this reverse pained me less than an interview later in the evening with my house master, who rounded off a stern admonition by saying reproachfully, "And I understood, Beecham, that you were fond of music!"

The holidays that followed my first term were at Christmas-time, and I went in for an orgy of opera-going on which I spent all my available pocket-money. To make my meagre supply meet my avid need I patronized the gallery, and most nights I was the first to arrive at its door, generally in company with another youthful enthusiast. The sensation of the moment was *Cavalleria Rusticana*, which seemed to announce a new star in the sky of Italian music and a potential successor to the veteran Verdi. But the dazzling promise of Mascagni's early days has never been fully fulfilled, and he is but one of the numerous young men of my generation who, either from some defect in themselves or a hostile element in the genius of the age, have disappointed an expectant world. A great deal now, as in previous ages, is laid to the charge of the time spirit; but I prefer to remember what Goethe once said to Eckermann on this score: "Everyone accuses the present age of immorality, but I see nothing in it to prevent a man being moral if he wants to be so."

No healthy and well-constituted boy, however, can be unhappy long at a public school, for in spite of its detractors it remains the best and most original of British institutions. A French historian has attributed many of our successes at the expense of his own countrymen in every part of the world, during the lengthy duel between the two nations in the eighteenth century, to the larger proportion of our youth which had been trained at an early age to exercise authority and cultivate initiative. If this be so, then the legend that the public school has played a leading part in the consolidation of our Empire is not wholly without foundation, as the order of capacity or talent essential for such an achievement is precisely that which ranks superior in its estimation to others that are purely intellectual. And having adopted the creed that the formation of character is of greater value in the long run than the enlightenment of mind, it preaches the doctrine that, as nine tenths of the world's practical affairs are carried on by men in association with or opposition to other men, the expanding spirit, influenced and dominated by a daily routine which is wholly masculine, reaches the gateway to maturity the better for being unweakened by the condoning conditions of home life. Such a system has its undeniable limitations, as any that is distinctly lopsided is bound to have; and Matthew Arnold has somewhere quoted a foreign observer of our rule in India to the effect that the English are just but not amiable.* Perhaps this was the commentator's way of suggesting that our disposition and manners were lacking in that ease and grace

---

* Essay on Falkland.

impossible of acquisition save through frequent association with the softer and more pliant half of humanity. But during the last twenty years no one can accuse us of any lack of easy tolerance. Indeed, it is likely that a fair percentage of the world's present troubles proceeds from our excessive indulgence in an over-prolonged mood of acquiescence; and it may interest those on the lookout for historical coincidences that it was during the same period when my country seemed to have forgotten its old instinct for clear decision and rapid action that the public-school tradition was the persistent object of a destructive criticism. But, whatever may be its merits or demerits, it is assuredly one of the rare examples found among us of an idea worked out with complete logic and consistency. For while most modern nations at some time or other have admitted the necessity of making work and religion compulsory in their schools, it has been left to the Englishman to discover and proclaim that games are not only of equal importance but worthy of an even greater measure of respect and veneration.

As time went on I became not only reconciled but attached to my life at Rossall. Occupying a bleak and isolated position on the North Lancashire coast, several miles away from any town and with few houses in the district, the place was not without charm of a grey and gloomy kind. Although little to the liking of that type of individual (everywhere in the majority) that is distressed or ill at ease if every leisure minute of the day is not spent in the pursuit of strange sights and novel experiences, it was not an unsympathetic *milieu* for the budding artist or philosopher, for whom a crowded calendar of activity is of small use. Indeed, for most young people a reasonable allowance of obligatory boredom is by no means an evil, especially if the outlets for serious mischief are few and far between. The mind, if there is anything in it, is reduced to the extremity of thinking occasionally for itself, and it is probably during these periods of enforced tranquillity, which so many of us keenly resent, that the bulk of the worth-while thought given to the world has had its birth.

It was in the summer of 1893 that my father took me with him on a visit to the United States. This was a great event in the life of an obscure member of the Lower School, and I was an object of envy to masters and boys alike. We sailed on the *Campania*, then the largest ship afloat, and on board was a distinguished party of artists all bound for the Chicago Exhibition, a celebration which had been advertised to the world as the greatest of its kind that ever had been or would ever be again on this earth. Among the group was Ben Davies, then at the height of his reputation, and at the usual concert of the voyage I played his accompaniments as well as those of the other vocalists. His was a voice of uncommon beauty, round, full, and expressive, less inherently tenor than baritone, and, like all organs of this mixed genre, thinning out perceptibly on the top. Later on, the upper notes disappeared entirely, but the middle register preserved to the end of a prolonged spell of singing days most of its former opulence and charm. We reached New York towards the end of August and went to stay at the old Astor House, at that time one of the leading hotels of the city. The temperature was tropical, and in my search for cooling drinks I made acquaintance with the ice cream soda, which I at once decided was every bit as good as any nectar served to the dwellers on Olympus. But mosquitoes, which were and still are the terror of my existence, beset me day and night, and I was hardly sorry when my father gave the sign to set out for Chicago. There we put up at an hotel on the lake which enjoyed a welcome breeze for the greater part of the day, and for two weeks gave ourselves up to the delights of the magnificent entertainment we had come to view. Since that time I have seen dozens of the same kind of event but never anything to compare with this. Years afterwards, whenever I ventured to repeat this opinion, my hearers would pooh-pooh it on the grounds of my extreme youth at the time or the impressions of a mind new to such a spectacle: but I had only to produce photographs of the various pavilions, notably those representing New York State and California (the latter housing the most brilliant display of the products of the earth ever contained under one roof), for all of them to come round to my view.

Our itinerary of travel was not extensive, owing to my father's preoccupation with business in two or three large cities, but we managed to squeeze in a trip to Niagara and another by pleasure steamer up the Hudson River to Albany, from where we went on by train to Boston. At the last moment he found it impossible to get through his work in time to catch the boat to England which we had planned to take, and I was obliged to return alone. The assemblage on board was this time far less glamorous than on the voyage westward, and I was beginning to think that the inevitable concert which I helped to organize was going to be a distinctly dull affair. But one day a fellow passenger approached me and with a slight air of mystery inquired if I knew that one of the world's greatest singers was on board and had not been asked to take part in it. I told him it was no fault of mine and begged him to produce this gift from the gods. He went off in search of his friend and returned after a while to announce that the latter would meet me in about half an hour in the big salon, which would probably then be empty, as most of the passengers would be dressing for dinner. Just before the appointed time I went below and awaited the arrival of the illustrious stranger with some excitement, for although I had had the opportunity of meeting and playing accompaniments for a fair number of well-known singers, I had not yet met a star of the very first magnitude. Presently there entered one of the largest men I have ever seen. So prodigious was his bulk that he could scarcely walk at all, and supported himself on two sticks. At first I hardly knew what to say, his whole appearance being so utterly unlike anything I had ever associated with public performance. Then he began to sing, having selected as his opening number the "Abendstern" from *Tannhäuser*, and, inexperienced as I was, I knew at once that here was something quite phenomenal. There being no one else in the room, and finding that I had knowledge of most of the baritone songs from the popular operas, he went on happily for quite a time, to my wonder and delight. The voice was of great range and uncommon power, and, like that of Plançon, rolled out in immense waves of sound with the easiest production and the most consummate control. At the very height of his career, his companion afterwards informed me, he had been obliged to quit the stage because of this unfortunate physical over-growth which the medical science of the day was impotent to reduce. He sang at the concert to an audience as astonished and enchanted as myself, but only on that one occasion, nor did I see him again until the moment of landing at

Liverpool, when I caught a glimpse of a huge and unwieldy object being assisted down the gangway by a small contingent of stewards and deck-hands.   But some forty years later, while conducting a series of concerts in Stockholm, I went to a representation at the Royal Opera, and in one of the intervals walked around the foyer to inspect the memorials to singers of a bygone day.   There in the centre were two statues, one of Jenny Lind and the other of my ship companion, Carl Frederick Lundquist, the greatest baritone voice that ever came out of Sweden.

I got back to school a week or two after the term had begun, and my friends were agog to hear of my adventures.   I think I must have disappointed them more than a little, for I then suffered from a disability which has never wholly left me, the incapacity to talk very much about an event which has made an impression on me until some time after it has happened.   But I had my albums of pictures to show, and these were more convincingly descriptive than any oral accounts that I could have given them.   The winter holidays I passed much the same way as in the year before, crowding into one brief month all I could in the way of opera and concert-going to make up for the slender musical diet of the previous twelve weeks.   Yet it would be hardly just if I were to convey the impression that there was a total dearth of music worth hearing at Rossall. Now and then some artist of minor celebrity would pay us a visit, and in the following year, 1894, we had a really grand festivity, the Jubilee of the school, which included in its programme of entertainment several choral and orchestral works of importance.   For these a large contingent of the Hallé Orchestra was brought from Manchester and I was enrolled as a temporary member in the percussion department. It was also about this time that I began to play the piano at the school concerts, and when in 1896 I became the captain of my house I was permitted to have an instrument of my own in my study.   But as this departure from precedent began and ended with me, I could never ascertain from the guarded comments of my superiors whether it was rated a success or not.   Prompted more by the urgings of one of my form-masters than by any overpowering aesthetic impulse, I let myself in for playing the big drum in a military band.   Rossall was the first school in the country to found a Cadet Corps and to practise all the operations and manœuvres of a miniature army; and my chief recollection of this quasi-patriotic effort was tramping up and down the country on what seemed like endless and fruitless quests, clad in a tight and ill-fitting uniform and burdened with a gigantic object which every five minutes I longed to heave into the nearest ditch.   Probably like most other people I have passed the greater part of my life doing things I have not wanted to do, but I cannot recall any task which ever irked me more than this rash association with the Rossall Cadet Corps.

I took part in nearly all games, but with a well-calculated absence of zeal, as I saw that a fuller absorption in them would rob me of many of the hours I preferred to give to books and music.   This coolness of mine towards the supreme value of athletics was regarded by nearly everyone with mixed feelings.   My prowess at the keyboard was in one way recognized as an asset to school prestige, but that anyone should choose to devote days and weeks to the practice necessary for an adequate rendering of a difficult piano piece when he might be winning life's greatest crown in a football or hockey team was the subject of a fairly general if compassionate disapproval. It was not as if I were wholly without capacity for sport. I was strong, active, and exceptionally quick on my feet, and on those infrequent occasions when I did turn out on the playing-fields displayed an aptitude which perhaps was overestimated because of its unexpectedness. Accordingly it was not until my last year that, influenced a little by mob psychology and rather more by the entreaties of my house-master, I agreed to propitiate the offended deities of the establishment by the sacrifice of some of the precious time I might have spent profitably in other ways. My virtue was rewarded by a place in the school cricket eleven, and it may surprise those who associate artistic temperament with high emotional disturbance to learn that my chief value to the side was a cautious stolidity which, although unproductive of many runs, enabled me to keep my wicket up for hours. It was not very exciting for me, and it must have been definitely unattractive to the spectator, but I found some compensation in observing the exasperation and recklessness produced in the opposition bowling by my defensive tactics. If we fail to find enjoyment in some tedious effort that has been forced upon us, it is always a source of comfort that others involved in it may be suffering even more.

6

OXFORD (1897–98)

THE CLOSING PHASE OF MY SCHOOL LIFE WAS NOT UNLIKE THAT WHICH I had known five years earlier before leaving home. Once more the itch for change began to torment and divert my mind constantly to other places and other pursuits; I had outlasted my time at Rossall and was moving away daily from all that was in its capacity to give me. It was inevitable in those days that to any young person whose main concern was music England could not be expected to compare favourably with the Continent. For there it was that all those semi-legendary figures from Palestrina to Wagner had lived and laboured, and my own country in point of musical prestige was as nothing compared with Italy, Germany, Austria, or even Russia. But unquestionably it was Germany above all which attracted and influenced the youth of my generation. After 1871 it had become the political leader of Europe, its population had increased almost as rapidly as that of the United States, and its commercial expansion was beginning to be a bogey to those who for half a century had been indulging in the dream that Great Britain had been chosen by a kindly Providence to remain for all time the workshop of the world. The numerous travel agencies, the uniformity of currency, and the non-existence of passports made access to every part of the Continent, except Russia, cheap and easy: and I had already seen something of it owing to the rather exceptional circumstances of my home life. My mother had become an almost chronic invalid, my father spent much of his time abroad during my summer holidays, and my only brother was nine years younger than myself. I was allowed therefore to go off, with friends generally, but by myself occasionally, to neighbouring lands such as

France, Belgium, Switzerland, and Scandinavia, where I had the chance of viewing some of those famous cities whose riper culture contrasted pleasingly with that of our own in the North and Midlands.

With few roots in the past and of comparatively mushroom growth, Lancashire had been about the last county in England to be touched by civilization, its history until the beginning of the nineteenth century being almost a blank. Prior to the great Industrial Revolution it had played an inconspicuous part in national affairs, and it would be hard to name more than two or three of its sons who had won celebrity in any line of public activity. Even at the close of the century it presented an oddly mixed picture of modernity and feudalism, a genial equalitarianism in the middle and lower classes being set off by a profound reverence for the old county families. The true Lancastrian delighted to remember that the head of the House of Stanley had once been King in Man and had held his court in the beautiful medieval city of Chester. Having tea one day at the house of a leading lawyer of the district, I noticed a singular object which occupied the central position on the main wall of his library, a small cigarette in a largish frame, and learned that this had been offered to my host during some public celebration by one of the most venerated notabilities of the county. It had been preserved in this way as a choice family heirloom to be handed down to future generations; and if regarded as a manifestation of the higher Toryism I find it even more affecting than that historic exploit, eighty years earlier, of the author of *Waverley*, who, after a banquet in Edinburgh, carried off in his pocket the wineglass from which the Regent had been drinking, and arrived at Abbotsford only to find that during the ride he had sat on and broken it to pieces.

But it was not only upon the musicians among us that Germany exercised a powerful spell. For half a century the reputation of its schools and universities had been spreading far and wide; young Englishmen had started going to Heidelberg and Göttingen instead of to Oxford and Cambridge, and towns like Dresden and Munich contained literally scores of institutions at which our girls scratched the surface of those alien arts and elegancies which guileless parents had been led to believe were vitally essential to the making of the perfect English lady. The study of Italian literature, which had been fashionable in the days of Hazlitt and Peacock, had given way to that of German, and the bolder speculations of Schopenhauer and Nietzsche were ousting from favour the innocuous ruminations of Huxley and Spencer. It is hardly surprising then how compelling for me was the lure of such a land, with its century of opera houses playing the year round, its dozens of symphony orchestras, and an artistic life generally that seemed to exist in like degree nowhere else. There was my goal, and I must reach it somehow or other.

But in my calculations I had reckoned without the rigid conservatism of my environment. My father, outside the conduct of his own business, was a man of pathetic simplicity and uncertain judgment. When any matter arose in connection with his family which demanded careful consideration or firm decision he would call into consultation either his lawyer or the clergyman whose church he attended—more often the latter, who was his most intimate friend. This worthy person was quite aghast at the idea that any member of his congregation should wish to pursue his studies abroad and marshalled all the forces of argument, social, instructional, and religious, against the horrid plan. Of course, I must go to an English university and tread the safe path of orthodoxy: any other course would lead surely and speedily to disaster and damnation. My father, who knew as little of the realities of the case as his spiritual adviser, was impressed and alarmed by the stream of warning poured into his ear, and resolutely set his face against any such dangerous departure. I was given the choice of Oxford or Cambridge, and as some of my closest school friends were going there that term I chose Oxford.

There are three or four ancient spots which in their combination of urban and rural charm are among the greater glories of England, and of these the most wholly delightful is this home of lost causes. It is also one of the half-dozen small cities left unspoiled in the world, where an artist, a philosopher, or a scholar might care to pass his declining days; and I trust that none of my friends in the place will doubt my affection for it if I say that my brief residence there was so much lost time for me. The main trouble was that I could not bring myself to understand why I had been sent there at all. For my father had often intimated how much he looked forward to my succeeding him in our family business, and in that case the scholastic routine of Oxford seemed to provide the least useful preparation thinkable for such a career. Had I been intended for Politics, the Bar, or the Church, with London as my probable base of activity, there might have been social advantages as well as a specific course of training for any of these professions. But my future lay elsewhere, nor did it add to my content that the town musically was a backwater if compared with any of the centres I had visited abroad.

It is not out of place, I feel, to vent here a few casual reflections upon our system of higher education which have been passing through my mind for some years. Three and four centuries ago Englishmen were entering universities at an age when nowadays we should expect to find them still tied to their mothers' apron-strings. There may be pious devotees of modern learning who will fail to be impressed by this admitted precocity, but it is unlikely that any unprejudiced critic can be found anywhere to allege that Tudor or Stuart scholarship was inferior to our own. As I see it, a boy now is sent to some preparatory institution at seven or eight, remains there until he is twelve or thirteen, passes on to a public school, where he continues the self-same curriculum, reaches the University when he is eighteen or so, and gives up three or four years more to a course of study which differs only in minor detail from that of the two earlier periods. Something like fourteen or fifteen years out of a lifetime spent in one unvaried groove of instruction. To my way of thinking, this is excessive, and prompts the feeling that the average Englishman remains in tutelage far too long. Formerly the gifted section of our youth was to the front in political life, dedicated to the task of empire-building in distant lands or writing dramatic masterpieces, at a stage when its descendants have hardly begun to think seriously about such matters. I have frequently wondered why so many of my countrymen carry on even into middle life the appearance as well as the mentality of the schoolboy, an unchanging immaturity which separates them sharply from the males of most other nations, and if the cause of it is not to be traced to the absorption in a monotonous scheme of work and play, which to judge by results must proceed at an incredibly slow rate of progress. It may be that the general decline of genius and talent among our people is due partly to an educational stagnation that has debilitated its intellectual life and fostered that spiritual sterility which for nearly a generation has been slowly creeping over every part of the Empire, and which even the most superficial observer cannot fail to note and lament.

However, if the present system is to be maintained, then surely some of its more obvious limitations and defects could be overcome by the inclusion in the syllabus of a few subjects of real interest, such as, for instance, the female sex.   Whatever differences of view there may exist among foreigners as to the merits or demerits, the virtues or vices of the Englishman, there is general agreement that he knows less about woman and her ways than the masculine creature of nearly every other civilized country.   Several years ago I read in a novel by a Spanish writer whose name I have forgotten a suggestion that every university ought to have at least one "Chair of Amoristics", and I cannot imagine why this admirable idea has been adopted nowhere.   What a heaven-sent boon it would be to both sexes, and how the unhappy effects of an over-indulgence in Hellenic and Hebraical research could be relieved and lightened by the diversion to a topic which, after all, occupies the mind of the ordinary man more than anything else in the world!   George Moore has related how once he passed an idle hour in a club-room scrutinizing about fifty men sitting there in silence, and how he could not fail to recognize by the expression on each face that its owner's thoughts were lingering unmistakably upon the image of a woman.   And yet, while fourteen years are given up to the construction of Latin verses or the examination of Greek roots, all the knowledge about the most important mystery on earth has to be gained by every young person going unaided his or her own sweet way, as if we did not all know what wise old Samuel Johnson had to say long ago in disapproval of self-educated men.   The more I think about the foundation of such a Chair, the more I am taken with the notion.   And what a charming relaxation it would be for those of our elder statesmen, who upon retirement must find time hanging rather heavily on their hands; especially those who, having forfeited the smile of fortune, are obliged to suffer unwilling elevation to the chillier temperature of the Upper House!   How such a change of occupation would have appealed, for instance, to the distinguished author of *The Pathway to Reality*, whom a grateful public, upon the outbreak of the last war, rewarded for his admirable services at the War Office, which included the establishment of our Territorial Army, by clamouring for his removal on the ground that he had spent a portion of his youth at a foreign university.

As I wanted as much spare time as was possible for music, I lived outside my college, Wadham, in Walton Street.   There I could play the piano as much as I liked without over-disturbing my neighbours; and it was about the same time that I began to compose, mostly songs and little pieces.   Indeed, my first term was almost crowded with one activity or another, for I attended faithfully a large number of lectures, appeared at college concerts, and played in its football team, this being perhaps my most surprising achievement, as I had never attained this dizzy height at Rossall.   During the Christmas vacation I went over with a friend to Dresden for a round of opera performances, parties, and dances on the ice, and, looking back over the years, I have no doubt that it was this sympathetic experience which was the initial cause of my backsliding from the virtuous resolution I had formed to make the best of my stay at Oxford. For in the following term my attendances in chapel and classroom grew less, my concentration on music greater, and I was so haunted by memories of the happy time I had spent in Dresden that, hearing of the production of a new opera shortly to be given there, I absented myself for a whole week from the university to go over and see it, a crime of the first magnitude against college discipline and one which, had it been discovered, would have brought about my instant expulsion. A trip to Italy during the spring did nothing to correct this refractory state of mind, and the sight of the cradle of the Latin race, instead of stimulating the keener pursuit of my classical studies, only the more convinced me of the futility of my existence at Oxford. I struggled through the summer term with difficulty, and then begged my father to let me go down and gratify my earlier desire to pass on to some Continental capital, where I could improve my modern languages, equip myself better for a business career, and revel in that fuller musical life which was wanting at home. At first he was not disinclined to listen to me, but once again the shadow of the priesthood crossed my path, my plea was rejected, and I had to resign myself to settling down quietly, anyway for a time, in a provincial district, and comforted only by the hope that something better might one day turn up. By an odd chance it was the frustration of these cherished plans that brought about my introduction to that branch of musical work which years later was to be the substance of my whole career.

Having a good deal of time on my hands, I commenced the formation of an orchestral society in my birthplace, St. Helens, collected all the amateur forces that were available, added the leaven of a solid professional contingent, and burst upon my fellow townsmen with a series of classical concerts. At once I realized that here was the medium of musical expression which I had vainly sought in the piano or any other solo instrument. I bought loads of scores, studied them voraciously, and found to my agreeable surprise that I had little difficulty either in grasping their contents or in committing them to memory. This unexpected discovery that I and the orchestra seemed meant for one another inspired me with a confidence in my capacities which I had not felt before, and without which I could not have ventured so boldly to grasp an opportunity of facing as conductor a large and famous body of musicians which was offered me shortly afterwards. My father, who was Mayor of the town that year, had decided to add to the regular public functions a concert by the Hallé Orchestra and its conductor Hans Richter. Richter had only recently come to Manchester, and his appointment had not been made without considerable opposition from many who wished to see Englishmen holding the few big posts in the country. In those days he enjoyed a commanding prestige which owed more to his personl association with Richard Wagner than to a talent which had decided limitations. A few things he interpreted admirably, a great many more indifferently, and the rest worse than any other conductor of eminence I have ever known. But his readings of Beethoven and Wagner were considered sacrosanct, and from them there was no right of appeal.

For this particular concert there had been chosen a programme

composed mainly of the works of these two masters, and the town and
district hummed with excitement at the coming event.   Almost at the
eleventh hour the devastating intelligence arrived that Richter could not
appear; my father was in despair, his magnificent entertainment seemed
threatened with disaster.   He consulted me as to what was to be done,
and I made the suggestion that I should take the absentee's place.   When
he had recovered from the shock of this audacious proposition he communicated with the authorities at Manchester, who were equally aghast
that a boy hardly twenty years of age, and an amateur at that, should
dare at a moment's notice to step into the shoes of their incomparable
chief.   Fortunately for me, the principal violinist flatly declined to play
at all, insisting that another conductor of experience and reputation should
be engaged; and my father, who until that moment had been in a state of
vacillation, arose in paternal wrath and put him down.   He had now
perhaps begun to realize, being the astutest advertiser of his day, that
what had at first looked like a possible reverse might be worked up to a
definite advantage.   Anyway, he politely informed the recalcitrant leader
that he might go to the devil, that his son was going to conduct and no
one else: and if the Hallé Orchestra did not wish to play, it could stay
away and he would send to London for another.   I went in person to
Manchester and interviewed the business manager of the Society, J. A.
Forsyth, who was polite and neutral about the whole matter, and the
concert took place without any of the hitches expected in most quarters
and hoped for in some.   Many years were to go by before the Hallé
Orchestra and I were to meet again, and it would have required an unusual
gift of prophecy to foretell in that year of 1899 that one day I should be
connected with it for a longer period than with any other in England, save
those of my own creation.

It was difficult to say along what road I should have travelled 'had I
remained longer in Lancashire.   Perhaps I should have settled down
permanently in business or adopted later on some career, political or
diplomatic, that with us has always been regarded as safe and respectable.
One thing, however, is quite certain: never in the minds of either my
familiars or myself was there even the vestige of an idea that one day I
might take up music as a profession.   But before long an event happened
to upset the calculations of everyone.   A serious difference of opinion
between my father and myself led to my leaving his house; I went to
London, and for the next nine years I neither saw nor heard from him.

7

BAYREUTH AND YOUNG GERMANY (1899)

IT WAS DURING THE SUMMER OF THE SAME YEAR THAT I PAID MY FIRST
visit to Bayreuth, and it may be imagined with what excitement I had
been looking forward to this celebration, which inspired as much enthusiasm in the musically devout of the end of the nineteenth century as did a
pilgrimage to some shrine such as that of Thomas à Becket at Canterbury
in the Middle Ages.   I journeyed by slow steps through Bruges, Brussels,

Cologne, Frankfurt, and Nuremberg, suitably preparing my mind for the great experience by a re-study of the music dramas I was to hear under ideal conditions, as well as an extensive dip into German history, folk-lore and lyrical poetry, and after about ten days reached the little Franconian capital on an evening early in August. The town was hot, stuffy and packed, the only accommodation I could secure was inadequate and uncomfortable, and a large number of the visitors seemed to be from my own country. This was an unwelcome surprise, for I had vaguely imagined that I should find myself in the pure atmosphere of an undiluted Teutonism, and the prevailing sound of my own tongue gave the place something of the tone of a holiday resort at home that dulled a little the edge of my expectations. With the splendid snobbery of youth I declined to believe that this accustomed crowd of knickerbockered sportsmen, gaitered bishops, and equine-visaged ladies could have any real affinity with the spirit of the mighty genius who had completed on the stage the task which Walter Scott a century earlier had begun in the novel, the reconstruction of the age of chivalry and romance. I coveted the happiness and applauded the prejudice of the royal Ludwig, and had I been a millionaire would have waited until the close of the Festival and engaged the company to play its programme all over again for the benefit of an audience of one, myself.

There were signs too that Bayreuth was ceasing to be the inviolate shrine of the Wagner cult and that the German public was beginning to lose some of an earlier faith in its artistic integrity. The air was filled with the din of controversy over the policy of Wahnfried as well as the quality of the performances at the Festspielhaus, and the redoubtable Felix Weingartner was to the front with a pamphlet in which he vigorously attacked both. The malcontents quite unambiguously proclaimed the decadence of the Festival, accused Cosima of having handed over the splendid musical machine of her husband as a toy for their son to play with, deplored the engagement of singers who had little knowledge of the true Wagnerian style, as well as conductors whose addiction to slow *tempi* weakened that force and liveliness which Richard had always demanded in the rendering of his music, and, worst of all, clamoured loudly for the removal from the chair of the youthful Siegfried, whose left-handed direction was denounced as feeble and uninspiring. Naturally the Wahnfried circle responded to its critics with the counter-accusations of intrigue and jealousy, and, so far as I could judge, seemed for the moment to be having the better of the argument. The personal prestige of Cosima, a remarkable woman of considerable attraction and indomitable will, still ran high, and if she did not know what Richard's true intentions and wishes had been, then no one did.

My own sympathies veered towards the opposition camp, as the representations I heard were distinctly disappointing. Although I had not seen the *Ring* before, and could not therefore judge where in detail I found them wanting, the singing, playing and stage production all fell below the level I had previsioned. The inevitable crowd of cranks and faddists swelled the ranks of worshippers and the bookshops overflowed with literary curiosities, some of them linking up the music dramas with every recent "ism" in philosophy, politics, science and even hygiene; one bright effort going so far as to allege that *Parsifal* was less of an art work than a piece of propaganda for the higher vegetarianism and not to be comprehended fully unless accepted as such. It was something of a relief to escape from this unidyllic environment into the country for a change of air during a pause in my cycle of performances, and as I had been told of a little Spa, Alexanderbad, some twenty miles out where one went to drink the steel-water springs and take walks in the pine woods all around, I went, and remained there for the rest of my visit, going into Bayreuth only on the days of performance.

There was a fair sprinkling of persons of my own age, but, with the exception of a few Americans of German extraction, no foreigners but myself, and I struck up acquaintance with some students and young naval officers, who manifested the keenest interest in everything English. There was a curious duality of outlook in all of them, a genuine admiration of Great Britain, its institutions and customs, coupled with a firm belief that Germany was destined in the coming years to supersede it as a leader in world affairs. They spoke with an assurance, even a note of fatalism, that made a deep impression upon me and set me wondering whether my conception of the Fatherland as a vast academy given up mainly to higher abstract thought and artistic endeavour was altogether accurate. There was little of that sort of thing in these young men, who, though educated and knowledgeable enough, were severely realistic and practical beyond the imagining of their opposite numbers at home. In the friendliest and most amiable fashion they would discuss with me the coming struggle between our two countries without ever entertaining the slightest doubt as to the result. Every empire has its day, they argued; the previous centuries had seen the rise and decline of Spain, Holland, and France, and England's turn must come. And who was there to fill its place but the wise, noble and gifted nation whose development had been the outstanding event of the nineteenth century? Step by step it had climbed up the ladder of achievement, and now its strength was concentrated and poised for heroic enterprise. I inquired if there was not room enough on the earth for two equally great powers to co-exist side by side in friendly rivalry, but the answer invariably was that there never had been two cocks of the walk of similar ambition who sooner or later could avoid coming to blows. They introduced me to the writings of modern German historians, notably those of von Treitschke, who saw in the new Empire the fulfilment of the dream of the great Hohenstaufen emperors that it was the mission of Germany to rule over a Europe dominated by Teutonic arms and culture.

All this seemed a long way off from the Goethean conception of it as an international home where all branches of knowledge, art, and learning could flourish in peace, and I consoled myself with the reflection that my companions after all were extremely young and might undergo many spiritual and mental changes before the day of reckoning arrived. Their vision was bounded by an horizon purely European, and Western European at that: and not one of them looked to the rapidly growing community across the Atlantic as another potential competitor in the race for world supremacy, or to the possibility of a military resurgence in the East. About the intellectual superiority of their own country over mine they were equally convinced, and, pointing to the much greater number of universities, State-supported theatres, opera houses and other institutions founded and maintained for the higher education of the people, contrasted all this wealth of cultural resource with the comparative poverty of it in England. Here they were on less assailable ground, for I had no answer to the challenge that while we possessed the greatest group of dramatists the world had ever seen, the Empire could not show one theatre given up to the regular representation of its pre-eminent contribution to art.

I had gone to bed early one evening, quite fatigued by a bout of political dialectics which had gone on most of the day, and waking also early the next morning went for a long tramp across the charming and rolling country that lay on every side of the Spa, during which I enjoyed two of the pleasantest coincidences that ever came my way. I had taken with me a small score of the Beethoven Fifth Symphony and the *Fruit, Flowers and Thorn Pieces* of Jean Paul Richter, and, reaching a pretty valley, sat down to read awhile. Suddenly I heard the call of a yellowhammer quite near me, repeated several times and with a short interval between each utterance. Presently it was answered by another from the opposite side of the valley, and this delightful duet went on for several minutes.*

Continuing my walk a mile or two further, I saw in the distance the outline of a small town, and on approaching discovered it to be a choice example of the walled city of medieval days, Wunsiedel, and none other than the birthplace of Jean Paul himself. Nothing on the face of it could be more strikingly at variance than the spirit of the little group I had left behind me in Alexanderbad and that of the sentimental humorist of ninety years earlier: but paradoxically there was a reconciliation between these seeming opposites. For clearly poets and musicians, as well as politicians and philosophers, had all this time been bending their energies to the rediscovery of a national or racial uniqueness in themselves, an aim that was a total reversal of the outlook of the eighteenth century. There is nothing distinctively German in Handel—indeed, he is above all others the accepted internationalist of music—or in Gluck, Mozart, Haydn, or even Beethoven, although in the latter we have some premonitory hints of the great breakaway from the broad European tradition that was to be initiated by Weber and consummated by Schumann.

I have often thought that if we are seeking an insight into one whole side of the Teutonic nature, we can find it more fully revealed than anywhere else in the art of Robert Schumann. According to Nietzsche, he and his contemporaries, including Mendelssohn, were merely an episode or interruption in the orderly flowing tide of German musical history; but while this may be true or not of the others, it is an entire misreading of Schumann's place in it. Far more completely national and unmistakably representative than any before or since is his, the genuine voice in song of his countrymen; and all that is best in the German soul is enshrined here as a witness to the world of what has been and in days to come may be again. Poetry and romance have been acknowledged to be more fully present in this music than in any other, Chopin's and Schubert's excepted.

---

* Everyone is aware that the habitual song of the yellowhammer is identical with the motto theme of the first movement of Beethoven's C Minor Symphony. But it is sometimes varied, and on this occasion the second voice of the duet answered with the last of the four notes of the phrase a third above, instead of below the preceding three.

But it is not these qualities in themselves that constitute its especial character, for all the really great men possess them in larger or smaller measure. It is the individual expression of them which sets Schumann so widely apart from his fellows and which takes the form of an intimate approach that salutes us, not so much as an audience to be conquered by rhetorical argument as a friend to be talked over by gentle persuasion. Queen Victoria used to complain that Mr. Gladstone would insist on addressing her as if she were a public meeting, and we are affected, though not disagreeably, in the same way when we listen to other composers. But it is a ceremony, sometimes a very formal one, and during its performance we are seldom forgetful that its author is addressing himself to a thousand or two others besides ourselves. There is none of this platform manner about Schumann, who has accomplished the miraculous feat of clothing exquisite and delicate fancies in subtle and secret phrases that each one of us feels to have been devised for his own particular understanding. To meet this ingratiating simplicity and confidential intimacy in an artistically sophisticated community is the rarest of phenomena. They are to be found almost exclusively in culture's more primitive stages, and typical instances are the earlier Gothic sculpture and the ballad poetry of all nations (notably that of Scotland), of which a lingering echo can be heard in the more local verse of Robert Burns. The sentiment that inspired them was nourished by the fireside rather than in the market-place, and was the most valued possession of that older Germany, land of toys and the Christmas tree, for whose people, perhaps more than any other, home was the centre of the world. But it was already evident to me that to regard this facet of German inner life as illustrative of the whole people at the close of the century was just another youthful illusion, which I had better discard at once; and fortifying myself by a fresh glance into the soothing wisdom of Jean Paul, I returned to Alexanderbad for breakfast and another prolonged debate with my companions on the future of the young empire.

The austerity of purely masculine society was tempered by the presence of two charming American girls whose forebears had come originally from the vicinity, and as their conversational acquaintance with the language was hardly better than mine, we made a little group of our own, to which we joined a young naval lieutenant who spoke English admirably. We played games, took walks, dined together, and made music afterwards in one of the large sitting-rooms of the hotel. One evening in the middle of a lively talk punctuated with a good deal of noisy laughter a diminutive baron who had been sitting with his massive wife on a sofa at the opposite end of the room jumped up suddenly, rushed forward, and shaking his fist furiously in the face of one of the girls, treated us to a violent harangue of which I could hardly follow a word. The lieutenant, who seemed highly amused, informed us that we were being accused of having spoken slightingly of the lady during one of our hilarious moments, and I hastened to assure the irate husband that not only had we not mentioned her name, but up to that moment had been unaware of her existence. This, however, he appeared to take as a fresh insult, for he stormed away all the more vigorously, and I was at last obliged to request our friend to tell him that if he did not cease at once and return to his seat I should be under the disagreeable necessity of

conducting him to it against his will.   This intimation of belligerent action,
if necessary, produced the desired effect, for he drew himself up with
immense dignity, turned right about face and strutted away in the direction of the door, his baroness well behind him in true German fashion.
Naturally the girls were rather upset by this untoward event and
retired earlier than usual, while the lieutenant and I stayed up to consider
what ought to be done next, it being finally decided that he should seek
out the enemy in the morning, explain to him the enormity of his offence,
and demand an apology.   That night I was haunted by dreams of a
sanguinary encounter carried on in the best Heidelbergian style, and for
the first time felt that there might be something after all in the much-
discussed project of a universal language, which should be made obligatory
upon the whole civilized world for the avoidance of needless misunder-
standings.   But evidently the baron had had time to think again over
the matter, for upon the visit of my emissary he professed willingness to
be convinced that his wife might have been in error and had not been the
inspiration of some of our cachinnatory outbursts.   This little unpleasant-
ness removed, we all got together, celebrated our reconciliation, and
remained on the best of terms during the remainder of my stay.

The series of performances at the Festspielhaus coming to an end, I
started on my homeward journey, loitering for a few days at Nuremberg
to better my acquaintance with the churches and other buildings I had so
much admired when first passing through.   I had intended to spend a little
time at Munich and Strasbourg and go on from there to Paris, but finding
that my funds had almost melted away through an indulgence in hospitality at the Spa much larger than I had anticipated, I abandoned this
part of my tour and returned by the way I had come.

By one of those contrarieties or perversities of human nature which
may really be natural and normal if we only understood them better,
I was less interested during my Bayreuth visit in the music of Wagner,
with which I was abundantly familiar, than in that of Brahms, which
was almost unknown to me.   Whether this was owing to a recoil from
the unnatural atmosphere of a place where idolatry and eccentricity were
so blatantly ubiquitous, or nothing more than the simple attraction of a
musical style wholly unlike the one which had been filling my ears for
weeks past, I do not know.   But upon my retirement to Alexanderbad I
took with me a large bundle of the Hamburg master's work, and devoted
most of my spare time to the study of it.   I formed then the opinion which
I have since been unable to vary: that Brahms was essentially a romantic
composer, as far removed as is conceivable from the true classical spirit
and generally at his best in smaller forms.

8

LONDON IN 1900

MY FIRST FEELING ON ARRIVING IN LONDON WAS ONE OF RELIEF AT HAVING
escaped from a condition of living which was becoming each day less
sympathetic to me.   My duties in our smooth-running and highly

organized business had been of the lightest, and the opportunities for serious work in other directions altogether limited. I was expected to fit in with and settle down to a routine through which the current of life flowed lazily and insignificantly, when I felt the growing need of getting to grips with something more arduous and absorbing. Thanks to an earlier knowledge of the larger world outside, I had reached a maturity beyond that of most of my generation, and what I wanted was some exacting and whole-time task to which I could devote a constantly increasing energy which had not yet found the right outlet for its full exercise.

Just as it is hard for those who have lived in comfortable circumstances to accept a lower standard of living when it is suddenly thrust upon them, so is it, in most cases, no easy problem for a young man who is without preparation for a specific career to decide what he can best do if thrown back largely on his own resources. But in mine no difficulty of choice was present, for I had one definite accomplishment at least—music—and that it had to be in one form or another. For many years I had worked in a general way, and with fair zeal, at the piano, a few other instruments, and the various arts of composition. I had read dozens of text books, histories and biographies, and knew backwards the *Grand Traité* of Berlioz. It was time to gather up all these loose threads and bind them together in a solid bundle of efficiency.

In public accounts of my career has frequently appeared the assertion that I am almost entirely self-taught and, beginning as a rank amateur, have attained a professional status with some difficulty after a long and painful novitiate. Nothing could be more remote from the truth. It is possible that at the age of twenty I might have failed to answer some of the questions in an examination paper set for boys of sixteen in a musical academy; but probably I should fail with equal success today, and I venture to say that a tolerable number of my most gifted colleagues would do no better. On the other hand, owing to my travels abroad and wider associations with musicians here and there, my miscellaneous fund of information was much more extensive than that of bthers of my age.

But even in childhood I had been taught those rudiments of the art which still go by the nonsensical name of theory, and at school I worked regularly with a master who was a man of excellent taste and scholarship. At Oxford I continued the same line of study with John Varley Roberts, the organist of Magdalen, who scanned and criticized all my earliest essays in composition. Varley Roberts, who was then getting on in years, was a bluff outspoken Yorkshireman of the old school, simple, thorough, and imbued with the belief that nothing of much consequence had happened to music since the death of Beethoven. A true son of his native county, he was a first-rate choral trainer, and his choir at Magdalen, the best in Oxford, equalled in reputation that of King's College Chapel at Cambridge. For all so-called voice producers and their contending views on how or how not to sing he had a healthy and old-fashioned contempt which he delighted to air on every suitable and unsuitable occasion. There coincided with the period of my residence a mild wave of interest in a subject which in most quarters is as much of a fixed science as table-rapping, and during one term we had a convocation of eminent authorities from all over the country for the exchange of ideas. At the various meetings where lectures were delivered and treatises read, Varley Roberts was regularly present, together with a large contingent of his choir-boys; and when the proceedings were terminated and the participants had departed whence they came, he called his flock together and addressed them in this refreshing style: "Now, lads, you have heard a great deal about the voice in the last few days, but I've got just this to say to you and don't you forget it. All you've got to do is to stand up, throw your heads back and sing; all the rest's humbug."

During the year I spent in Lancashire I was introduced by Steudner Welsing, my piano master, to a young professor of composition at the Liverpool School of Music, Frederic Austin, who as time went on developed into one of the most versatile and accomplished musicians of the day. With him I further pursued the straight path of knowledge to my distinct advantage, but more on the aesthetic than on the technical side. For this was my first encounter with a wholly modern and up-to-date type of musical mind, adventurous, impressionable, and yet coolly analytical and tolerant. The brief association I enjoyed with him had the beneficial result of sweeping out of my mind the lingering cobweb traces of the rigid scholasticism to which I had bowed grudgingly at Oxford, so that by the time I left for the South I was culturally emancipated enough to be able to accept or reject whatever came to me with greater self-confidence. At the same time, to make sure that there should be no gaps in my armour of instruction, I went to see Sir Charles Villiers Stanford and, laying my case before him, asked if he would take me as a private pupil. He explained that he had little time for such work outside the College of Music, and passed me on to his chief assistant, Charles Wood, with some of whose compositions I was already acquainted.

During the previous year an enterprising and audacious scheme had been launched at New Brighton, a popular resort a few miles from Liverpool on the other side of the Mersey, where an orchestra of about sixty players, under Granville Bantock, gave weekly concerts with the programme of each given up to the work of a single British composer. There it was that I heard the music of all those men who were then looked upon as the leaders of the English musical renaissance—Parry, MacKenzie, Stanford, Corder, Wood, Wallace, and Bantock himself. There was a good deal of genuine interest in and enthusiasm for this prolific native movement, and in certain circles and journals nearly everything produced by it was hailed as a masterpiece. Now and then I come across cantatas or oratorios on the back pages of which are Press notices of some piece written during the last quarter of the century, and I have to rub my eyes twice before I can credit what I am reading. All our geese were swans, no longer need we suffer from any complex of inferiority, we had caught up with our neighbours of Italy and Germany, and the future of the art was in our hands. The names of Brahms and Parry were coupled together in a fashion that suggested an equality of achievement in the two men, and any adverse criticism from abroad was dismissed derisively as prejudice or jealousy. In short, a cheerful wave of musical chauvinism was sweeping over the land, and all of us to a greater or lesser degree were borne along upon it.

With Charles Wood I worked steadily and industriously for over two years, submitting to him every imaginable kind of exercise, fugues, choral pieces accompanied and unaccompanied, orchestral fragments, one grand opera (of which I myself wrote the libretto), and another in a lighter vein. The manuscripts of these early efforts disappeared years ago, and I have offered up many a prayer that they remain eternally missing. The declining days of Grieg were saddened by the remembrance of a string quartet written in extreme youth which too had been lost, and the haunting dread that it might be discovered and published after his death by some injudicious busybody was the one dark shadow in a happy and contented life.

I sometimes wonder if the present generation can possibly realize how different is the world it is inhabiting and accepting as a matter of course from that of fifty years ago. Gibbon in the *Decline and Fall* has reminded us that in his time, the latter half of the eighteenth century, the transport facilities from Rome to London had remained unchanged since the days of the Emperor Hadrian, and modern historians have had their say about the striking transformations wrought everywhere by the discovery of steam at the beginning of the nineteenth. But the inventions which crowded upon us at its close are perhaps too near to be appraised as justly, and we have yet to learn whether some of them are to be regarded as blessings or curses. The society in which I was brought up knew nothing of the telephone, the motor-car, the gramophone, the aeroplane, the submarine, the radio, or even modern journalism. In the London of 1900, horse-drawn buses and hansom cabs still provided the chief means of getting about, supplemented by a semi-underground railway that was a veritable portent of dirt and gloom. But apart from little inconveniences like these life for some of us was unquestionably more spacious and agreeable. The sense of security was universal, and no man in his senses doubted for a moment that the British Empire, which was then about one hundred and fifty years old, was destined to remain just where it stood for another thousand or two at least. The National Debt was small, the income tax was negligible, a golden sovereign purchased twice as much as did its paper equivalent twenty years later, and most important of all, Parliament sat for only half the year, thus enabling the executive part of the Government to get on with its duties quickly and efficiently. The Diamond Jubilee of Queen Victoria in 1897 seemed to British people everywhere to be not only the close of one great imperialistic era but the beginning of another that was to be still more glorious; and even the disquieting revelations of Mr. Rowntree of the deplorable conditions in which about one-third of our population actually existed failed to wound the national pride or disturb its tranquil complacency.

Only a few minds of a more inquiring turn scanned the future with a tinge of anxiety and recalled the prophecy of a great philosopher that we were drawing near to that era of war on a scale that future generations would look back upon with wonder and admiration. One of the most outspoken of such uncomfortable fellows (for so they were regarded) with whom I came in touch was Sidney Whitman, the historian of the House of Habsburg,* who, knowing his Europe through and through, was under no illusion about the purpose to which the colossal military forces being trained in nearly every land would ultimately be devoted. I had met Whitman at a house where I was playing the piano, and as he had

---

* His best-known work is *Austria*.

professed interest not only in my performance but my share of a brief conversation we had had on foreign affairs, I followed this up by calling on him with some articles I had been writing on various musical subjects and upon which I was anxious to have his opinion.   As I was tolerably well pleased with them myself, I was rather chagrined to be told that they were on the whole windy rubbish, that my style was painfully ornate and high-flown, that I must be suffering from a lengthy period of over-feeding at the tables of the nineteenth-century romantic writers, that what I needed most was a complete change of diet, and that many of the paragraphs which sought to deal with the mere technical problems of my art might have been interpolated without incongruity into a novel by Disraeli. But my literary excesses might be cured, or at any rate eased, by a solid course of eighteenth-century prose-reading, and if at any time I still found myself hankering unwholesomely after the picturesque, there were the Jacobean dramatists to show me how it ought to be done.   Of the great contemporaries and successors of Shakespeare I knew comparatively little, as neither in my home nor school had they any licensed place in the libraries. But shortly afterwards I was enabled to remedy this state of deplorable ignorance through the lucky chance of an invitation to spend a few weeks in the Portuguese home of Sir Francis Cook.

Montserrat, a few miles from Cintra, once the home of Beckford, author of *Vathek*, and noted by Byron in the first canto of his *Childe Harold*,* is a splendid palace whose gardens are world-renowned for containing almost every tree, shrub and plant known to botany.   But the chief attraction of the place to me was a large and first-rate library where I found everything of the periods that I had been advised to study and first made acquaintance with that noble company whose work, according to Swinburne, makes every other period of English literature seem half alive.   During my stay I must have read scores of volumes beginning with Marlowe and continuing to Shirley, and if I had a preference at the moment it was probably for Beaumont and Fletcher, and more particularly those plays in the joint collection which through their unity of style are manifestly the work of the latter.   There are few better antidotes for a stubborn mood of melancholy than an escape into the radiant world of this brilliant and neglected genius whom the second of our great poet-critics with intent to rebuke once styled the English Euripides.   And whenever I renew my acquaintance with the easy flow of his nervously animated verse and the perfect music of his lyrical numbers, I recall the judgment of Dryden that it was in the twin "bards of passion and of mirth" that our language reached its summit of perfection.

---

* *Childe Harold*, Canto I, Stanza XXII:
        "There thou too Vathek! England's wealthiest son,
        Once formed thy Paradise. . . ."

The stanza No. XIX containing a description of the scenery around Montserrat is among the half-dozen best in the First Canto:
        "The horrid crags by toppling convent crowned,
        The cork trees hoar that clothe the shaggy steep,
        The mountain-moss by scorching skies imbrowned,
        The sunken glen, whose sunless shrubs must weep,
        The tender azure of the unruffled deep,
        The orange tints that gild the greenest bough,
        The torrents that from cliff to valley leap,
        The vine on high, the willow branch below,
        Mixed in one mighty scene, with varied beauty glow."

Unaccountably brief in the history of every nation is the lastingness of any achievement of supreme merit in one especial domain of Art; and in none is this more strikingly exemplified than in that of poetic drama. Athens, England, Spain, France and Germany have all conformed to some high and inscrutable decree that no human power can control or resist. A short sixty years saw the birth, growth, and decline of the English cycle of greatness, and hardly more that of the Greek; while the duration of each of the others is even less, although France might be said to have had the semblance of a silver age in the nineteenth century. Like certain freak performances of nature, they appear seemingly from nowhere, breathe out their short-dated lives, and vanish to return no more.

There are some who, having dwelt awhile on high mountain tops, like to make their descent by gradual stages so that the contrast may not be too sharp between the air which they are leaving behind and that on the plains below. In similar fashion I avoided a too rapid plunge from the poet altitude of 1600 to the prosaic flatland of 1700 by stopping at the half-way house of the heroic drama of Davenant and Dryden, which like most transition phases is more singular than satisfactory. I had little regret therefore on reaching a solid earthy level where men no longer toiled vainly to bend the bow of Ulysses and were resignedly content to entrust their fancies to a prose as perfect as the verse of the great age. But it is less the change in the medium of communication between author and public which had been slowly taking place over fifty years that is so impressive as the transformation of outlook over the whole kingdom of letters. The masters of the Elizabethan and Jacobean era were still good Europeans, true heirs of the Renaissance, and each one of them (paraphrasing Ancient Pistol) might have said, "The world's mine oyster which I with my pen will open." They traversed with colossal strides the surface of all lands, drawing material as well as inspiration from every quarter to which their insatiable curiosity led them, and were in the fullest sense of the word—universal.

With the dawn of the eighteenth century we are made profoundly conscious that the literary mind of England has contracted to a bounded nationalism, that the Reformation has now fully accomplished its task, and that our small island is no longer a part of Europe. Henceforth the whole country is to become and remain for the best part of one hundred years a vast parish, and, with small concern for what is going on outside its borders, is to find happiness in cultivating no garden but its own, and in exploring no delights other than those of England, home, and beauty. It is owing to this splendid parochialism that the eighteenth century is the most truly English of all in our history and that its literature attains a genuinely classical perfection denied to that of more than one period of incontestably loftier aim.

Most of the other acquaintances I made during my first year in London happened to be of an ultra-radical, socialistic, and anti-imperialistic colour, little Englanders to a man. This was in its way another fresh world to me, and for a while I was attracted by the writings of Blatchford, Kropotkin, Bland, and other leaders of the school. It was through my association with an elderly harpmaker, George Morley, a man of considerable culture with whom I played chess and billiards, that I began to frequent the meetings of the Fabian Society, where lecturers would expound to us the full gospel of the new creed.   One evening there was an address on Shelley, and the speaker, while professing great admiration for his genius, deplored that the poet, as the son of a Sussex squire, had been born to the evil enjoyment of unearned increment; for in the kingdom of heaven on earth that was at hand there would be no room for men of such breed.   That evening on my return home I reviewed in my mind the many distinguished names in letters (going back no further than Chaucer) who, had they been born after the establishment of this arid social system, would never have been allowed to write at all.   Gathering together all the Society's books, pamphlets, and leaflets, I hurled them into the fire; and as I watched the pile burning away merrily I remembered how Voltaire had once said that while a philosopher had the right to investigate everything once, there were some things that only a fool would wish to experience twice.

9

FIRST OPERA COMPANY (1902)

IT WAS ABOUT THE BEGINNING OF MY THIRD YEAR IN LONDON THAT ONE day I heard of a new opera company which was about to go on tour in the suburbs, with a cast of artists nearly all well known to me.   I resolved to try my luck with the management, and with a full score under my arm marched down to its offices, where I found a score of other persons in waiting.   Hours went by and I was beginning to think I should never obtain even a glimpse of authority, when suddenly the attention of us all was drawn to signs of what was unmistakably some sort of a scene going on in the inner room, accompanied by a very ineffective improvisation on a piano conspicuously out of tune.   Presently the door was flung open and a portly choleric individual appeared and called out: "Is there anyone here who can play the piano?"   Several of those present at once answered in the affirmative.   "But do any of you know *Faust* without the music?" continued the apparition, and to this there was no reply.   It dawned upon me that here might be an opportunity of penetrating the stronghold; so I meekly raised my voice and said: "I think I know the opera."

"What part of it?" sternly demanded my questioner.

"Any part of it."   Gazing at me incredulously, he said, "Come in," and in I went.

It appeared that a singer who had been sent there with a recommendation for the part of Marguerite had neglected to bring a copy of the piece with her, and this oversight had kindled the official wrath.   I played through those portions which were required for the trial, and was about to take my leave, when the now partly pacified impresario said, "Wait a bit. I want a word with you—besides, there may be others out there who have forgotten their music"; and so it proved to be.   After the singers had left he enquired: "Why did you come here?"

"I have an opera with me which I hoped you might hear with a view to performance," said I.

"Good God, what an idea!" said he.   His astonishment seemed so profound that I hardly knew how to continue the conversation, and was thinking of a fresh opening, when he went on, "How many of the pieces I am giving do you know?"—handing me at the same time a prospectus of his season. I looked at it, informed him that I was familiar with all of them, and he asked me if I had ever conducted. I told him exactly what I had done, and he suggested that I try my hand at opera. Naturally I jumped at the idea, still nourishing the hope that it might lead to the production of one of my works. As it was now about lunch-time, he invited me to come back in the afternoon and talk it over, and when I returned I found him quite alone. He explained that he had given orders that no one should be admitted as he wanted to have a little private singing, declaring himself to be the possessor of the finest tenor voice in England. I was made to sit at the piano and accompany him for the rest of the day in long extracts from operas that contained his favourite roles, and every time there was a brief pause he asked for my opinion as to his performance. Naturally I allowed my enthusiasm to grow with each effort, and the result was that before I left I had been offered and had accepted the post of one of the two conductors of the new company, with instructions to start at once on the rehearsals which were taking place at the "Old Vic".

The tour lasted about two months; we visited such outlying places as Clapham, Brixton, and Stratford, and I enjoyed myself hugely, conducting in addition to *Carmen* and *Pagliacci* that trilogy of popular Saturday-nighters dubbed facetiously "The English Ring"—*The Bohemian Girl, Maritana,* and *The Lily of Killarney.* But all the fun and excitement I extracted from the experience (that inveterate old joker, G. H. Snazelle, who was playing Devilshoof, succeeded in setting fire to the stage as a farewell gesture on the last night) could not blind my soberer perceptions to the truth that if there was one especial way in which opera should not be given, then here it was in all its rounded perfection. Some of the singers, of course, were excellent, and I have never heard Marie Duma's rendering of Leonora in *Il Trovatore* bettered anywhere in the world for tone quality, phrasing and insight into the true character of the role. But of attempt, even the slightest, at production there was none, and both scenery and dresses were atrocious. Some of the principals brought their own costumes along, but the detached spectacle of one or two brilliantly clad figures only threw into more dismal relief the larger mass of squalor in the background. The chorus, which was composed mainly of veterans of both the sexes, was accurate but toneless, and the orchestra quite the most incompetent I have known anywhere. I could not help comparing the wretched conditions under which great works of art were being presented to the public with the care, preparation and even luxury bestowed upon any of the half-dozen musical comedies or farces then running in the West End. Sometimes I would feel a touch of astonishment that we had an audience at all for the motley kind of entertainment we were offering, and at others an uncomfortable twinge of conscience, as if I were an accomplice in some rather discreditable racket, which among a community more critical and knowledgeable would have provoked an instant breach of the peace.

The inferiority of the orchestral performance would be an impossibility today in England, so incontestably higher is the general level of playing. But at that time, outside the few great orchestras such as the Covent

Garden Opera, the Queen's Hall or the Hallé of Manchester, where at least
the technical accomplishment was first rate, the average player was
hardly equipped to tackle any music except that of a simple and straightforward kind.   The musical culture of the country had for generations
been almost entirely choral, and the instrumental side had been relegated
to an obscure background from which it was only just beginning to emerge.
Sir Edward Elgar has told us how during the earlier days of his career he
once conducted a country town orchestra and overheard an elderly fiddler,
who was timidly attempting a rather high passage, murmur to his desk
colleague, "You know, this is the first time I have been up here."   But
already there were signs of a new and different spirit abroad which during
the next few years was to yield gratifying results, chiefly owing to the
wisdom of the colleges of music in creating student orchestras where
young instrumentalists could be familiarized at an early age with a substantial portion of the classical repertoire.   Gradually the old and slightly
tatterdemalion world of orchestral playing was rejuvenated by the invasion of a new type of player, who had not only a better knowledge of
his instrument but a wider fund of general instruction.

None the less, I have always considered that this rather uninviting
initiation into professional life was of the greatest service to me.   To be
pitchforked into such a chaotic welter and be forced to make something
tangible and workable out of it is incomparably more useful to the young
conductor than to take command of a highly trained body of experts,
accustomed through long routine to fulfil their respective tasks with ease
and celerity.   Indeed, the youthful or comparatively youthful musician
should not be allowed, except on some rare occasion, to conduct an orchestra of the front rank at all; and if he does I am not sure which of the two
parties to the transaction suffers the more from it.   It is almost impossible
that he can teach it anything, and it is more than likely that its accustomed discipline will speedily relax under a leadership that has neither
experience nor authority.   Further, the unhappy young man will have to
decide between the alternatives of assuming an air of omniscience as
comical as a child preaching in a cathedral pulpit, or an abnegation of any
effort at real direction; either of which will be equally acceptable to that
collection of humorists who make up the personnel of nearly every first-
class orchestra of the world.   For there is no other company of human
beings engaged in a communal task that can match it for instant and
accurate valuation of competence or incompetence, be it in a conductor,
singer, pianist or any other executant whose craft has been daily under its
argus eye year in and year out.   Be it in the opera house or the concert
room, I would in nineteen cases out of twenty abide by the verdict or
accept the opinion of a great orchestra far more confidently than I would
that of either the Press or the public.

It is only fair to an institution in which I have so many good friends to
explain a little this passing allusion to the Press.   There are, in every
country where music is seriously cultivated, a few really remarkable men
of keen sensibility, wide learning, and brilliant intellect whose writings
are a delight and stimulation to all those who read them.   Any one of
these is in himself as much of a force as a great virtuoso or combination of
instrumentalists.   But even the most highly gifted intelligence does not
always remain unaffected by the long and continued prod of subtle and

intangible influences that emanate from every point of contact in a large musical circle, and it is only too obvious that during the last twenty years criticism generally has concentrated more and more on the material values of music and less on the spiritual. In other words, it has been and still is concerning itself almost exclusively with that which it calls technique, with little regard for anything else. In so doing it has mistaken the means for the end, the essential for the quintessential; and the result is that we have a standardized technique in every branch of the art, before which all have agreed to bow, save one dissenting group, the really musical. For we have reached a stage where we are confronted with the paradoxical situation that, while never before have there been so many musicians who are credited with impeccable mechanical excellence, there have also never been so many dull and uninspiring interpreters.

What has been forgotten is that technique is not an independent entity separate from the music itself. If someone plays Mozart or Schubert to me in a way I dislike, it is meaningless and irrelevant if an apologetic friend assures me that he is quite competent in Liszt. And if I reply that his technique is not equal to the task of interpreting satisfactorily the two other masters, my criticism is regarded as either a libel or an insult. I therefore have to explain that my idea of technique includes a good deal more than playing mere notes accurately or even brilliantly. There is, for example, the choice of tone for a particular piece and the creation of a definite mood or atmosphere through the calculated control of a fixed range of dynamics. Are these important branches of the art of the keyboard to be considered as coming under the head of technique? If not, then under what other? For without a mastery of them no execution has for me the slightest interest or value. And it is precisely the want of the capacity to do these things that makes in my estimation the mere sounds produced by many public performers so superficially musical as to give the minimum of pleasure. Again, accuracy, although excellent in itself, is not the only thing which is essential. The great Rubinstein was not always accurate, he made mistakes; yet no one in those days suggested that he had a faulty technique. But in our present year of grace he would certainly have been severely admonished for a simple little slip and perhaps told to go away and practise before he ventured on another public appearance.

Some years ago I took my own orchestra, which already knew the work sufficiently well, through a series of sectional rehearsals of the *Ring*. Every department, even double basses, had to go over each phrase with care and attention. As all the players were of recognized accomplishment, the performance was of a clarity, sonority and accuracy that I have never heard equalled anywhere, save for a single break on the trumpet in a passage that unfortunately is familiar to every amateur in the world. This little misadventure, which the same player would probably not repeat in fifty years, filled the bulk of the critical Press with an unholy joy. Nothing else in the rest of the representation seemed to have the smallest interest for them, and there was hardly a word of appreciation for the remainder of a four-hour spell of flawless playing. No; they had discovered a spot on the sun which their noctalyptic vision had so magnified as to make them doubt whether the latter was really there at all. And so I venture the modest opinion that the worship of the so-called impeccable execution has been a little overdone and that it is time that some measure of attention be given to the spirit and character of the music itself. After all, there is nothing easier to achieve than dead accuracy if one really sets about it. For there does exist one branch of work where it is of more importance than anything else—the making of records for the gramophone. Here the purely intellectual and technical elements take precedence over the emotional, owing to the cardinal necessity of securing a perfect balance adjustable to the peculiarities and limitations of the microphone and the disc. Here no one, conductor, pianist or violinist, can let himself go for a single moment. Every bar is the bondservant of a tyrant to whom the correct playing of each note, a flawless pitch, and a discreet scheme of dynamics are the supreme considerations. In a public performance there are moments when a conductor is impelled to make exceptional demands upon his players for the full realization of the grandeur and eloquence inherent in the work he is striving to interpret; and sometimes vaulting ambition overleaps itself and tests to straining-point the limits of that unsleeping control which the true Apollonian spirit maintains should never be violated. It is without doubt a fault, but surely one more excusable than a persistent discretion which never takes a risk or soars above the middle height of adventure.

But returning to my first encounter with opera, the most valuable lesson I learned was, that while all the music which sounded right and effective in the theatre had a character or quality possessed by none other, it failed to make anything like the same appeal when heard outside it. To apply the term "dramatic" and to be content with such a definition would be inadequate and misleading. The symphonic work of Beethoven more than that of any other composer is essentially dramatic, and if anyone be doubtful on the point, he need only listen to it after a course of Mendelssohn, Schumann, or Dvořák, all of whom wrote quite good symphonies in their way. Yet Beethoven's theatre music is not one quarter as vital and telling as that of Mozart. The Fifth and Sixth Symphonies (particularly the latter) of Tchaikovsky have a distinctly dramatic quality, but of all the Russian composers he is the least successful in opera. What is this intangible element in the music itself which must be half the battle already won for any piece that has to dominate the stage? And how many works do we not know which are admirably constructed and have both capital stories and excellent music, but which fail to hold the public attention really interested and absorbed? It is not easy to answer this question; but it may be a highly developed inner visual sense in the consciousness of supremely gifted writers for the theatre like Mozart, Verdi, Wagner, and Puccini, that sees as in an ever-present mirror the progress of the drama running through every phrase, word, and action, and simultaneously evolves the right sort of music to go along with it. But whatever is its nature, there is no doubt about its existence, and the realization of it was to me at the time important enough to send me back to a reperusal of the operatic efforts of my countrymen, who so far had failed to produce a single work that could hold its own with even the dozens of second-rate pieces turned out by the composers of France or Italy.

It could not be owing to any inherent incapacity for the theatre in our people, who during a period of several hundred years had been giving to the world one of the few great schools of drama known to civilization; but it might conceivably be traced to the predilection among our musicians themselves for those foreign masters like Bach, Beethoven, Mendelssohn, and Brahms, who are a complete antithesis to all that has to do with the essential spirit of it. As I have already indicated, German influence was everywhere omnipotent, while at the same time it was overlooked that the Germans were not really a theatrically gifted people. Their dramatic literature could not compare with that of several other great European nations, and even in the field of opera their composers, outside Weber and Wagner, had produced very little of genuine originality. It therefore seemed to me that until our musicians realized all this more clearly, turned their backs on their Teutonic models, generated a more wholesome respect for the composers of other countries, and (more important than all else) began like the Russians to cultivate a style and idiom of their own, they had better return to the safer and easier task of writing oratorios and cantatas for the thousands of choral societies up and down the kingdom, just as their forefathers had been peacefully and ineffectively doing for the past two hundred years.

10

A FOREIGN INTERLUDE (1904)

MY COLLEAGUE IN THE CONDUCTOR'S CHAIR OF THE OPERA COMPANY WAS an Italian, Emilio Pizzi, an excellent musician who for a few years back had obtained a fair success with a short opera produced by some courageous *entrepreneur* in the West End. He was a friend of the celebrated librettist, Luigi Illica, part author of the "books" of *La Bohème* and *Tosca*, collaborator with nearly all the composers of modern Italy, and an old admirer of English literature. Pizzi suggested that if I were contemplating another opera it might be a good idea to ask this past master of the craft for a suitable libretto. Possibly he had something already sketched out that might do, for, being a man of fiery energy, he never sat and waited until a fresh commission came along, but always had half a dozen subjects on the stocks, to be completed when the call was sounded. We communicated with Illica, who replied that he was sure he had the very thing I was looking for: a three-act tragedy on the life of Christopher Marlowe. Nothing could have happened more pat to my mood, for I had just finished rereading all the plays of the founder of the Elizabethan drama, of whom a contemporary wrote, "His raptures were all fire and air", and I was deeply under the spell of their rhetorical magnificence. At the same time I could discover nothing in the life of Marlowe himself of the slightest romantic interest, and I surmised that the Italian poet proposed to draw largely upon his own imagination in framing the plot of a fairly long lyric drama. And so it turned out to be: a very charming and creditable effort with about one-quarter fact and the rest pure fiction.

Although he was able to let me have at once an outline of its scenes and episodes, Illica could not settle down for a little while to work on the text itself, as all his available time had to be given up to Puccini and their new opera *Madama Butterfly*, which was to be produced the following year. Too much absorbed in the prospect of my coming task to take on any other effort of composition, and yet unwilling to remain musically idle during the period of waiting, I set out to find some fresh job of conducting, but without success. There seemed to be no opportunities anywhere, and I was soon forced to the conclusion that if I wanted to continue before the public in this capacity, the only thing to do was to hire an orchestra and give concerts on my own account, at the moment an enterprise quite beyond my means. I next considered the formation of a choral society for the performance mainly of Tudor music, of which I had made a special study while working with Charles Wood, and although this project did materialize eventually, it was through the initiative of another than myself. One evening, at the house of my friend the harpmaker, I met a young man who had not long been back in London from Paris, Vincent d'Indy and the Schola Cantorum. He too was full of the subject of ancient choral music and thought it might be fun to collect about a dozen persons together, sit round a table and sing it for our own amusement. This we did, but in a very casual fashion, and a few months later my new friend, Charles Kennedy Scott, proposed that our little group be increased to a size large enough for public concert appearance. The reconstituted body was christened the Oriana Madrigal Society, and under Scott's masterly direction acquired during the next few years a technical skill, an eloquence of expression and an insight into the music it was called upon to interpret that placed it an easy first among the small choirs of the kingdom.

Not long afterwards I came into possession of a moderate-sized estate, the gift of my grandfather, which enabled me to reconsider my plans for the future. But before committing myself to any definite line of action, I decided first to go for a lengthy stay on the Continent which might stimulate my ideas and broaden my outlook. I had been working pretty hard in London for over three years along a single track, and I should be all the better for a renewal of acquaintance with those great musical centres, in one of which during my Lancashire days I had wanted so much to make my second home. More particularly I felt the need of enlarging my knowledge of orchestration, something which Charles Wood had always told me could be taught only by a master hand. I made my way to Paris, and sought the advice of Messager, who sent me on to Moskowski. The latter was at the outset somewhat at a loss to know what to do with me and insisted that I already had as much proficiency as the average musician of my years. But that was not good enough for my ambition, and our argument ended by my inventing a system of study which proved to be of equal interest to both of us. I used to select, or myself write, a shortish piece of two or three hundred bars and orchestrate it in the different styles of, say, Haydn, Bizet, Tchaikovsky or himself, and very soon, I think, he extracted as much amusement from this pleasant game as I derived instruction. Anyway, he always maintained that it was an excellent plan, and I know that, assisted by his wide experience and refinement of taste, I learned much from it that later on I was able to put to useful purposes.

One evening I went to hear Grétry's *Richard Cœur de Lion* at the

Opéra Comique, and, at once attracted by this delicate and delightful music, set out to acquire all I could of the composer's work as well as that of his contemporaries.   To my surprise, there was very little of it in print, a mere handful of piano copies in the big music stores, and, as for full scores, they were to be found only in curiosity shops.   It took me several months to compile a complete set of the operas of Méhul, and I never succeeded in collecting more than half a dozen of Dalayrac, Monsigny, and Isouiard together.   This music is markedly individual in that it owes little or nothing to any ancestry but that of the popular song of old France, which in turn took its character from the idiom and accent of the language.   In the case of Grétry there is a lightness, a grace and a melodic invention surpassed only by Mozart, while in that of Méhul there is a vein of simple and chivalric romance to be found in no other composer of the day except Weber.   But indeed the whole of the school has a refinement and distinction that never fails to fall fragrantly on the ear, and offers to the musical amateur, who may feel at times that the evolution of his art is becoming a little too much for either his understanding or enjoyment, a soothing retreat where he may effectively rally his shattered forces.   Having plenty of time on my hands, I spent some of it in the Bibliothèque Nationale, transcribing those works which had gone entirely out of publication, and when I left Paris in the summer for Switzerland I had a small company of young men still working at the job.

It is perhaps unusual for a young man who has spent half a year in the most brilliant and celebrated of European cities to take his leave without saying a single word about it, and among my patient readers there may be some who will wonder why.   Was I insensible to its attractions or out of temper with its atmosphere?   Had something occurred to lower its credit in my eyes?   Was I unhappy there or did I dislike the cooking?   My reticence is due to none of these hypothetical causes, for as towns go Paris to me is as good as any other.   But the fact is I do not like living in them at all.   By far the greater part of my first thirty years was spent in the country, and when I came to settle finally in London it took me several months to become habituated to its air, noise, and smells.   But what of the churches, the palaces, and those other objects of interest which some people talk about as if they were the whole place itself?   All very admirable in their way, but in the case of huge overgrown communities like London or Paris, just ornaments of microscopic size on an immense and shapeless mass.   In Oxford, Exeter, Winchester, or Chester the structures of beauty and shapeliness have another relationship to their surroundings and form an integral part of the main municipal plan.   But if one looks down from the air upon London, the general impression is one of endless streets of small interest, and that portion of it which has any claim to aesthetic value, or which can avoid the imputation of ugliness and vulgarity, is but a tiny fraction of the total sum.   For myself, I can rarely be brought to associate most great architectural monuments exclusively with their locality, and this presumably is because their connection with our present-day life is entirely different from what it was with that of the past.   For a while the inevitable centres of social activity were the cathedral and the royal palace or residence of the chief notability of the district; in the smaller towns it was the city hall and later on the municipal theatre or opera house.   With us it is the hotel de luxe, a fitting symbol of the transient character of our day; and our inability to conceive and plan large urban areas in which the average citizen can take a personal interest or pride is due to the gradually evaporating esteem for those institutions, secular as well as ecclesiastical, which offer better opportunities for self-praise in terms of architecture than the ephemeral temples of a transitional age. And yet there is nothing so important to the mental, moral and physical content of any aggregation of human beings as the laying out of the area in which it lives and works, with an eye not merely to the facilities of communication but to the regular gratification of those instincts in the universal consciousness which cry out for order and symmetry. Of this the ancient world had the fullest understanding, to the extent of treating it as a matter of course; and beauty was not looked upon as a casual curiosity to be acknowledged on stated occasions only, after the style of our modern religion. It was an element which ran through the whole life of the city and affected the daily thoughts and actions of each dweller in it.

I established myself for the months of July and August in Lucerne, where I hoped to put in a good deal of work on *Christopher Marlowe*, of which by this time I had received the full script from Illica; and to vary the routine of composition I took up the study of another instrument. I had already some practical knowledge of half a dozen others, all of the orchestral family, and although I had no ambition to achieve a mastery of any one of them, I had already found that some working knowledge of the mysteries of an oboe or trumpet was of practical use if confronted with a performer apt to allege as excuse for his own shortcomings that this or that passage could not be played in a certain way. On one occasion at least I found myself in the fortunate position to demonstrate by personal illustration that he was mistaken. It was the trombone which I decided to add to my collection, and, purchasing one, started work on it with vigour. After a few days there was a general protest from the other occupants of the *pension* where I was residing, and I took a studio in the principal music shop of the town, where other instrumentalists, mostly pianists and violinists, went for their practices. Here too I was such a disturbing factor in the house of harmony, and my presence so plainly undesired, that I retired to a remote corner of the cathedral graveyard, the quietest and most secluded spot in the place. Once again I was requested to take myself elsewhere because of complaints that I interfered with the choir meetings, and I was finally reduced to the extremity of hiring a small boat and rowing to the middle of the lake, where at last I could let myself go on what by that time I had discovered to be without question the most unpopular medium of musical sound in the world. Many a time since I have wondered, but have always forgotten to ask, how other persons learn these instruments; whether they are provided with padded and sound-proof cells in isolated premises, or whether under the guidance of skilful experts they are enabled from the beginning to extract from them effects that are less of a public nuisance than my self taught efforts would appear to have been.

In September I went down to Milan. There I met Illica, and a few days later went off with him to his house at Castellarquato, a tiny town about half-way between Piacenza and Parma on a spur of the Apennines. Here I stayed about a week discussing not only Marlowe but every other subject that touched upon the writing and production of opera. The opinions and experiences of the man who had written libretti for opera composers such as Puccini, Mascagni, Giordano, and Franchetti, the most successful of the day, were naturally of extreme value to me; and I was interested to learn, among other things, that even the most cunning hand may sometimes miscalculate its intended effect. *Madama Butterfly* had been given its first performance the previous spring, but not with the unqualified success which had been anticipated. The authors had withdrawn it from performance, remodelled portions of it, and were now waiting to submit the revised version to the public for a fresh verdict. This took place a little later on at Genoa, and from entering the field as a doubtful starter *Madama Butterfly* became not only a certain winner, but perhaps the most reliable gate-money draw of the last fifty years.

Hearing of my interest in old music, Illica reported the presence of many manuscripts in the village church, some of them attributed to Palestrina, and in the great convent of Borgo San Donnino, situated about six or seven miles away,—literally hundreds of the sixteenth, seventeenth, and eighteenth centuries. The wealth of such material in Italy must be immense, and it may be that some day, when the people of that country have time to think of something besides the revival of the Roman Empire at the expense of half a dozen other nations, they may devote a tiny portion of it to the unearthing of some of these treasures for the benefit of the rest of the world. Even in those days I found, as I had done in Germany, though not to such a rampant degree, the same itch for imperialistic expansion, noticeably among those of my own generation. During a conversation with some of them at the University of Bologna one fiery spark said to me with fierce conviction: "Malta is ours and we are going to have it!" If there are any who think that the latter-day policy of Italy is the exclusive creation of the Fascist Party, they are mistaken; and that it was twenty years earlier in the heart and brain of young Italy is something to which I can bear witness.

From Castellarquato I went by slow stages through Parma, Modena and Bologna to Florence, where I spent the whole autumn. I expect that if a plebiscite were taken among the people of every civilized nation as to which is the most attractive town in Europe, there would be a decided majority in favour of Florence. While it is large enough to support a social life of vitality and interest, it has escaped the peril of uncontrolled growth that has irretrievably ruined so many other haunts of old-time beauty; and while its artistic interest is inexhaustible and its rural surroundings elegantly cultivated, it has at the same time a touch of homeliness and intimacy wholly absent from its exotic rival Venice or the present capital of the kingdom.

There I worked away steadily and fruitfully, with time to spare for the consideration of what I should do on my return to England. Everything I had undertaken up to that moment seemed to be little more than the tentative labour of a journeyman at his trade; but I was now beginning to have a clearer idea of what I could and could not do, and the time had come to put it to the test. So about the close of the year I packed up and started homeward, stopping only at Bologna for a few days to buy a quantity of its furniture of the seventeenth century which I had seen and admired a few months before on my way south.

II

A REAL BEGINNING (1905-6)

DURING MY TRAVELS ABROAD MY MIND HAD BEEN TURNING MORE RE-currently than before to thoughts of conducting, for I had begun to wonder if it might not be easier to bring myself to the notice of the London public in this way than to wait for the uncertain chance of having my compositions played by someone else. With the exception of the two months' opera season of which I have written I had done nothing in this line since I left the north of England five years ago, and I often recalled the keen delight it had given me in those far-off days to handle the giant instrument of the orchestra, how fully I had felt at home with it, and how I had seemed to find little difficulty in expressing through it my own personality. After all, nothing very disastrous could come of it, for in those days conductors were much less common than now, concerts were fewer, and a new departure, even a modest one, might not be unwelcome.

My opening essay was given at the Bechstein (now Wigmore) Hall with a body of forty players drawn from the Queen's Hall Orchestra, and the programme included several of the eighteenth-century French and Italian works which I had collected on the Continent. A qualifying note of modernity was Cyril Scott's pretty ballad for voice and orchestra, *Helen of Kirkconnel*, sung by Frederic Austin, who not long before this had thrown up his old job in Liverpool to devote himself wholly to the profession of a singer. My chief sensation both during and after the performance was one of definite disappointment with myself: for at hardly any moment during it had I the conviction that I was obtaining from my executants the tone, style, and general effect I wanted. Somehow or other the sound of much of the music was strangely different from the conception of it in my brain, and, though my friends did their best to make me think I was mistaken and the newspapers were sympathetic, I felt I knew better, and I knew I could do better. But first I must find out what was the matter. I returned to the study of a large number of well-known scores, attended during the next few months nearly every concert given at Queen's Hall, and found that in many instances I experienced the same sense of dissatisfaction on listening to performances under other conductors. Years before I had not been troubled in this way; everything had sounded grand and perfect, and I began to be alarmed. Was my ear beginning to be affected or—more awful reflection—had the actual sound of the modern orchestra begun to distress me as it did increasingly an ultra-fastidious friend of mine in Paris? But one evening I listened to a highly unsatisfactory rendering of some famous piece, of which I knew every note, and now there could be no doubt where the fault lay. At one moment the brass instruments were excessive, at another inadequate; the wind and horns strident or feeble, and the strings feverish or flaccid. Briefly, there was no true balance or adjustment of the component parts of the machine, and it began to filter through my consciousness that if here was the source of trouble in a flagrant instance like this, it might turn out to be the same in fifty others less obvious. My curiosity well aroused, I followed with a keener ear everything I heard, and formed a conviction which the passage of time has only strengthened. The supremely important factor in any choral or instrumental ensemble is the relationship between the different sections of the forces of play.

During the years I had been poring over hundreds of scores there must have crystallized in my mind definite impressions, less of interpretation than of the co-ordinated sound of the various combinations for which they had been written. These I determined to submit to the test of performance without delay, in a series of concerts devoted to a period of music where accuracy of execution, purity of style, and the harmonious balance of parts were all essential to its correct and effective presentation. I then considered the practical side of my enterprise: what players I should engage, whether I should be able to have enough rehearsals for my needs, and if there would be the slightest public interest in it. Among the principal members of the two leading London orchestras there had been more than a suspicion of scepticism and condescension when I had broached my plan; and as for the chances of an audience, the manager whom I had placed in charge of its business end quite cheerfully expressed the view that as no one knew even the names of most of the composers I intended to play, not a soul would dream of buying a ticket. For a short while I vacillated in a state of uneasy indecision from which I was rescued by two fortuitous circumstances.

One day I had a visitor, Charles Draper, the foremost clarinettist in the country, who together with a few other first-class men in their respective lines had recently founded a chamber orchestra. Having heard something of my projected concerts, and my difficulties over players, he had come to offer me the services of this new group. I went to one of its rehearsals and, immediately impressed by a superior refinement of tone which I had not found elsewhere, decided that here might be an instrument capable of answering the demands I should make upon it. But what of the daunting prospect of playing to what would look like an unending vista of empty seats? This was enough to damp the ardour of an even more sanguine spirit than mine, and I invited my pessimistic manager to spend a day with me in the country to talk the matter over. After lunch we went for a long walk across the fields, discussing the problem from every critical angle, and on the way back came across no less than three horseshoes. This extraordinary occurrence made such an impression on both of us that, flinging prudence to the winds, we drew up our prospectus, sent it off to the printer, and two days later advertised the series. Contrary to nearly everyone's expectation, there was considerable interest in the concerts; the originality of the programmes, the appearance of a fresh body of players containing some of the best-known names in the profession, and a conductor almost unknown to central London, all exciting a fair amount of attention. The orchestra played excellently throughout, and I had the satisfaction of sensing that, through its ability to grasp my intentions, it was well within my power to realize in the concert hall that which I had conceived in the study.

Draper and his companions were as gratified by the success as I myself and professed anxiety to continue the association with me. This was pleasant enough, but to turn a temporary connection into a permanent partnership would require a more solid interest in common than the limited number of public performances on which I could afford to speculate. We should have to go out together to secure engagements; no easy matter, for very few individuals had use for an orchestra of even moderate size. It could be split up into small groups of anything from three or four to ten and rented out to musical societies here and there, and this is how most orchestral musicians at that time made or augmented their incomes. The really good instrumentalist had as little lack of work then as now, and on the whole extracted more amusement from it. His routine was less mechanized, we were still in the pre-radio-cum-recording age, and there was an incomparably greater amount of living music given in private houses. If anyone wanted to hear Caruso or Paderewski he had either to go to the opera house and concert-room, or procure an invitation to a big party for which they had been engaged. Naturally, the second alternative was available only to a limited number of amateurs, and the rest had to be satisfied with a less lavish class of entertainment or the making of music for themselves, mostly in the way of chamber work.

But the employment of an orchestra *en bloc* for any purpose but appearance in a public building was a novel idea, and a hostess who thought nothing of spending a thousand or two on a handful of famous artists for the entertainment of her guests was not yet awake to the possibility that there might be some other attraction which they would endure for five consecutive minutes, with moderate attention and (possibly) in comparative silence. Something therefore had to be done about it, and I took it upon myself to disseminate the doctrine by and large that the orchestra was the thing of the future, that all the best music was written for it, and the sooner people made up their minds to come and hear it, the better for their aesthetic salvation.

Many delicately minded persons have been known to express disapproval and even abhorrence of what they term my proselytizing or publicity methods, on the score that they are undignified and incompatible with the spiritual delicacy of the true artist. This sort of thing, they protest, should be left to the vulgar hand of that odd product of our latter-day culture, the press agent, or that still more fantastic curiosity, the gossip-writer. With delicious hypocrisy they contrive to discern an inseparable gulf between performing the dirty work of life for oneself and paying someone else to do it. But the main reason why I have never made use of such allies is that whenever I have gone out to seek advertisement or notoriety it has been less to promote my individual interests than to advance some cause in which the welfare of hundreds of other persons was as much involved as my own.

I soon discovered that with the degenerating methods of modern journalism it was almost useless to give interviews save to one or two responsible papers. Sometimes the reporter was incapable of taking down or reproducing with even partial accuracy what I had said, and at others the script would be so mangled as to deprive it of the least sense and logic. The only fairly safe method of communicating one's ideas to the public was by writing articles, giving addresses, or creating controversies during which a few well-calculated indiscretions of opinion might have the effect of ruffling the sensibilities of an appreciable section of my compatriots. I think it was Disraeli who said somewhere that the best introduction into society for any young man was to fight a duel: and certainly almost the only telling means of launching an innovation is to arouse a heated argument about the desirability or propriety of it. Without the creation of some such sharply defined issue it has become nowadays impossible to set anything decisively on foot, owing to the colossal complacency fostered in the man in the street by the unceasing stream flowing daily from the world's press in praise of his intellectual and moral perfections.

It is for this reason that the scheme for a National Theatre languished among us for so many years. It was about the time of which I am writing that a German-Jewish banker in London made the intriguing discovery that while we possessed the finest group of dramatic authors the world had yet known, the opportunities of seeing their work existed nowhere. He communicated his views to a public even more astonished (but for the different reason that it was a stranger even to the names of some of its most illustrious countrymen) and contributed the handsome sum of £75,000 towards the building and endowment of a theatre where the best plays, old and new, could be given year in and year out for the pleasure of those who had any desire to see them. The proposition was hailed as a noble one, received the blessing of Cabinet Ministers, leaders of the Church, universities, schools and every other cultural body in the Kingdom, and for the next three decades did not advance a single step further. Only during the last few years has a definite effort been made to fulfill the design of the benevolent alien, but, it should be hardly necessary to add, entirely in the wrong direction. A site of inadequate dimensions was acquired in a location sufficiently removed from London's hub to make it inconvenient for the bulk of its inhabitants; and, should any structure ever be raised on it, it will prove to be just one more of those quaint "follies" with which the eccentricity of Englishmen with more money than discretion has dotted our helpless countryside.

The necessity to be up and doing for a set purpose marked for me the boundary line separating for ever a life of contemplation from one of activity. Up to this time I had lived quietly, seeing few friends, reading, ruminating, and applying myself almost as much to the study of other arts as to the practice of music. But these tranquil days were over; I was to be no longer a musing spectator of the life around me, but a busy actor on its scene, armed with a miscellaneous fund of information that might rival Sam Weller's peculiar knowledge of London, a reservoir of stored-up energy, and a belligerency of utterance of which I had not hitherto suspected the possession.

12

AN OLD-TIME PERSONAGE

SOME OF THE IMMEDIATE RESULTS OF THE CHANGE IN MY WAY OF LIFE were the making of many new acquaintances and the reappearance of others not seen for years. Among the latter was Victor Maurel, whom I have always regarded as one of the half-dozen supreme artistic personalities of my time. He had recently settled in London and was endeavouring to found a private academy for advanced operatic students, the sort of experiment likely to meet with success nowhere. Singers may be divided into two classes, those who are born and those who are made.

The former, who are to be numbered on the fingers of both hands, are only too well aware of their unique place in the universe, while the latter, who are legion, are equally unaware of their limitations. Geniuses like Patti or Chaliapin make their appearance no more than once in fifty years and seem from the outset to be endowed with a natural instinct for singing, acting, and all else that has to do with their craft, to which the technical lore of the school has little to add. But the vast majority must work laboriously to attain even a condition of competence, whether it be in subduing the intractability of the voice itself, removing, in Bacon's phrase, "a stond or impediment in the wit", or mitigating the disability of corporeal mediocrity. Formerly the aspiring neophyte had only two fields of activity open to him, the opera house and the concert room, in both of which he really had to know how to sing, and no nonsense about it. In the days of Rossini at the academy of Bologna the minimum course for male students was seven years and for female five.

During the past thirty years the economic position of the young person with a voice has undergone a radical change, and thanks to radio, revue, and other channels of employment it is now possible to earn a substantial livelihood with the barest amount of preliminary training. It is no uncommon experience to see some raw student starting a career on the strength of what someone has told him is the finest voice of the day and a few months of spasmodic study. And although he may have some vague intention of settling down sooner or later to a more serious course of work, hardly anything ever does come of it, with the result that before long he is surprised to find that his voice shows signs of wear and tear from the want of an adequately prepared physical foundation. As for the elaborate apprenticeship necessary for a solid and enduring stage success, of which the pervading essential is an intimate acquaintance with roles from the various angles of music, text, period, deportment and gesture, I have met all too few willing to submit themselves to it. A certain British singer about whose capacity to interpret a part he was coveting I betrayed some hesitation endeavoured to win me over by the engaging assurance that he was a natural actor and equally at home in everything that he played. While natural acting in the case of a superbly endowed artist would mean the sharpest differentiation between the rendering of such widely differing characters as Lohengrin, Romeo, and Don José, to my genial and complacent friend it was simply the duplication of himself as known in ordinary life throughout the whole of his repertoire. In other words, he was never for a single moment any of the above-mentioned heroes of romance but always and unmistakably John Smith.

But even if there could have been found half a dozen youngsters of vision and industry, I doubt if Maurel ever had the capacity to teach anything that might have been of use to them. Like every other great artist, his method, if he ever had one, was wholly personal and incommunicable to others. I attended many of the lessons he gave, often played the piano for him at them, and could not fail to be amused by the obvious bewilderment of the average pupil when listening to the queer medley which the master innocently conceived to be practical instruction. He would ramble on for hours about this or that knotty problem of art and how it might best be solved, some of which might have been of interest to a writer on aesthetics; and he would declaim eloquently about the potentialities of "*la voix*" in terms that might have been understood by a voice producer of experience or singer of mature accomplishment. Even the vocal fragments he would throw in to illustrate his text were of negligible help, as here too the technique of his craft was too individual to admit of much analysis.   For instance, he occasionally startled us by an effect of sustained tone which, increasing gradually to a fortissimo on an ascending passage, was executed in a single breath and with an apparently natural ease that I have heard equalled only by Caruso and Battistini. But as this is the kind of trick that usually owes more to some physical peculiarity than to vocal cultivation, it is outside the province of imitation.

I use the word "occasionally" in connection with the state of his voice at that time, which was one of serious decline, with only here and there traces of the splendid and flexible organ I had heard ten years before on the Continent.   Like that of Chaliapin, Plançon, or Gilibert (he who accomplished the fabulous feat of bringing tears to the eyes of the world-weary Edward VII), it was of an unforgettable timbre, differing as much from the ordinary baritone as a Chinaman from a Hottentot, and, as with nearly all the truly great singers I have known, remarkable less for volume than quality.   Both he and Chaliapin achieved celebrity and prominence in their profession at an early age (Maurel was, I believe, one of the leading baritones of the Paris Grand Opera when only twenty-two), and perhaps for that reason sang themselves out sooner than others like Journet and Santley, whose voices at sixty-five and seventy respectively still retained much of the vigour and brilliance of their best days.   Even more than Jean de Reszke, was Maurel a magnificent type of the human animal.   Tall of stature, with a striking physiognomy and an almost feline grace of movement, he was in *Don Giovanni*, in *Figaro* as Il Conte, or in *Ernani* as Don Carlos, the incarnation of the *grand seigneur* of the romantic novelist's dream, and in roles where nobility of bearing was essential he has never been approached by any of his successors.   Added to these external attributes was a keen and inquiring intelligence which he brought to bear on anything he studied for performance combined with an inexhaustible industry.   During one particular week spent in his studio we did nothing each day but repeat over and over again two little songs, of which every phrase and syllable was sung fifty times in attempts to achieve variations of accent, inflection, and verbal point.   He would appear quite early in the morning clad in multi-coloured pyjamas, a resplendent dressing-gown, and a silk top hat, which he rarely removed even in the more animated moments of our work.   He too loved the old French operas of the eighteenth century, and this, the chief *trait d'union* between us, brought about a delightful event which has never been repeated in my experience.   Among his pupils was Mrs. Emile Mond, a woman of taste and scholarship, in whose house we gave a performance of Grétry's one-act opera, *Le Tableau Parlant*, with a cast which included Maurel in the principal role, a few singers imported from the Paris Opéra Comique, and Mrs. Mond herself.   Shortly after this he left England for America, where he remained for the rest of his life, and I did not see him again for some years, by which time every remaining vestige of his voice had vanished.

But apart from his historical importance as the central operatic figure of his generation, Maurel was of added interest to us as about the last genuine specimen of that theatrical tribe which has suffered such a melancholy change during the last fifty years. Formerly an actor or singer was recognizable as such a quarter of a mile away; and though the members of certain other professions such as parsons or prize-fighters might have claimed the same distinction, none of them vaunted it in such conspicuous fashion. Today he is indistinguishable from men of common make in appearance, speech and manners; and, in true accordance with the spirit of the time, aspires to own as little individuality and to be as much like his neighbour as he can be. But the ancient type of player was a creature apart from the rest of his kind, proud of an originality mani-fested not only in physical divergencies, but in a mentality which had remained unchanged for centuries. The prime function of anyone who seeks to divert the public of a theatre is to create illusion, and the greater the performance the greater the illusion. As time goes on the life of the player becomes more and more itself an illusion, through an ever intenser absorption into the realm of fantasy in which its working days are passed. For this reason everything that the mummer of old did or said, his massive movements and picturesque postures, his orotund periods and sententious phrases, were all reflections and echoes of the dream world peopled by the creations of the great playwrights. This dramatic tradition which had held the stage since the production of Marlowe's *Tamburlaine*, had been rooted in the mixed soil of tragedy and romance and had followed pretty generally the Aristotelian precept that the actions of great men (in the material sense of power and position) are of more interest than those of their lesser brethren.

For over three centuries the European theatre as represented by Shakespeare, Fletcher, Calderon, Racine, Molière, Goethe and the rest was mainly an upper-class affair in which the principal personages were seen strutting authoritatively on the larger stage of life, and the men whose daily occupation was to deliver the speech and portray the actions of princes, cardinals, and fine ladies came to look down on the middle and lower classes of society as something belonging to an inferior stratum of civilization. But with the triumph of the bourgeois drama of which Ibsen was the progenitor and Shaw the heir, this grandiose and spacious art gradually yielded to one of modest gesture and prosaic speech, much as the easy and familiar style of Hazlitt and Hunt superseded the ornate and weighty periods of Johnson and Gibbon. Forced to reproduce the actions and utterances of the suburban villa in place of those of the royal palace, the actor step by step declined from the exalted height where his spirit bathed daily in the sunshine of reflected greatness to that flat-land of commonplace existence which most of us endure and do not despise. The process of descent is now accomplished, and an artistic community formerly as separate from the common herd as the Quakers or the Mor-mons has achieved a colourless and unimpressive uniformity. Of all the personalities of this ilk who vanished one by one from the scene of their glory forty and fifty years ago, the most characteristic and complete was Maurel. Poetry and fustian, inspiration and bathos, intellectual maturity united with childlike naïveté, all were present in him, and such were the merits and demerits of the player of a day that is dead. The mould is shattered and will not be repaired in our time.

It soon became clear that if the New Symphony Orchestra was to compete successfully for public favour with its elder rivals, the Queen's Hall and London Symphony, it must evolve from a small into a large body of players. This was accomplished satisfactorily during the summer of 1907, and I was enabled to start the autumn season with a series of concerts in the ampler accommodation of Queen's Hall with programmes this time devoted almost wholly to unknown modern works. The public likes to label a musician just as it does an actor and to confine him in a special corner of its own choosing. I am sure that it must be a painful shock to thousands of the other sex when some adored idol of the stage, who has been playing for long years romantic parts like Monsieur Beaucaire or Sydney Carton, suddenly betrays their trust by leaving the dear, wonted path for some deplorable aberration such as Dr. Jekyll and Mr. Hyde. Similarly I fear that my rapid transition from a delicate and fastidious classicism to a robust and uncompromising modernism may have wounded the feelings of those who had begun to look upon me as the champion of the neglected music of a half-forgotten age. But my orchestra, now enlarged to ninety musicians, was calling out for stronger fare than Paisiello or Zingarelli could provide, however charming these were in their own way; and my own inclination was at one with its need.

At the conclusion of our first concert a stranger of arresting appearance was brought into the artists' room and introduced to me. It was Frederick Delius, who, arriving from France a few days before, had been struck by the novel look of our programme and had come along to see what was going on. With fine and ascetic features that might have been taken for those of a distinguished ecclesiastic had it not been for the curiously eager and restless expression both in the eyes and mouth, he spoke with decision and emphasis and a slight North-country accent. Praising the performance, he told us that the purpose of his visit to England was to investigate the orchestral situation, as a German friend of his, Fritz Cassirer, who earlier in the year had produced his opera *A Village Romeo and Juliet* at the Komische Oper in Berlin, wanted to give some concerts in London. An eminent authority whom they consulted had advised them that there were only two orchestras available, and here to his surprise was a third, playing the music of his own day and, from what he could observe, really liking it. On this he commented in characteristic fashion: "London is the only town in the world where a first-class band like this can give such a set of concerts without one of its leading musicians being aware of its existence."

A few days later he came to see me again, this time with Cassirer, and engaged the orchestra for a trial concert in which the principal pieces to be played were his *Appalachia* and *Ein Heldenleben* of Strauss. With the exception of the piano concerto, an early work given a few weeks before this at a Promenade Concert, nothing of Delius had been heard in London for seven or eight years, and musical circles were keenly interested in this almost legendary figure who, although born an Englishman, had been living abroad for over twenty years. He had reached the age of forty-five, had written a long string of works of which hardly any of us had yet heard a note, and had now turned up again like a traveller from distant parts with a trunk full of rare curiosities. I had dipped only casually into a few of them, but enough to compel the instant recognition of a musical intelligence not only different from but actually antagonistic to any with which I was acquainted. Then came the performance of *Appalachia*, throughout which my dominant emotion was wonderment that music like this could have remained unknown for years, when any number of inferior compositions were being given daily with the printer's ink scarcely dry upon their scores. The piece made a deep impression on everyone, but in all that was written or said about it, its two outstanding qualities were hardly noticed. Whether it was or was not an authentic set of variations, whether it was too short or too long, or whether Delius had been well- or ill-advised in writing the choral finale just in the way he had done, were all points of secondary interest. What should have been evident at first hearing was the remotely alien sound of it, a note in English music stranger than any heard for over two hundred years, and the masterly and personal use of the orchestra. The instrumental combinations, notably those in the variations that depict nature life in the woods and swamps, were a revelation of what the orchestra could be made to utter, and although forty years have passed since it was first put down on paper, the whole work still astonishes by its variety of atmosphere, loveliness of tone, and the unorthodox exploitation of those *tutti* moments which are handled by most composers old and new in such depressingly stereotyped fashion.

It seemed that if there was one thing above all else for the orchestra and myself to do at once, it was to acquire all of this music that we could lay our hands on, make it as much our own as that of the lesser eighteenth-century masters, and play it often and everywhere. It was too late to make any change in our pre-Christmas programmes, but I found a place in the first of the New Year for *Paris: the Song of a Great City*, which though written as far back as 1899 had not yet been given in London. Wrought in the form of a colossal nocturne, this audacious experiment (the greatest yet made) in musical impressionism won more immediate and general acceptance than any other of the composer's works played during this period; and thirty-three years later, in the spring of 1941, when I gave it at Carnegie Hall, the boldest and acutest of American critics declared that Delius wrote better for the orchestra than anyone else.

13

ENGLISH CHORAL MUSIC (1907)

THE QUESTION HAS OFTEN BEEN ASKED WHY THE ENGLISH MORE THAN any other people are given up so earnestly to the practice of choral singing. I have read many answers to it, of which the least plausible is that of a distinguished British historian who declares that solo singing is favoured in an aristocratic society and communal or choral in a democratic. This certainly will not do, for at the time this opinion was uttered the country where, after England, choral music flourished most widely was Imperial Germany, and those in which it was and still remains the most backward are the two great republics France and the United States of America. There may be something, but I do not venture to say how much, in the rather extreme view of another writer that as we have produced fewer solo singers of rank than any other country of importance the public takes such little pleasure in listening to them that it prefers to make music for itself. Lastly, there is the sadly cynical observation of one to whom any rejoicing of the heart in tuneful numbers is a harrowing ordeal, that concerted singing does have one clear advantage over other kinds, inasmuch as it enables a man to let off all the emotional steam with which he may be seething, without hearing in the glorious welter of noise around him either the sound of his neighbour's voice or that of his own.

With all respect to the views of those eminent persons I fancy that the true origins of this indulgence of ours are of an antiquity and respectability that make them worthy of our esteem and sympathy. As most people know who have any acquaintance with the history of art, the inhabitants of my country during the fifteenth and sixteenth centuries were more given up to music-making than those of any other in Europe; and in castles, cottages, theatres and outdoor shows it was cultivated to the full. But with the triumph of the Long Parliament, dominated by Puritans, plays were forbidden, masques abandoned, the maypole and the hobby-horse disappeared from country fairs, nearly all music except psalm-singing was discouraged, and in less than fifty years from the passing of the great and pleasure-loving Elizabeth the gayest and most melodious community in the world had become the saddest and most silent. The Merrie England of the Middle Ages was no more, the spiritual and cultural unity of the people was disintegrated and has never been refashioned. For the rest of the seventeenth century its contribution to the development of the Arts was as nothing if compared with that of its Continental neighbours, and abdicating its old-time leadership it seemed content to take no part in the two revolutionary movements of the time, the rise of Opera and the growth of the Orchestra. One attempt after another was made to introduce and establish Opera, but without success; and while in France, Italy, and Germany it became and remains the most popular branch of music, in England it has always been the occasional entertainment of a small minority. Although the love and practice of choral singing departed from high places, the memory of its great days lingered in the heart of the populace: but alas, it had nothing to sing. The happy pagan strains of its forefathers no longer appealed to a breed whose main intellectual nourishment was the stern sublimity of the Authorized Version, and who pined for a new vocal strain that would satisfy the religious as well as the artistic longings of a regenerated spirit. Their prayers were answered by the coming of the mighty Handel, who, seizing upon the dramatic stories of the Bible and making the chorus their real protagonist, blazed the trail for the whole of that revival of mass singing which has played a far greater part than anything else in our musical history. For a century and a half the words "song" and "Handel" were almost synonymous, and with just reason; for since his time mankind has heard no music written for voices which can even feebly rival his for grandeur of build and tone, nobility and tenderness of melody, scholastic skill and ingenuity and inexhaustible variety of effect.

But the tide of the movement did not rise to full height until the rapid transformation of the North from a drowsy Arcadia to the busiest industrial area of the universe. The bulk of its new population was Nonconformist, shunned the theatre and all other garish pleasures, but swore by the Bible and loved to sing. Life was grim and tedious in its hideous towns, and as there was little that their consciences permitted them to do in the way of amusement, the choral societies grew in size and numbers until they became social gatherings as much as artistic institutions. By the close of the century there were nearly five thousand of them up and down the land, many of high excellence, and tidings of their exploits had spread over the earth.

Although England is a smallish country with an apparently homo-geneous people, there are striking contrasts between the voices of one part and another in a dozen obvious instances; and of some interest to the biologist should be the distinctive dissimilarities between two choirs living only a few miles from one another, traceable without doubt to ancient racial differentiations that time in most other directions has ironed away. It is no insult to the musical intelligence of the South to say that in simple vocal endowment it does not enter into serious competition with the North, although the capital possesses one or two notable exceptions to this rule such as the London Philharmonic Choir, which the genius of Kennedy Scott has lifted to a higher cultural level than any other in the kingdom. It is the region beyond the Trent where the traditions of the craft are best maintained and its practice most widely diffused, especially in Yorkshire, whose singing is as serious and dour a business as its cricket. I speak of the attitude towards it and not of the performance, for nothing can exceed the solid brilliance of the sopranos or the rich sonority of the basses, particularly those of the Huddersfield district, who in range and power outrival all others, the Russians not excepted.

As for the chorus masters, those who made of these raw masses of vocal material (entirely amateur) instruments for the interpretation of great music as flexible and subtle as a fine orchestra, they were totally unlike any other class of musician alive. A small percentage only of them had received an orthodox musical training, the vast majority being almost wholly without knowledge of any branch of the art except their own. Their acquaintance with the orchestra was negligible, as may be gathered from an occasion when a celebrated member of the guild, apologizing for his maladroit handling of some instrumental passage in an oratorio, said with mixed pride and humility, "I knaw nowt about band, but I can mak choir sing"; and "mak choir sing" he certainly could. What most of them did have were a perfect ear, a refined sense of vocal tone, an apprecia-tion of the meaning of words, and the potentialities of them as carriers of sound, an accomplishment handed down from Tudor days. Often too they were men of character with a distinct capacity for saving an awkward situation of the sort that occurred at a northern festival during my boy-hood. The choir had learned under its trainer some stirring piece of the martial sort by a popular composer of advanced age who for some years had not been seen in public. The committee out of courtesy asked the veteran to conduct his own work, and to their surprise as well as em-barrassment he accepted the invitation. But owing to some mistake at the last moment in his travelling arrangements, he arrived only an hour or two before the performance, had a hurried rehearsal with the orchestra, and came face to face with the choir for the first time on the platform. It may have been temporary fatigue or permanent loss of vigour, but to the general consternation the old gentleman began his piece at about half the pace the choir had practised it, and for the first quarter of a minute the chaos was complete, some of the choir going on, others hanging back, half the orchestra following the conductor, and the rest racing after those singers who were in advance. All at once the audience, which was beginning to palpitate with anxiety, was electrified by the sight of their beloved chorus-master rushing wildly from the wings on to the stage and roaring out at the top of his voice, "Tak naw nawtice of him, tak naw nawtice of him, sing it as you've larnt it." And in some miraculous fashion the choir, after a few bars of lightning readjustment, struck a common *tempo* and sang on brilliantly to the end, dragging in their wake both conductor and orchestra like captives bound to a triumphal chariot.

The reputation of the Birmingham singers was hardly, if any, less than that of their northern brethren, so that in accepting an offer to conduct the concerts of the City Choral Society for the season of 1907–8 I looked forward both to a pleasant time and an instructive experience. But I had not been in active charge more than a few weeks before I began heartily to regret my appointment, for I found myself in the very centre of a fierce internecine struggle in which all the musical institutions of the town seemed to be taking an animated part. The most belligerent if not the most influental of the opposing groups had constituted itself the champion of an out-and-out modernity, to the extent of treating the performance of any work not written within the twenty previous years as a serious misdemeanour. The classics of the nineteenth century were proclaimed to be obsolete, and, as for the older masters like Handel and Haydn, the mere mention of their names provoked fiery outbursts of anger and resentment. I have to admit that there was partial justification for this intransigency of attitude and that some of the grievances were not outside reason. For one cause or another, the most likely perhaps being the proximity of London, the development of the instrumental resources of the city had lagged behind that of Manchester, Liverpool, and the Scottish centres, and it was only at the Triennial Festival or some concert of a visiting orchestra that the public had the chance of hearing works with which other audiences had long been familiar. But unfortunately the level of performance at the first named event, into which was crowded during three or four days as much new music as the normal ear could absorb in ten, was rarely higher than adequate, as the time and facilities for rehearsal were never anything like sufficient. Over everything hung what Berlioz once described as the fatal disability of all English musical institutions, the curse of the *à peu près*, and often the proceedings resembled a race meeting more than an artistic celebration.

It might have helped a little if for the Festival there had been a conductor who combined enterprise with a liking for novelty; but the master of the show was the conservative Hans Richter, for whom the world of creative effort had stopped about 1895 and who on one occasion had advertised the limitations of his taste and knowledge by declaring that there was no such thing as French music. Hence it sometimes happened that a composer was asked or preferred to conduct his own work, usually with disastrous consequences; for the poor wretch, who seldom had the slightest aptitude for the use of the baton, succeeded only in giving the public the least favourable impression of it. It was also through this failure to find the necessary time for rehearsal that the classical portion of the programme had become stereotyped and narrowed to half a dozen popular favourites, which appeared and reappeared with a regularity that drove the progressives to a pitch of ungovernable fury. But here their zeal overshot the mark and hindered them from realizing that the real trouble with the classics was not that they were overplayed, but virtually unknown.

The powerful reaction at the beginning of the present century against Handel was aroused less by the man and all his works than the tiresome iteration of a few of them, as well as the unsatisfactory conditions under which they were given. While in the composer's time the number of voices and instruments was each about the same, the growth of choirs from thirty-five or forty to anything between three hundred and two thousand singers destroyed this harmonious balance, and our sight as well as hearing was offended by the incongruity of vast masses of choral tone insufficiently supported by orchestral accompaniment. To redress this glaring inequality recourse was had to the organ, without reflecting that it too had changed out of recognition during two hundred years in character and size. The inevitable result was that the two elder members of the triple alliance worked nervously in dread of their new partner, who in the quieter movements rarely furnished a tonal contribution that blended with their own, and in the louder generally overwhelmed them with a deafening clatter of reverberatory thunder. The general effect was one of a monotony with which the public grew the more impatient as its enjoyment and appreciation of the richly varied colour scheme of the modern orchestra increased; and an ill-directed attempt to restore Handel's own instrumentation, shorn of those additions which men like Mozart and Mendelssohn had made by way of concession to the taste of their day, augmented rather than diminished the tedium of the performance. It is unsafe to dogmatize about composers who worked and lived in an age so distant from our own, but of one thing I am fairly sure: If Handel, who was the greatest impresario as well as artist of his day, were confronted with the gigantic crowds of singers that now strive to interpret his music, he would at once cut them down to a quarter of their bloated dimensions or rewrite the orchestral portion of his scores for the largest combination of instruments he could lay his hand upon. There is an heretical belief in many quarters that eighteenth-century composers were frail and delicate creatures who liked tenuity of sound and should be treated today with tender concern. This is against all historical evidence, particularly in the cases of Handel and Mozart, both of whom revelled in resounding splendour of tone, as we know well from the complaints of the former and the correspondence of the latter. The bubbling delight of Wolfgang Amadeus on discovering no less than forty violins in the Mannheim Orchestra, a larger quantity than can be found in any like combination today, is but one piece of proof out of a hundred that these great men were not anaemic epicenes but creatures of overflowing vigour and passion.

Before accepting the engagement with the Society I had no knowledge of these local conditions, and at the time of discussing programmes with some of the committee I had been innocently impressed with their enthusiasm over my suggestions of old and little-known choral pieces. There was no one I knew to warn me that this particular organization was regarded as the very stronghold of reaction by the insurrectionists, and that I as its conductor would be attacked as the master criminal of the conspiracy to put the musical clock back a hundred years or more. It was bad enough to inflict on them works like *The Seasons* of Haydn or the *Dettingen Te Deum* of Handel; but when it came to a Mass of Cherubini and a selection or two from my minor French and Italian masters of the seventeenth and eighteenth centuries I was made to feel that I ought to be banished for ever from the society of all decent people. But for these little troubles I found compensation in some new acquaintances, notably Granville Bantock and Ernest Newman, two of the outstanding figures in English musical life.

Had he been born and lived in any other country, Bantock by this time would be one of the most popular composers of the day. His genius, which is lyrical and dramatic, has been to a large extent thwarted by the non-existence among us of those institutions which alone could have given it the scope and opportunity to flower easily and organically into ripe maturity, as well as by the restriction for performance to the concert hall and cathedral, two settings which in time invariably diminish the native warmth and vigour of the born man of the theatre. For none who has heard his *Omar Khayyám* can fail to perceive where is the rightful home of music such as this. The flow of genial melody, unmistakably of the "stagey" sort, a solid but lively handling of the orchestra, and a by no means too common capacity for passing swiftly and easily from one contrasting mood to another, all indicate a gift that could have presented the Opera House with half a dozen pieces of the quasi-romantic type, a welcome addition to a repertoire that is gradually thinning away to nothing. With an artistic nature of the mediumistic order he contrived to absorb most of the influences of his day with surpassing rapidity by making such use as he thought needful of any one of them and purging himself with equal facility to pass on to others. The sumptuous Orient, the radiance of Antiquity and the mists of the Celtic twilight, each of these has taken possession of and controlled him for an appointed season; and his achievement is a palace of art in which the many chambers have been designed and occupied by their builder one at a time. Having the quick penetration of the true lyrical writer for reaching the heart of a poem and re-creating it in fitting and telling turns of melody, his songs are among the best we have had from a British composer for over a century, and when I recall the texts of *Ferishtah's Fancies* and the Sappho Songs I cannot help believing that Bantock's settings of them will remain unchallenged for some time to come.

To the Anglo-Saxon public certainly and to many others probably, the name of Ernest Newman is familiar as the keenest and wittiest writer on music of the past fifty years. Critics, like politicians, are frequently accused of inconsistency when they change their opinions, but why they must be denied a privilege enjoyed by everyone else I have never understood. Ernest Newman has changed his about as much as any other man, for which praise rather than blame should be accorded him. It is too much to ask of the profoundest intellect that it should have an equal understanding of every school or individual composer at a single given moment, or to expect that a keen study of or deep affection for one of them should not beget a temporary impatience with some other. Only advancing years bring the calm spirit of reconciliation and cool mental insight which can discern signs of association or likeness where formerly appeared nothing but opposition or dissimilarity. But none has comprehended more truly or interpreted more sympathetically in his critical work the music of the particular period with which he was for the moment intimately concerned than Ernest Newman. And when we add to this enviable faculty that lucidity of style, indefeasible logic and pretty knack of phrase-turning that have placed him among the best writers of modern English prose, it is not surprising that he has attained the commanding position which he occupies today. Of late years he has been pursuing an inquiry into the anatomy of musical works analogous to the fingerprint system of police departments like Scotland Yard or the Sûreté in Paris, which I fancy he has inherited from that band of commentators who half a century ago caused such wrath and dismay among orthodox scholars of the Elizabethan and Jacobean drama by placing a note of interrogation against the authenticity of half the plays in the accepted canon. One of the disadvantages of this method is that it is easier to deny than affirm, for while there is a fair unanimity as to who did not write this or that doubtful work, there is equal disagreement as to who actually did. If the fingerprint process yields such negative results in the case of literature it is even more subject to fallibility in that of music. The great composers in their masterpieces are inimitable, but few things are easier to turn out than plausible copies of their second-rate manner.

14

FREDERICK DELIUS (1908)

THE UNEXPECTED ADVENT OF A NEW CONDUCTOR AND A FULL AND FIRST-class orchestra devoting themselves largely—nay, almost aggressively—to the introduction of unfamiliar compositions naturally excited the curiosity as well as the hopes of many of the rising young English composers, who were clamouring for a wider recognition as well as a more studied performance of their work. Until this moment almost the only chance of a hearing was to be found in the Promenade Concerts, which ran nightly during August and September and included in their programmes not only all the standard repertoire of the great masters, but a large mass of modern novelty. But the immense amount of music played, and the necessarily limited time for rehearsal, did not make this otherwise admirable series always the best vehicle for bringing forward new and frequently intricate pieces under really favourable conditions. Also at this time of year most of our knowledgeable amateurs were out of London, so that the bulk of the native effort was to be heard in the off-season only.

As nearly all the men who sought my company or co-operation were about my own age, none of them had reached that maturity where it was possible to take stock of their achievement; but their ability and promise were never in question at any moment. Arnold Bax from the beginning revealed an all round technical accomplishment of the highest order; Vaughan Williams was already striking out that individualistic line which was eventually to mark him as the most essentially English composer of his time; the rare and charming personality of Cyril Scott was fully present in his smaller pieces; and there were half a dozen others of almost equal capacity, if of less originality, such as W. H. Bell, J. B. McEwen, and Frank Bridge.

But the most picturesque and singular figure of the hour was undoubtedly Joseph Holbrooke. His talent was electric and absorptive. Liszt and Richard Strauss were his models, and he gravitated by instinct and with ease to the fantastic and the macabre in his choice of subject. Under the conviction that my mission in life was to serve the contemporary muse, particularly his own, he hastened to get in touch with me. At our first meeting he inveighed loudly and bitterly against the neglect of his work and the apathy of audiences, and then produced from his pocket an immense string of Press notices and a list of performances which flatly contradicted all that he had been saying. Having satisfied himself that I was the sort of collaborator he was looking for, he confided in me that he was working on a musical experiment that would prove to be the event of the year. He had been approached by a stranger who had written a long narrative poem of metaphysical character entitled *Apollo and the Seaman*, which he wanted to bring to public attention in the most telling fashion. This was to be effected by taking Queen's Hall, rigging up an immense screen to separate the platform from the auditorium, and throwing on it by means of magic-lantern slides the poem, stanza by stanza; all the while an orchestra, concealed behind the screen, played music illustrating the succeeding moods and episodes of the story. Upon my asking what sort of orchestra he proposed to use, he replied that the poet had suggested a few strings and pipes, something soothing, pastoral and economical. But as the piece was in places really stirring and dramatic, he (Holbrooke) did not see how he could limit himself to such a primitive scheme of colour.

It was agreed that when he had finished a good part of his score he would bring it to me to see if I would co-operate on the executive side of this odd enterprise, and a few weeks later he turned up with an enormous manuscript which contained, in addition to a choral section requiring about two hundred and fifty voices, nearly all the orchestral instruments I had ever heard of and a few that I had not. Among the latter was the sarrusophone, used mainly in French military bands, a species of bass bassoon, and capable, according to my friend, of yielding lower notes of extraordinary sonority. One of these at least he urged we must have at any cost, but since he could not find it in England he had determined to go over to Paris to look for it there; and as about this time I had received an invitation from Delius to spend a few days at his house near Fontainebleau, I proposed that we set out on the voyage of discovery together.

It was a raw December morning when we met at Victoria Station for our outward journey, and I was impressed not only by my companion's choice of apparel, which was of the sort most people wear only at the height of summer, but by his supply of luggage, which consisted of one small bag, hardly bigger than a modern woman's vanity-case. On the way to the coast he chatted gaily about the inherent affinity of all Englishmen for the sea, but was so ill during our crossing that he needed two days' complete rest in Paris before we could start on the hunt for our sarrusophonist. This did not prove so easy as anticipated; there seemed to be very few of the species about, and these either could not leave their jobs or shrank from facing the rigours of a winter trip. But we finally heard of a likely quarry in an outer suburb of the city, and after a tiresome search up and down the district, for no one knew the exact address, we ran it to earth on the top floor of a tenement building of which the stairway ascent was as long and painful as that of Martial's lodging in ancient Rome.

Enshrined in a tiny apartment and surrounded by, indeed almost buried beneath, dozens of weird-looking instruments was an equally diminutive old man of gentle and venerable appearance to whom we made known the reason of our visit. To our intense relief he accepted our offer of an engagement with alacrity, declaring that such an event would be a worthy climax to a long career spent in the service of the Republic, and going so far in his enthusiasm as to toy with the idea that Providence had chosen him out as an apostle to convey a special-branch of Gallic culture to the less enlightened shores of Great Britain. Our mission accomplished, I went on to Grez-sur-Loing, a small village lying about five miles south of the Forest of Fontainebleau, the home of Delius and a spot of some antiquity. A church of the thirteenth century, together with a ruined castle of the twelfth, adjoined the house of the composer, of which the front entrance opened on to the little main street. Once inside, however, nothing met the eye except a long garden sloping down to the river and a country landscape beyond it fading away in the distance.

Of all the men in any walk of life that I have known during a career spent almost as much in other countries as in my own, Frederick Delius is the most remarkable. His biographers have styled him an Englishman, born of German parents settled in Yorkshire in the early part of the nineteenth century, and this is correct so far as it goes. But it does not take us nearly far enough in probing the problem of a highly complex personality, and the truth is that Delius was of no decided nationality but a citizen of all Europe, with a marked intellectual bias towards the northern part of it. His family was almost definitely of Dutch origin, and some time in the sixteenth century had changed its patronymic from Delij or Deligh to a latinized form of it, a common enough practice at the time. A member of it was numbered among the chaplains of Edward VI of England and others are traceable to Spain, France and Germany. But whatever were the diverse elements that united to make up the interesting amalgam of Frederick, anything less Teutonic would be hard to imagine. His earthy solidity and delicate romanticism were English, his uncompromising logic and analytical insight French, and his spiritual roots went down deep to that layer of far northern culture which, half Icelandic, half Celtic, gave birth centuries ago to the beautiful folk-music of Scotland and Ireland and in the nineteenth century to the boundless imaginative genius of Ibsen.

A portion of his unsettled youth he spent on an orange plantation in Florida, to which he had been sent by anxious parents striving to head him away from the dangerous lure of the Continent, and where, anticipating Dvořák by some fifteen years, he discovered the potentialities of Negro music. After his return to England and a period of study in Leipzig, which it is hard to believe was the slightest benefit to him, he made his way to Paris, where he lived for about twelve years, and upon his marriage moved out to the house at Grez, which he occupied until his death in 1934. By his own account, France was the only country in which he found it possible to work and live at ease, for it was there alone that he could enjoy that constant and prolific intercourse with intellectual equals which has always been one of the more attractive features of life in the French capital, as well as a social independence and immunity from unwanted intrusion hard to find on the other side of the Channel.

It was inevitable in a musician of such highly and narrowly original type that he should seek associates outside his own profession, and it was mostly men of letters and painters who formed his intimate circle during those earlier years, of whom the more notable were Strindberg, Sisley and Gauguin. Of the work of the last-named he possessed a splendid example which hung on the walls of his studio at Grez for over twenty years. But in the financial chaos in which so many found themselves nearly lost just after the war he disposed of it to Sir Michael Sadler, at that time Principal of the Sheffield University and an ardent Gauguin collector, for a price some fifty times more than he had paid for it. For there was nothing in Delius of that vague indetermination associated traditionally with musical genius; in practical affairs he was as hardheaded as any to be found in his native county, and his knowledge of the world, both men and women, was searching and profound. Coolly cynical where the majority were concerned, and chary of sympathy or encouragement for those who in his opinion were not deadly in earnest over their job, he was frank and cordial with the few to whom he was genuinely attached. In general company he loved passionately to provoke highly controversial discussions on every subject imaginable, and in these he was seen at his social best; for his uncanny gift of penetrating the heart of the matter and hitting the nail on the very centre of its head often gained him the advantage over men who had the reputation of being experts in their particular callings.

After a while I discovered that his entire philosophy of life was based upon an ultra-Nietzschean conception of the individual. The individual was all in all, a sovereign creature who perhaps owed certain perfunctory duties to the State in return for mere protection and security, but certainly nothing more to anyone but himself and the vital needs of his task. This, of course, means that Frederick from the Anglo-Saxon point of view must be reckoned a supreme and complete egoist, and such he was, unquestionably. He chose to give little to others, but then he asked for no more in return. "My mind to me a kingdom is," sang old William Byrd, and so it was with Delius, who knew as well, if not better than any man I have known, exactly what he wanted and went after it with a simplicity and celerity that were models of direct action. But this self-centred, self-sufficient, and self-protected spirit had its noble and idealistic side, for it lived on earth but to look steadily into its own remoter depths, bring to the light the best discoverable there, and to translate it into terms of music with hardly a care that it should be acclaimed by others or even noticed at all. Never did I observe any occasion when he lifted a finger to advance the cause of his own work; and not once in our subsequently long association did he ever actually ask me to play anything of his, although he knew well enough that I was ready to do so at any moment.

This unique character made a deep impression upon me and actively influenced my life for several years. It was not that I shared either his views or sentiments—indeed, more often than not I heartily disagreed with both—but that for the first time in my career I had encountered a personality of unmistakable stamp, full, mellow and unchanging, to whom nothing in the world was ambiguous or equivocal. It is related of Goethe that he preferred the conversation of Englishmen to that of his own countrymen, for the reason that the former, although often complete asses, were at the same time almost always complete men. Delius in his own way was a complete man, carved by nature in a clear and definable piece out of the rough and shapeless store of her raw material; a signpost to others on the way of life, a light to those in darkness; and an unfailing reassurance to all who strove to preserve their faith in those two supreme human virtues, honesty and independence.

At the time of our meeting I was just beginning to emerge from a psychological condition which for many years I had dimly sensed was alien to my real self, and from which I did not quite know how to escape. Keats has told us that the imagination of the boy is healthy as much as that of the grown man; but that there is an intermediate state when it is likely to go astray in any errant direction. This period began for me about the time I went to Oxford, lasted for at least seven or eight years, and was essentially one of unrest, indecision and self-questioning. Life led me tentatively to more than one point of attraction but held me to none; and, devoted as I was to music, I was at any time capable of turning to some other career. I was distrustful not only of my ability but of my good fortune where anything that had to do with music was concerned, for during the few years previous to these events I had suffered two setbacks in my work. From the time I arrived in London I had industriously continued my piano studies with the settled intention of appearing sooner or later as a fully fledged professional. But this, the lesser of my two ambitions, was wrecked for ever by a mysterious mishap to one of my wrists of which I never ascertained the actual cause. Whether it came from overstrain in practice, from the blow of a cricket ball or some other accident unnoticed at the moment, I do not know, but from a certain day I became incapable of playing longer than fifteen or twenty minutes without a species of cramp or partial paralysis numbing and rendering impotent the lower half of my arm. Every effort of medical science to remedy my misfortune was unavailing, and this disability has remained with me to the present time. I was hardly more fortunate with my creative endeavours, which I had begun with the highest hopes of success, for here too I encountered a mortifying reverse. My dream was to become an operatic composer on a grand scale, and I had made two or three full sized experiments in that direction. But the longer I laboured, the more dissatisfied I became with the inadequacy of my effort, and I gradually came to realize that the task was beyond me, at any rate for the time being. Had I been wiser and more experienced I should soon have recognized that my small inventive capacity could without difficulty have found its natural medium of expression in forms other than the mighty machine of opera, and that if my ambition had been under better control I might have developed eventually into a moderately respectable composer of songs and small pieces. But at that time I was unmindful of the sound Daedalian maxim that middle flights are safest for tyros, and as it seemed a case of "Aut Caesar aut nihil" I chose the latter alternative.

After these disappointments it was an agreeable surprise to find strangers from so many different sides hailing me as an orchestral conductor of talent for whom there was a definite future. The encouragement I received was enough to satisfy almost anyone else than myself, but I was still a little reluctant to devote the whole of my energies irrevocably to a single occupation until I could bring myself to believe that I might achieve a success in it that would compensate for my failures elsewhere. That I did take the final plunge was due mainly to the convincing council and constant conviction of Frederick Delius.

15

"APOLLO AND THE SEAMAN" (1908)

ON RETURNING TO ENGLAND I BEGAN WITH ARDOUR THE TASK OF REALIZING in rehearsal and performance the artistic problem of *Apollo and the Seaman*, and it soon became evident that the most important personage in the whole scheme was the manipulator of the magic lantern. As both orchestra and conductor were behind the screen it was clearly impossible for them to follow the text of the poem, and the only alternative was for the poem to follow the music. This involved the co-operation of someone who possessed a knowledge of it as well as a turn for mechanics, and I sought the assistance of William Wallace,* whose easy familiarity with nearly every known art and craft had long marked him out as one of the most versatile characters of the day. He responded to the invitation with such alacrity and enthusiasm that I could not resist the suspicion that his interest had been aroused as much by the singularity of the enterprise and the prospect of an hour or two's light entertainment as by any curiosity of an aesthetic kind. The author of the poem, Herbert Trench, an agreeable personality with a mind almost childlike in its placid imperturbability, devoted himself to the labour of forming a gigantic social committee; and although I never learned just how many of the peerage he managed to lure on to it, the number must have been uncommonly high, for at almost every rehearsal he would break in upon us to announce with triumphant satisfaction that he had "bagged another Duchess".

This was not the only diversion to hinder the speedy mastery of a vast and intricate score. The band parts, which had been copied with reckless celerity, teemed with errors of every sort; between the first reading and the performance I corrected over a hundred in those of the wind and brass sections alone, and as much of the instrumentation was heavy and strenuous our first impressions were not those that one passes on lightly to any composer seeking sympathy and approval from his interpreters. In the midst of it all arrived the venerable sarrusophonist, who at once became an especial object of interest to the rest of the players and the

---

* This richly endowed personality was a doctor of medicine by profession, although he refrained from actual practice. Joseph Holbrooke, in his entertaining work *Contemporary British Composers*, tells us that Wallace was the composer of the first English symphonic poem, and adds, "He is very Scotch, with all that race's faults and virtues, but I am glad to chronicle his name, as there are so few Scotch composers one can point to with any pride and not one of them lives in his own country, lovely as it is."

recipient of an excess of hospitality which for a few days deprived us of his company. Meanwhile it had been discovered that he had brought over the wrong set of instruments (there seemed to be as many in the family as there are names in a Biblical genealogy), which further delayed his participation in the proceedings: and even when the right ones did arrive they were to my ears almost inaudible in the sea of sound that surged about me. But as the composer professed to hear every note, although I never believed him, I could say no more and only hoped that on the night itself we should have a better return than this for all the trouble we had taken in enticing the stranger to our shores.

The eventful day of the first performance arrived; the final rehearsal held in the morning went smoothly enough, and even the magic lantern, which had had its little troubles, played up well. At that time I lived in the country a few miles out of London, and it was my habit on concert days to spend the afternoon there getting as much fresh air as I could before the evening. But the cab which had been ordered to take me from my house to the station failed to arrive, so that I missed the train by which I was to travel. The next one did not arrive in London until a few minutes before the concert; there was a dense fog on the line, all efforts to obtain a motor-car were unavailing, and I saw the elaborate schedule of preparation which we had worked out to the last detail going for nothing. In order that the performance should begin in an atmosphere of impressive mystery, a time-table had been drawn up under which at eight o'clock the doors of the hall were to be closed to further admittance. At one minute past the lights were to be half lowered, at three minutes past further lowered, and a minute later the lowest pedal note on the organ was to begin sounding as softly as possible. On the fifth minute the hall would be plunged into complete darkness, the organ would cease, and a soft blow on the cymbals would give the signal for the appearance on the screen of the first lantern slide, Apollo himself. With all these delicate operations in danger of being reduced to chaos, it may be imagined with what anxiety I awaited the coming of the train. To my joy and relief it steamed into the station hardly a moment late, and as if conscious of the importance of the occasion went on to London without any loss of time.

It was just six minutes past eight when I arrived at the hall and found everyone in a high state of worry and excitement. All had gone according to plan with the exception of the final tap on the cymbals, the cue for which I myself had to give, and the result was that the audience, who had been sitting in complete darkness for what seemed to them an age, seeing nothing and hearing only the weird rumbling of the thirty-two-foot pedal note, had begun to feel decidedly uneasy. There was a feeling that something had gone wrong, and a slight apprehension of danger was brewing; very soon there might have been a panic. I dashed to the platform, and on seeing me the cymbal-player, who had worked himself up into a fine condition of nerves, smote his instrument, not discreetly as arranged, but with terrific force. Simultaneously an immense head of the god flashed on the screen and everyone in the audience jumped half a foot in the air. The inevitable reaction followed almost immediately, and with one of the heartiest bursts of laughter I have ever heard in a public building the crowd resumed its normal equilibrium. If anyone at this moment could have taken a peep behind the curtain he would have been edified by the unusual spectacle of nearly four hundred performers, also in darkness save for their carefully shaded desk-lamps, directed by myself in shirt-sleeves and encouraged from time to time by the appearance of the composer, bearing in hand a huge can filled with beer, from which he drew frequent and copious draughts.

On the whole this remarkable experiment went off satisfactorily on both sides of the dividing line, and the only accident of any consequence I noticed on ours was that which befell our aged friend from across the Channel. Excited and bewildered by his novel surroundings, he missed his first important lead and after several wild efforts to come in at the wrong place, which were promptly suppressed by his adjoining colleagues, gave up desparingly and remained tacit for the rest of the evening. On the other, not all the skill and coolness of my friend William Wallace were equal to preventing his slaves of the lamp from resisting the temptation to vary now and then the settled sequence of the lantern slides. When the ethereal flight of Apollo across the daffodil fields was being read by the audience, the orchestra was illustrating it with thunderous explosions from trumpets, trombones, and drums, and the lurid description of the dead uprising from below lost something of its grandeur and terror through synchronizing with a handful of instruments which bore some resemblance to those pipes which the poet had once conceived should be the continuous musical background to his text.

But in spite of these minor mishaps everyone seemed happy about it all, the authors at having in their opinion produced a new art form, the audience at having been present at an exhilarating experience, and the newspapers and wits of the town at having something to write and make merry about. The following day I received a letter from Herbert Trench, containing many pleasant things about the performance and one note only of personal criticism. Everything had gone better than he had anticipated with the exception of the orchestral rendering of what he called the "Hell Section" of the work. This he craved leave to think had never sounded so eerie and stupendous since the opening days of rehearsal. I replied that I was entirely of the same opinion, but refrained from suggesting that it may have been my ill-advised correction of the hundred odd mistakes in the wind and brass parts that was largely responsible for the decrescendo in his enjoyment.

As for our foreign guest, he returned to his native land covered with glory. The fame of his Odyssey had penetrated not only the quarter where he resided but the whole of artistic Paris; honours were showered upon him, and a famous artist was commissioned to paint his portrait, which was exhibited in the Salon during the forthcoming season. Somewhere among my keepsakes is a picture postcard on which is depicted the old gentleman sitting with a look of radiant happiness on his face, and holding in a close embrace his beloved sarrusophone, the instrument which had played such a picturesque if silent part in the episode.

16

A HAPPY YEAR (1908–9)

THE TWELVE MONTHS THAT LINKED THE SUMMERS OF 1908 AND 1909 ARE among the pleasantest in my recollection.   I was now fairly launched on a flood-tide of activity wholly congenial to me; I felt completely at one with my musical kind and was accepted as a leader in a vigorous and progressive movement.   It was, in fact, a short transition period separating the stage of youthful experiment from the larger and more spacious days of big enterprises that lay closely ahead of me, but of which I had as yet no inkling.   Surrounded by a delightfully enthusiastic set of companions who looked upon me as the principal mouthpiece of their message to the world, life for the time being seemed altogether worthy of praise and enjoyment.

In July I went over to Norway to meet Delius, with whom I had planned a long walking tour in parts little frequented by the average tourist, and reaching Oslo (then Christiania) about a week in advance of him was lucky to find a dramatic festival going on at the State Theatre. Until six months or so prior to this my knowledge of Scandinavian authors had been of the slightest, being limited to a few Ibsen plays which I had seen in London and a novel or two of Björnson.   But influenced by Delius, who spoke each of the languages of the three kingdoms like a native and seemed to know their literature better than that of his own country, I had prepared myself for the trip by reading everything I could lay my hands on that had been translated, from the classical comedy of Holberg to the contemporary novels of Jonas Lie and E. P. Jacobsen.

It was lucky for me that I was in pretty good physical condition at that time, thanks mainly to tennis and long country rambles, for Delius proved to be a first-class mountaineer and a pedestrian of untiring energy.   One morning we got up at half past five after a decidedly troubled night spent in a cattle-hut, climbed on to the Josteldalsbrae, the largest glacier in Europe, walked across a long arm of it, and, stopping for hardly five minutes on the way, reached our destination about half past eight in the evening.   This was one of the high-lights of our tour, and the only thing that marred the total enjoyment of one of the grandest sights in the world was the frequent thought of bears, which, according to my companion, had an unpleasant habit of appearing suddenly on the glacier to the discomfiture of the unarmed traveller.   But as he passed on this unwelcome information to me quite casually and admitted that he had never caught sight of one on any previous occasion, I forgot my uneasiness in the contemplation of this marvellous sea of ice stretching for a hundred and twenty miles and taking on gradually a richer hue of gold as the sun sank lower and its rays grew longer.   So when we got down to the tiny hamlet where we were to lodge that night he was almost as startled as I to see lying in front of the inn a huge specimen of the tribe, which had wandered down only an hour or two earlier from the glacier in search of food, and had been shot by one of the farmers who had been on the lookout for it.

Almost as unforgettable was the ascent of Galdhöpiggen, the highest mountain in the country, on the top of which we spent two or three days and where we encountered in the dining-room of the little hostelry one of our countrymen. He was absorbed in the task of assimilating an immense plateful of some unappetizing sort of meat which he dosed with frequent extracts from a bottle of Worcester sauce, and the appearance of our national condiment in this remote spot filled us both with such astonishment that we were moved to inquire how he had got hold of it. He told us that he had been climbing this mountain for the past four successive years and on each occasion had called for the piquant accessory without which the enjoyment of any kind of fleshy viand was out of the question. But no sympathetic response had been made to his repeated inquiries until the present season, when the landlord welcomed him with a complacent grin on his face and a bottle of the precious stuff in either hand. Now at last he could feast his eyes upon one of the finest panoramas of the Northland, untroubled by the recurring sensation that there was something wanting to complete his happiness, and deeply impressed we hastened to express our appreciation of a remarkable example of British persistency.

In the lower land of the dales, wherever there was an available stream, Delius would procure a rod and sit peacefully fishing for hours ; and it was during these periods of relaxation that I would lead him to talk about his music and the correct interpretation of it. So far he had never been present at either rehearsals or performances where I had given any of his works, and I was not yet sure that I had been doing the right thing by them. The scores, especially the printed ones, were vilely edited and annotated, and if played in exact accordance with their directions of tempo, phrasing, and dynamics could not help being comparatively ineffective and unconvincing. Accustomed to the scrupulous care which the modern composer lavishes on this side of his task, and without which no adequate presentation of any piece of an intricate character is possible, I was amazed at this revelation of indifference or ineptitude on Delius' part, for it seemed that having once got down on paper the mere notes of his creations, he concerned himself hardly at all with how they could be made clear of ambiguity to his interpreters. I gathered from what he said that, as he seldom left his retreat at Grez to venture into the active world of music-making, he had been content to rely upon the advice of some fellow composers, who were in closer touch with the executive side of it. He never told me who they were, but it was distressingly obvious that they possessed more zeal than insight. I knew that he was wholly wanting in talent as a public performer, for some months earlier I had with agonized anxiety watched him endeavouring to conduct his *Appalachia*. In one of the slow variations which was in four-four time he contrived, I never knew how, to beat five to the bar throughout; and to compass this extraordinary feat had practised the motions of conducting in front of a looking-glass for six weeks beforehand. The only other time he dared venture to appear in this role was at a Three Choirs Festival concert at which I was unable to be present, much to my relief. But I was afterwards told by several who were there that the performance (the first anywhere) of his *Dance Rhapsody* sent shivers of excitement running down the backs of everyone sitting in the massive nave of the Norman cathedral.

There is an odd opinion current in many foreign places that the Englishman is a dull and humourless sort of fellow, although how it has obtained circulation, in face of the admitted fact that his nation has produced the most famous company of comic playwrights, novelists, essayists, and even philosophers, that civilization has yet seen, is beyond the understanding of anyone who has thought twice about the matter. Like every other popular notion, it is the reverse of true; and I venture to assume the pleasing privilege of informing a deluded world that whatever else there may or may not be in my country, there is more fun and laughter there to the square acre (save, of course, in the Celtic principality of Wales) than there is to the square mile of any other known area. Even if a man does achieve a gravity alien to the common spirit around him he is not able to keep it up for long. The opposing pressure from outside is too powerful and sooner or later forces him to renounce the worship of the goddess of gloom. The most serious creatures find themselves victims of the most ludicrous situations unless they exercise the greatest care to avoid them, and this is what Delius, who despite much wit and some humour was fundamentally a serious soul, could never succeed in doing. Everyone of strong personality has within him a centripetal ruling force, magnet-like, which draws from without into its orbit another like unto itself, whether it be rest or unrest, hate or love. There must have been in Frederick an element which invited visitations of the twin spirits of high and low comedy, for the moment he exchanged the safe sanctuary of Fontainebleau for the busy haunts of men was the instant sign for their appearance, and the incident of the *Dance Rhapsody* may be numbered among their most successful exploits.

How the piece ever came to be played at all in a sacred edifice remains a mystery to this day; nothing except possibly the anarchic operations of a swing band would have been less appropriate. Then the composer chose to incorporate into his score an important solo part for an instrument which, like Lucy, there were few to praise and very few to love, the bass oboe. As if these two errors of judgment were not enough, he must needs be persuaded into accepting the services of a young lady of semi-amateur status who had volunteered at short notice to see what she could do with it. Now the bass oboe, like certain other members of the single- and double-reed families, is to be endured only if manipulated with supreme cunning and control; otherwise its presence in the orchestra is a strain upon the nervous system of conductor and players alike, a danger to the seemly rendering of the piece in hand, and a cause of astonishment and risibility in the audience. A perfect breath control is the essential requisite for keeping it well in order, and this alone can obviate the eruption of sounds that would arouse attention even in a circus. As none of these safety-first precautions had been taken, the public, which had assembled in the sombre interior of an eleventh-century basilica, in anticipation of some pensive and poetical effort from the most discussed musician of the day, was confounded by the frequent audition of noises that resembled nothing so much as the painful endeavour of an anguished mother-duck to effect the speedy evacuation of an abnormally large-sized egg. Had the composer-conductor not been a figure of renown, of middle age, and of outward sobriety, I have often shuddered to think what might have happened. As it was, so successful proved the enterprise of the ministers of Momus that the wife of one of the leading ecclesiastical dignitaries, precipitately fleeing the church, decided it were better to absent herself from any of the subsequent performances rather than run the risk of losing a hardly won reputation for dignity and decorum.

When the autumn arrived we resumed our concerts, continuing the policy of previous seasons; and, stimulated by the optimism of the progressive sections in several provincial cities, ventured there on proselytizing missions, sometimes with happy but more often with dismal results. I had been led to believe that Manchester, which during the prolonged reign of Hans Richter had hardened into a veritable citadel of extreme musical Diehardism, was hungering for some variation from the unchanging round of Beethoven, Brahms, and Wagner. Profiting by the engagement of my orchestra for a concert given by the North Staffordshire Choral Society at Hanley, where Delius' *Sea Drift* was in the programme, I decided to take it on to Manchester, together with the full chorus, and to gladden the hearts of the new believers there. There were about four hundred of us on the platform of the Free Trade Hall, which when full held some two thousand six hundred, and there were actually present in the auditorium less than three hundred. In the vast single gallery which contained about half of the total capacity there was one solitary patron, and even he for some time escaped our notice. Having brought along with him all the full scores of the pieces we were playing, he had propped them up in front of and around him, and in this way made himself wholly invisible to those below.

Towards the close of this year differences arose between the orchestra and myself, mainly over the perpetual bogeys of the public musical life of that time, rehearsals and the deputy system, which led to the termination of my connection with it. As I was midway in the passage of a long season and any early adjustment of the breach seemed unlikely, I set about forming an entirely new body of players, there being no other established organization available. In nearly every orchestra that I have met in any part of the world there is to be found at least one person who combines a respectable business talent with an encyclopaedic knowledge of his own section of the musical community, and there was an admirable specimen of the kind in this one. He had been of the greatest use to me from the beginning of my regular concert career, as he knew the name, character, and degree of ability of every player in the town and seemed able to lay his hand upon any one of them at an hour's notice. This excellent fellow, Verdi Fawcett, belonged to a numerous family scattered here and there over the country, all orchestral musicians and each with a Christian name borrowed, like his own, from one of the great composers, ancient or modern. He placed himself immediately at my service as factotum, proving to be as indispensable and invaluable to me in this capacity as ever Figaro was to Almaviva, and within three weeks I had a completely new group of eighty, mainly young men not long out of the colleges, whose average age must have been well under twenty-five. Hearing that there was a violinist of uncommon dexterity in the restaurant band of the Waldorf Hotel, I went to dine there one night, and, following my request for a solo, he complied with the finale of the Mendelssohn Violin Concerto taken at a speed that made me hold my breath. I scribbled on a card, "Splendid, but the right tempo is so and so", indicating by a metronome mark what I thought it should be, and at once came back the answer, "Many thanks, I'll play it again for you a little later on."

At the close of dinner we were introduced, and I learned not only that he was barely twenty-three but that the instrument he was using had been made by himself. I offered and he accepted a prominent place in my new orchestra, and a few months later became its principal violin, a position he occupied for five years. This gifted and resourceful youth developed into the best all-round concert-master I have met anywhere, uniting in himself a technical faculty equal to any demand made upon it, a full warm tone, a faultless rhythmic sense, and a brain that remained cool in the face of any untoward happening. Such was the beginning of the career of Albert Sammons, whom many consider the best English fiddler of this generation.

Soon after this I gained another valuable recruit to the string section, in this case a mature artist of experience and celebrity. That there is a plentiful crop of competent players in England on that instrument of mixed sex, the viola, is due wholly to the example of Lionel Tertis. With a natural facility that might have made him the rival of a Heifetz or a Menuhin he has elected to devote his life to the exploitation of the resources of this hermaphrodite of the orchestra, and the instruction of a band of youth to replace the older type of player, who rarely atoned by making an adequate study of it for his customary failure on the violin. Tertis remained with us for about eighteen months, after which, unable to endure longer the strenuous routine, the long hours, and the close atmosphere of the Opera House, he resigned his position, and I do not think has ever been seen in an orchestra again.

17

A NEW ORCHESTRA AND SOME MUSICIANS (1909)

AS I HAVE INDICATED, THE NEW ORCHESTRA, OUTSIDE A VETERAN OR TWO, was an essentially youthful body, and its members differed conspicuously from the older type of orchestra player. Their executive standard was higher, their musicianship broader and sounder, and their general culture of a wholly superior order, much of it traceable to a solid all-round training and early contact with men and women of refinement in the great colleges of music. Filled with an enthusiasm and untiring appetite for work that would horrify the soul of a modern trade-union official, they regarded music as primarily an artistic pursuit, a joyous pastime which had not yet degenerated into an industry distinguishable from others of a mechanical nature only by conditions of higher pay for less labour. Not yet was a conductor confronted with the spectacle of a hundred men, calling themselves artists and demanding the respect due to such, downing tools in the middle of a phrase and executing a precipitate stampede from the platform on the first stroke of a clock striking the hour which announced the end of the session. Some years ago I was conducting a series of concerts in a certain foreign capital, and half an hour before the conclusion of the first rehearsal an individual with a stop-watch took up his position behind me and at regular intervals called out loudly: "Fifteen minutes more, ten minutes more, only five minutes left." I was obliged to inform the venerable society for which I was working that if this astonishing practice, so admirably calculated to assist concentration among the players as well as the conductor, was repeated on any subsequent occasion, it would be I who would indulge in the process of downing tools without a second's hesitation and leave the place for ever.

These rigid and unnatural regulations do not originate with the players themselves, at all events not those of the highest class, but with a type of mind that regards all musicians as children who must be protected against any of those stirring and spontaneous impulses to work when they are so inclined, impulses which are inseparable from a genuine artistic nature. It is unfortunately true that in earlier days there was, as in many other occupations, a certain exploitation of the humbler sort of musician on the part of employers of small sensibility or conscience. But the talented player never stood in need of coddling or guarding, being quite capable of looking competently after his own interests, nor does he today; and what he wants more than anything else is to be allowed to give vent to the unfettered expression of his best self, which if thwarted or over regulated will in time inevitably run to seed. Of course every thinking person knows exactly where all this regimentation is going to end. For generations in all Anglo-Saxon communities music has been maintained by the public spirit and liberality of private persons. It is a fine art, a luxury, and not an absolute necessity like food, drink, clothing, or transportation; and today this class is feeling keenly that it is not being given a square deal and that its sacrifices are being taken too much for granted and its goodwill abused. The next step in the game will be their retirement from the scene, leaving either to the State or to those more vitally and directly concerned the responsibility of shouldering the burden. As music is unlike most other businesses in that it is almost always run at a large financial loss, the task of meeting it will have to be sustained in one form or another by musicians themselves, for it is safe to prophesy that the State will not support that which is at the moment a wholly parasitic industry. In other words, music is something that people can get on without, and if it costs too much they will. I have for many years now been sounding warnings about the precarious condition of the entire fabric of music, how easily even the major orchestral organizations which are the greater glory of our modern artistic life could decline and disappear. They did not exist on any important scale fifty years ago, they are subject like all else to the various laws of development (down as well as up), economy, and public taste, and quite conceivably might return to that void from which they came.

The years stretching from 1900 to 1914 constituted the second phase of that national artistic evolution of which the first had been the period 1885 to 1890. The public was awakening to the realization that there might be Englishmen who had what the French call "the matter of music" in them, not only in composers, but singers and instrumentalists. But a large number of amateurs still nourished the belief that to hear adequate orchestral or operatic performances one must go abroad, to Vienna, Berlin, Munich, or Bayreuth, and one nervous Wagnerite, almost panic-stricken on seeing the inclusion of *Die Meistersinger* in the repertoire of one of my opera seasons, asked anxiously: "Do you think the orchestra can really play it?" A similar scepticism prevailed about solo artists, singers especially, who almost invariably renounced the lowly patronymics so wanting in romance and mystery for grand-sounding foreign names which were contentedly accepted by the public as evidences of the real thing. For this reason we had such adoptions as Melba, Nordica, Nevada, Donalda, or Stralia, and many others, all striving to conceal from a world which really knew all about them the inferiority of their origin, and sometimes ignorance of the actual birthplace of an artist led to incidents in which it was impossible for even the kindliest person not to take a little malicious delight.   One day an agent brought to me a new tenor who styled himself (let us say) Signor Amboni.   He was young, presentable, and had a voice of excellent quality and considerable volume.   Although I hardly ever made use of singers at my concerts I was impressed by the newcomer and interpolated him into one of them to sing arias from *Rigoletto*, *Manon*, and *Die Walküre*.   Everyone thought that my find sang well enough, but some of the Press fell foul of his pronunciation, averring that if only he would stick to his native Italian all would be well.   His French might at a pinch be forgiven, but his German simply would not do at all.   The following evening I gave a supper party at which Amboni was present and I observed some private hilarity between him and one or two others when the subject of this criticism was mentioned, the cause of which the rest of us remained in ignorance until the arrival later on of Fritz Cassirer, who had come on from another gathering.   On being presented to Amboni, he gazed at him in stupefaction for quite ten seconds as if he could not believe the evidence of his very short-sighted eyes, and finally gasped out: "Good Lord, it's old Hasselbaum!"   The Italian whose German pronunciation had been condemned as deplorable turned out to be a genuine son of the Fatherland from Mannheim!

The summer of 1909 was marked by three events all of capital importance to me.   The first was a performance of Delius' *A Mass of Life*, his *magnum opus*, which, though of quite ordinary length, had been heard nowhere in its entirety.   My old friends, the North Staffordshire Choir, had prepared it with great care and sang with splendid tone and flawless intonation many passages then regarded as harsh and unvocal, and which were assailed vigorously by upholders of the elder school of choral writing modelled on Handel and Mendelssohn.   After the quartette of solo singers had come forward several times at the end to acknowledge the applause, I brought out the chorus-master, a slight, elderly figure unknown to the London public, and I heard a young girl in the front row of the stalls ask her male companion who it was.   "That, my dear," he replied without an instant's hesitation, "is the librettist."   Poor Nietzsche, whose *Also sprach Zarathustra* had supplied the text for the Mass, had then been in his grave about ten years.

The next was the entrance into my life of Ethel Smyth and her opera *The Wreckers*.   Ethel Smyth is without question the most remarkable of her sex that I have been privileged to know.   I have been told that here and there in the world there have been observed a few examples of that same fiery energy and unrelenting fixity of purpose, and that almost unscrupulous capacity to accomplish the purpose in hand.   It may be, but they have never come my way, and I like to cherish the conviction that such a portent could have been hatched only by the England of the great Victorian age.   Unlike most artists, she was a born fighter and rebel, roused to controversy and reprisal on the slightest provocation, and hardly ever bore in mind the advice of the Boyg in *Peer Gynt* to "go round" rather than forward, preferring frontal attacks to flank movements whenever she could make them.*   This did not make her the easiest of colleagues, and her frequent efforts at direct action either in the theatre or concert hall hindered rather than forwarded the aim which everyone else wanted just as much to attain.   Efficiency itself in her own daily life, she demanded an equal measure of it from others on all occasions private and public. But the faculty possessed by many far less gifted of extracting from their co-workers the best which they had to give did not always seem within her power to exercise.

In after years a good deal of her unremitting militancy evaporated, but at the time of which I am writing it was gloriously rampant, receiving constant stimulus from her close association with the aggressive suffragette movement headed by Mrs. Pankhurst.   Into this Ethel threw herself with almost ferocious zeal, was seen in processions, wrote a marching song which sounded like a call to combat *à l'outrance*, and finally distinguished herself by hurling a large-sized brick through the front window of the house of the Home Secretary.   For this exploit and sundry others of a rowdy character she spent a few weeks in Holloway Gaol together with a chosen band of peace-disturbing accomplices, and there I went to see her one day.   I arrived in the main courtyard of the prison to find the noble company of martyrs marching round it and singing lustily their war-chant while the composer, beaming approbation from an overlooking upper window, beat time in almost Bacchic frenzy with a toothbrush.

The easy capacity to be led away to by-paths and side-shows which have no direct connection with her art has had the unsatisfactory effect of limiting this amazing woman's musical output.   But what there is of it has a distinctive quality that separates it from the rest of English music. The vigour and rhythmic force of portions of *The Wreckers* and *Hey Nonny No* equal anything of the kind written in my time, and hand in hand with these characteristics go a high emotion and delicate sentiment wholly free from rhetoric or bathos.†   Tempted at times by an infelicitous choice of subject, she has forsaken her own broad highway of simplicity and downrightness for some tortuous track, where she finds it fitting to make use of a scholasticism that weighs upon her natural style as irons do upon a prisoner; and in larger forms her aesthetic judgment is not always to be trusted.   In that charming little opera *The Boatswain's Mate*, the first act, with its mixture of lyrical numbers and dialogue, is perfect in style and structure.   But in the second this happy scheme is thrown overboard for an uninterrupted stream of music involving the setting of portions of the text that one feels would have been more effective and congruous had they been kept in speech as in the earlier section of the work.   Many a time during the past twenty-five years have I thought of suggesting that here was one of those cases where, as other eminent composers have

---

* *Peer Gynt*, Act 2, Scene 7:
    Peer: What are you?
    The Voice: The great Boyg.
    Peer: Make the way clear, Boyg!
    The Voice: Go roundabout, Peer!
    Peer: No, through!
    † As, for instance, in her songs such as *La Danse* and *Chrysilla*.

discovered, some effort of revision might be beneficial, but have always drawn back in apprehension lest I set in motion a volume of correspondence from her of self-justification, all expressed with a subtlety, ingenuity, and illusive logic that would have done credit to the dialectical brain of St. Thomas Aquinas. Undoubtedly her masterpiece is *The Wreckers*, which remains one of the three or four English operas of real musical merit and vitality written during the past forty years. This fine piece has never had a convincing representation owing to the apparent impossibility of finding an Anglo-Saxon soprano who can interpret revealingly that splendid and original figure, the tragic heroine Thirza. Neither in this part nor that of Mark, the tenor, have I heard or seen more than a tithe of that intensity and spiritual exaltation without which these two characters must fail to make their mark. But the ability to play tragedy with great and moving force has departed for a while from the English stage, and we must wait for a sign of its return before there can be the slightest hope of *The Wreckers* coming into its own.

Lastly, after nearly a decade, my father and I became reconciled, and until the end of his life remained on the closest terms of friendship. During the last few years I discovered he had been keenly interested in my doings and would slip unnoticed into a remote seat at my concerts and steal away before the end, lest someone should observe his presence and report it to me. He had been spending much more of his time in London than in the old days and had bought a house in Hampstead, to which, as was to be expected, he had added a large wing containing a picture gallery with a fine collection of Turners, Constables, Coxes, and DeWints. My recent experiences over the production of *The Wreckers* had strongly revived in me an interest that had lain dormant for seven years, although during that time I had been reflecting continuously upon the many-sided problem of operatic representation, not solely from the musical angle. My association with masters of their craft like Maurel had yielded me an insight into the technique of the stage and had begotten a desire to try my hand at a venture given under conditions where the various ideas and theories I had been forming could take living shape. But this sort of thing was unrealizable without powerful backing, which up to the moment had not been forthcoming. I approached my father, found his old interest in opera unabated, and obtained a mandate to draw up a plan of campaign. Nothing definite, however, could be determined for some weeks, as he was about to leave for the United States and I was setting out on a long tour with my orchestra in the provinces.

This took place during a September that lived handsomely up to its reputation of being the finest month of the year. Avoiding the large industrialized cities and visiting mainly pleasant and picturesque country towns like Cambridge, Norwich, and Chester, this event, in which the spirit of holiday was more present than that of work, was the most agreeable I have ever known. Whether it was equally gratifying to the gallant impresario who had taken us out I doubt, for the concert rooms were mostly smallish and, even when full, could hardly have met the evenings' expenses. But for us it was entirely delightful to roam around the kingdom, play football or see sights by day, and make music at night. In the North we touched Lancaster, where we found a hall whose walls were almost covered with inscriptions and directions, one of which, "It is strictly forbidden to use in this building the words Hell, Damn, and other Biblical Expressions", took the fancy of my players exceedingly, without compelling the accustomed observance of it.

On the way to our southernmost point, Torquay, we stopped at Cheltenham, where during the afternoon of the concert day I and some of the orchestra were invited to inspect one of the leading girls' colleges. As we arrived in a quadrangle to find a large number of young women drawn up in military formation, the principal came forward to meet us, and simultaneously a cheery looking girl, stepping briskly out of the ranks, embraced me heartily while the whole body of her companions cheered enthusiastically. I was a little taken aback, but, recovering my presence of mind, said to the principal, who was beaming with satisfaction: "What delightful customs you have in your college, madam, but may I ask who this charming young lady is?" The chief, drawing herself up with dignity, replied a little coldly: "That is your youngest sister." At the time of my quitting the family roof, some ten years earlier, she was only six or seven, and I had not seen her since.

18

FIRST COVENT GARDEN SEASON (1910)

TO ANYONE UNACQUAINTED WITH THE CHARACTER OF THE BRITISH PUBLIC it would have seemed beyond question that what it was craving more than anything else in the world at this time was opera. Over a period of ten years there had been carried on in and out of the Press an unceasing campaign for the establishment of an English opera, or perhaps more accurately an opera in English; and according to dozens of writers on the subject, both professional and amateur, we should never be a really civilized nation until we had one. The only existing institution of importance, the Grand Opera Syndicate, which gave us regular seasons in the summer at Covent Garden in French, Italian and German, was constantly assailed as being inimical to the interests of native music, and condemned on two further counts—insufficiency of repertoire and adherence to the star system.

For my part I never saw reason or justice in either of these indictments. The programme given was fairly large and representative, more so indeed than in some of the famous theatres on the Continent, and the so-called star system was nothing worse than the practice of engaging for each role that particular singer whom the Directorate thought best fitted for it, hardly a serious offence against music. Six opera houses running the whole year round could not have played all the works which newspaper-writers were convinced the public wanted to hear; and if this need were genuine, then clearly what was wanted was less the reformation or abolition of an institution that was doing excellent work in its own way than the creation of others to meet it. But as it is always more fun and less trouble to criticize than construct, nothing tangible ever came of this busy activity of tongue and pen.

In determining, then, the character of my own effort I had to take into consideration these two public aspirations—a more varied choice of fare, and the performance of English works, together with the engagement of a large number of English singers. The first was much easier to gratify than the second, for there were dozens, even hundreds, of pieces unknown then as now. That was purely a matter of selection, and should be simple enough in view of the clamour for anything and everything. But the production of operas by native composers on any scale was quite another matter. There were very few that could be given with any reasonable chance of success, and as for the singers, most of them had been trained for oratorio and other concert work and had little or no knowledge of the stage and all that varied accomplishment which is essential to a successful career on it. Furthermore, English voices are unlike those of most other nations; really robust tenors and true dramatic sopranos hardly exist among us, and high baritones are as rare as a perfect summer. The best among them are of comparatively moderate volume, pure and excellent in tone but lacking in power and brilliance in comparison with those of Italy, Germany and France. Care and discretion would be necessary in the planning of a scheme of work that would display them to advantage by the side of their rivals, and perhaps my ultimate goal would prove to be a building of smaller dimensions than Covent Garden or La Scala, something after the model of that admirable French organization the Opéra Comique. But as my advisers were strongly of the opinion that this my first important season should be given at Covent Garden, a theatre that had been associated in the public mind with opera for over two hundred years, there I went.

The programme was made up of *Elektra*, *A Village Romeo and Juliet*, *Ivanhoe*, *Tristan und Isolde*, *The Wreckers*, *Carmen*, *Hänsel und Gretel*, and *L'Enfant Prodigue*. This last-named piece was originally a short cantata which I transferred to the stage, and proved to be a capital curtain-raiser. I myself conducted the Strauss and Delius operas, while Bruno Walter, whose first appearance this was at Covent Garden, and Percy Pitt divided the others between them. With the exception of *Elektra* none of the other novelties and unfamiliar pieces met with popular success, although the general attendance was fairly good. *A Village Romeo and Juliet* was pronounced to be undramatic by the Press, although I myself have never been able to discover this deficiency in it. All the same, Delius has certainly a method of writing opera shared by no one else. So long as the singers are off the stage the orchestra plays delicately and enchantingly, but the moment they reappear it strikes up fiercely and complainingly as if it resented not being allowed to relate the whole story by itself. During the last act the curtain is down for about eight minutes, and there is heard a strain of haunting beauty; an intermezzo now known to every concert-goer as "The Walk to the Paradise Garden". But in the theatre it went for next to nothing, being almost completely drowned by the combining sounds of British workmen battering on the stage and the loud conversation of the audience.

When I revived the work some years later I introduced here a new stage picture so that this lovely piece could be played with the curtain up, the only way in an English theatre to secure attention. What the public does not see it takes no interest in, and I would advise all young composers, if they wish their music to be listened to, never to lower the curtain

for one second during the course of an act.   Better let it remain up with
the operations of scene-shifting and workmen in shirt-sleeves in full view,
for possibly a fair proportion of the spectators would leave the building
under the impression that these were actually a part of the entertainment.

Just as *A Village Romeo* and *The Wreckers* represented the living
English school, so the revival of *Ivanhoe* was an act of respect to a dead
English master, Sullivan.   It was essentially an affair of action and
spectacle, and the designers and machinists saw their opportunity and
went out boldly to grasp it.   I was guaranteed effects of wonder and
excitement that would outmatch the most thrilling Drury Lane melodrama, and tons of timber were ordered for the scenes of the tournament
and the burning of the Castle of Torquilstone.   In those days we had not
yet escaped from the cycle of ultra-realism in stage decoration and everything had to be as life-like as possible.   If there was a house on the stage
it must be a real house; trees and waterfalls must be the things themselves;
and artists as well as the public took a childish delight in going farther
than merely holding the mirror up to nature.   This phase came to an
end shortly afterwards when a celebrated actor-manager, nervously uncertain of the effect likely to be made on his cultivated audience by the
unassisted recital of Shakespeare's verse, was moved to enliven the
occasion by letting loose on the stage a brood of tame rabbits during
Oberon's magnificent speech in *A Midsummer Night's Dream*.   Naturally
against this rival attraction on the boards the unfortunate Bard had very
little chance.

I soon observed that the soaring ambitions of the scenic department
were reacting none too favourably upon the musical side of the work.
There were so many buildings, fences, trees, rivers and animals encum-
bering the stage that there was hardly any room upon it for the unlucky
singers; and as for the chorus and supers numbering nearly three hundred,
it was evident that if something were not done to accommodate them
better they would have to sing in the adjoining market.   But it is as
difficult to alter traditional methods in a theatre as to impose economy
on a Government department, and I waited and vacillated until the final
rehearsal, when the grand surprises were to be seen in their full glory.   The
burning of the castle was certainly an astonishing triumph as viewed
from the auditorium, but it was appreciated less by the occupants of the
crowded stage.   For regardless of the value of human life, huge chunks of
masonry flew in every direction, spreading terror among the attackers and
defenders alike.   There was almost a riot, and undoubtedly there would
have been no performance if I had not given my word to control the
enthusiasm of the realists.   All that day there was a depressed exodus
from the theatre of about as much wood and other solid material as
would have built a good-sized sailing yacht.

With the production of *Elektra* in London, the reputation of its composer reached its zenith.   Excepting the death of King Edward, which
occurred in the following spring, it was the most discussed event of the
year.   Some time had gone by since a new piece of Strauss had been
heard, the last being the *Sinfonia Domestica* in 1905, which had been
little more than a faint success.   About ten years had passed since *Ein
Heldenleben*, and the earlier Symphonic Poems had been overplayed.
None of the composer's operas had yet been given in London; the town

was in just the right mood for a new musical sensation; it expected it and most decidedly it got it. Weeks before the first performance newspapers vied one with another in drawing the most lurid pictures of what was going to happen on the stage; musicians took sides, and a small war raged with refreshing vivacity before a note of the score had been heard. Scholars fell foul of the libretto on the gound that Hofmannsthal had bedevilled the grand old story, although for my part I never saw much to choose between the Greek and the German in the way of horrors. The tale, even as told by the silver tongue of Sophocles, is one of the gruesomest in literature.

Some of this journalistic fever, which my advertising manager assured me was of untold value, occasioned embarrassment now and then to the theatre staff. As all know who are acquainted with the work, there is a modest procession of sacrificial victims, a few sheep generally, to prelude the first entrance of Clytemnestra. But from the accounts in some journals one would have thought that half the inhabitants of the Zoo were being rehearsed to take their part in the show. One day I received a letter from a farmer living about one hundred miles from London whose imagination had been fired by reading of these marvels, and under the impression that I was seeking voluntary contributions to my production in the way of livestock, he had arranged for the transportation to London of a fine young bull, which he claimed to be mild in disposition and seemly in behaviour. As the animal had already started on his journey there was nothing to be done but wait for his arrival, have him photographed for the satisfaction of his former owner, and as we could not employ him in the service of art, put him to the next best purpose.

Strauss's share of the work, taken as a whole, is his most characteristic achievement. Here he has the fullest opportunity of working that vein of grotesque and weird fantasy of which he remains the greatest master in music. On the side of pathos and tenderness he rises to a fairly satisfactory height, and in spite of inequalities of style realizes a unity which is lacking in his other stage works. The almost entire absence of charm and romance makes it unique, and if it is reported truly that Gluck in his austerity thought more of the Muses than the Graces, then Strauss might here be fairly said to have shown a preference for the Furies. The public was undoubtedly impressed and startled, and to satisfy the demand for further performances, I was obliged to extend my season. For the last night I invited Strauss to conduct, and he agreed to come provided I gave him two rehearsals with the orchestra. But in the middle of the first of them—that is after about three-quarters of an hour—he quitted the desk, expressing the highest satisfaction with the work of the players. So far as I could ascertain, musicians did not like the piece at all. One eminent British composer on leaving the theatre was asked what he thought of it. "Words fail me," he replied, "and I'm going home at once to play the chord of C major twenty times over to satisfy myself that it still exists." The curious thing about this little piece of criticism is that *Elektra* actually finishes with the chord in question, thundered out several times in repetition on the full orchestra.

There is in every large town of every country at least one individual who is the living terror of managers, conductors, pianists, or any other kind of artist. This is the single composer enthusiast. For this type of fanatic no other music except that of the object of his idolatry exists at all. If he thinks that it is being insufficiently played he writes long and frequent letters to the Press. He attends all concerts where any composition of the master is given, and if there is something in the performance that he does not like he fires off a volley of oral or epistolary abuse at the misguided and incompetent interpreter. He is always *plus royaliste que le roi*, and there is no escape from him; in other words, he is the world's greatest bore and its Nuisance Number One. As I had already suffered from the attentions of the leading Strauss devotee and watchdog in London, I was hardly surprised when he got in touch with me over *Elektra* in the following fashion.

Sir,
    Do you intend to imitate the cheeseparing habits of the Grand Opera Syndicate? What is coming over you? Last night from my coign of vantage in the gallery I counted your orchestra and could discover no more than ninety-eight players. As you well know, Strauss has stipulated for no less than one hundred and eleven. What have you done with the rest? Please reply at once.
Yours anxiously,
SYLVESTER SPARROW.

For the moment I felt like the unhappy Varus when the Emperor Augustus confronted him with the terrifying demand: "Where are my Legions?" Surely it was impossible for a company of them to have trooped out while I was conducting, without my observing it. To satisfy myself, I ascended to the exalted spot which Mr. Sparrow termed his "coign of vantage" and discovered the explanation of the mystery. From there it was impossible to see the full orchestra, some having been concealed in and under certain boxes, and greatly relieved I was able to send a reply that all was well and the temple had not been profaned.

Nothing matures or grows old more rapidly than music. The brilliant audacity of one generation declines into the sober commonplace of another, and an audience of today would not find it easy to realize how strange and bewildering the score of *Elektra* sounded to the public of 1910. About the middle of the work there is a short scene where two men—messengers—rush excitedly on the stage and after singing a few phrases disappear. At one of our later performances this episode occurred in the usual way and the opera went on. About five minutes later the same performers entered again, and without regard to what was happening at the moment in a scene of totally different character went through their parts and vanished exactly as before. I pinched myself to make sure I was not dreaming and, bending down to Albert Sammons, who was leading, asked: "Have those two fellows been on already?"

"Yes," he replied.

"Are you certain?"

"There is no doubt about it."

I put the same question to the leader of the second violins, and he was equally convinced that we had been treated to an unsolicited and highly original form of encore. At the close I went on the stage to discover the cause of this novel addition to the normal attractions of an operatic evening, and found the culprits in the company of the chorus-master, all three of them looking very ill at ease.

"Am I right in assuming that you took upon yourselves to repeat your scene this evening?" I asked frigidly.

"I am afraid you are," replied one of them.

"What is the explanation of this twice-nightly experiment?"

This question was answered by the chorus-master, who explained that a part of his duty was to take the cue for the sending on of the two singers from a passage in the orchestra.   On this occasion his attention had been distracted by the disagreeable task of forcibly expelling a rude and refractory chorister through the stage door into the street.   This being successfully accomplished, he returned to his post aglow with victory, and presently there came along something that to his flushed ear resembled the familiar phrase which was his lighthouse in the polyphonic sea of whirling sound.

"Now you go on," he called out to the singers.

"But we have been on," they answered.

"Then it was at the wrong place—you must go on again"; and as they seemed unreasonably hesitant he literally pushed them on to the scene.

I was relieved to find that a more agreeable manifestation of human weakness than artistic vanity was at the bottom of the mystery, and I discharged the offenders with a caution and the reminder that there was quite enough rough-and-tumble going on in the band without the actors joining in.   As I never heard a comment or received a protest from any member of the audience I concluded that this curious variation from the orderly course of performance had either passed unnoticed or had proved to their liking.   But I do not think that even an audience of savages in Central Africa would fail to notice in works like *Faust* or *Carmen* a repetition of the songs of Siebel or the Toreador during scenes with which they obviously had not the slightest connection.   I awaited anxiously the arrival of next day's mail, which I felt sure would bring me an explosive communication from my friend Sylvester Sparrow.   To my relief, nothing appeared, from which I gathered that the "coign of vantage" had not harboured its usual tenant that night.

19

OPÉRA COMIQUE AND HIS MAJESTY'S THEATRE (1910)

IN THE SEASON JUST CONCLUDED MY CONTINGENT OF NATIVE SINGERS had acquitted itself with gratifying credit, and the report that a new spirit was stirring in the town attracted back to England a certain number of others who, unable to find anything interesting to do at home, had been building up careers in a dozen different opera houses abroad.   The offer of His Majesty's Theatre for the summer months coincided happily with my plan to give an all-English season in a moderate sized house, and I drew up what I considered to be a widely varied repertoire of about a dozen operas.   This involved an unusual amount of labour, as most of them not only required careful translation but were wholly unfamiliar to my artists even in the original tongue.

I opened with *Contes d'Hoffmann,* for the main reason that it suited the particular talents of the more gifted members of my company, chief among them being John Coates, who took the leading part. Coates was among the half-dozen most interesting artistic personalities of the time in England—scrupulous, fastidious and conscientious in all that he attempted. His appearance on the stage was noble and animated, and his voice, although of moderate power, was flexible and expressive. His diction was admirable and his singing of English an unalloyed pleasure to the ear. Nine-tenths of the English-speaking vocalists whom I hear seem to have the smallest idea of the potentialities of their own language. Their ordinary speech may be articulate enough, but the moment they begin to vocalize they transform it into a strange medley which sounds German and Italian all mixed together in one jumble of complete unintelligibility. I went one evening with Delius to a concert in a smallish hall, where a well-known baritone was giving a group of his songs. At the conclusion the composer, on being asked his opinion of the performance, said blandly but annihilatingly: "Admirable, but what language was he singing in?" And yet we could not have been more than five yards at the most from the platform. Coates shared the capacity with a few others, such as Charles Santley and Gervase Elwes, of making English sound not only perfectly clear but beautiful as well, just as did at a later date his younger rival, Frank Mullings, in some ways the most remarkably talented of them all, and of whom I shall have something to say later on.

Hoffmann was a definite hit, the lyrical character of the music and the fantastic if slightly incomprehensible story appealing to everybody; and quite a fair portion of my daily post consisted of requests that I should furnish a detailed explanation of what it was all about. One of the oddest that I received was from a clergyman who lived in the country and was unable to spend the night in London. He could, however, come up during the day, and suggested that it would be very nice if the singers and orchestra would assemble for a quiet hour one afternoon so that he might hear, like Ludwig of Bavaria, the best parts of the work sung and played for his exclusive benefit.

The second piece in my programme, Massenet's *Werther,* was as much of a failure as *Hoffmann* was a success. In fact, it was a downright catastrophe, enjoying a run of one performance. It is always easier to comprehend the causes of a fiasco such as this after the event than to foresee them before. The representation vocally and instrumentally was far from bad, every note being sung and played quite accurately; the scenery was attractive, and a good deal of trouble had been taken over the whole production. The truth of the matter was that the artists taking part in it were temperamentally at odds with the style and sentiment both of the music and the story. Indeed, the two roles of Werther and Charlotte are outside the accomplishment of almost any Anglo-Saxon singer, who probably can never quite succeed during the performance in banishing from his or her recollection Thackeray's satirical lines about the well-conducted German maiden, who (after her lover's tragic death) went on tranquilly cutting bread-and-butter. But it was a favourite work of mine and in those early days I lacked the experience to gauge the capacities or incapacities of my artists, and frequently mounted operas more for the purpose of hearing the music myself than for giving pleasure to the public. The latter had moments of illumination when it appreciated this attitude of mine and generally rewarded it by absenting itself from the theatre altogether!

The third French work of my choice was the *Muguette* of Edmond de Missa, who had died a few months earlier. It was a fair example of that genre of piece which is peculiar to the genius of France; and which occupies a half-way stage between grand opera and the Viennese operetta or our English musical comedy. Starting in a humble way as a vagrant entertainment at fairs and in market-places, it was moulded into an art form by the powerful intelligence of Philidor and the inventive genius of Grétry, and is something eminently suitable to the aesthetic needs of the Gallic taste. The stories are usually well put together and frequently have genuine literary merit, while the music is scholarly, refined, and never too academic for popular enjoyment. During the nineteenth century it passed through the developing hands of Boieldieu, Auber and Gounod, and flowered into maturity with *Carmen*, *Manon*, and *Louise*. Without presuming to claim anything like equality with these master-pieces, *Muguette* is not an unworthy poor relation of the family. The text, founded on an English novel, *The Two Little Wooden Shoes* of Ouida, is simple and sympathetic, while the score is a pleasing trickle of pretty songs, duets, and choruses. I had hoped that our public would take to the little work and that its success would enable me to introduce others of the same description; but it was not to be. It failed to make an appeal, chiefly for the reason, so I was told, that no place in it had been found for that indispensable institution of the lighter stage in England, the blue-nosed comedian, and after a few performances it was also withdrawn.

I then took in hand a short Mozart Cycle which included *Il Seraglio*, *Le Nozze di Figaro*, *Così Fan Tutte*, and *Il Impresario*. Of the four works *Così Fan Tutte* proved easily the most interesting; few had ever heard of it, and fewer still seemed acquainted with the music, although it is equal in beauty to anything the composer ever wrote. As one lovely melody followed another until it seemed as if the invention of Mozart was inexhaustible, the whole culminating in the wonderful canon-quartette of the last scene, it was hard to believe that in our age of vaunted culture and education a work like this, then one hundred and twenty years old, was being heard almost for the first time in a great city like London. Admittedly it lacks the breadth and dramatic poignancy of *Don Giovanni*, the brilliant and acute vigour of *Figaro*, or the bright dewy freshness of *Il Seraglio*: nor do we find there any of those solemn intimations which are heard now and then in *Die Zauberflöte*. *Così Fan Tutte* is a long summer day spent in a cloudless land by a Southern sea, and its motto might be that of Hazlitt's sundial:

"Horas non numero nisi serenas."*

---

* "*Horas non numero nisi serenas* is the motto on a sundial near Venice. There is a softness and a harmony in the words and in the thought unparalleled. Of all conceits it is surely the most classical. 'I count only the hours that are serene.' What a bland and care-dispelling feeling! How the shadows seem to fade on the dial plate as the sky lours, and time presents only a blank unless as its progress is marked by what is joyous, and all that is not happy sinks into oblivion! What a fine lesson is conveyed to the mind—to take no note of time but by its benefits, to watch only for the smiles and neglect the frowns of fate, to compose our lives of bright and gentle moments, turning always to the sunny side of things, and letting the rest slip from our imaginations, unheeded or forgotten!"—*The New Monthly Magazine*, October, 1827.

In the next generation the German theatre was to be subdued by another spell, that of Weber, and the enchantment of wild places and old tales: and henceforth it was upon this road that music was to travel through Spohr, Marschner, and Meyerbeer to Wagner and the weighty magnificence of his later music.

History cannot be unwritten, and it is therefore idle to lament that the music of the nineteenth century has followed a course, especially towards the end of it, which has sometimes appeared to despair of human happiness. But when we listen to perfect beauty such as that of Mozart it is impossible not to regret that with him there passed out of music a mood of golden serenity which has never returned. In *Così Fan Tutte* the dying eighteenth century casts a backward glance over a period outstanding in European life for grace and charm and, averting its eyes from the view of a new age suckled in a creed of iconoclasm, sings its swan-song in praise of a civilization that has passed away for ever.

The unfamiliarity of some of my recruits with the character and style of serious opera sometimes led to incidents that helped appreciably to relieve the strain of our incessant labour during this season. In one of the Mozart pieces I was anxious that all the female parts should be undertaken by singers who had something of appearance as well as voice; and I allotted one of them which had always been a favourite with the greatest artists of the world to a lady who had achieved some celebrity in a less exacting branch of musical entertainment. The rehearsals went along merrily until one day I had a call from a male relative who announced that she wished to relinquish her part.

"Doesn't she like it?" I asked.

"Oh, she likes it well enough," he replied, "but I feel you have not been quite frank with us about it."

"What do you mean?" I said in astonishment.

"Well, you told us that it was the principal role in the opera."

"Isn't it?"

"How can it be when it is written only on the second line?"

I pointed out that it was not always the principal part which occupied the top line, reminding him of *Carmen*, where the heroine's part was to be found on the third.

"That's all very well for people who understand these things," he commented, "but you see Miss X has had a distinguished career in her own way and it might do her no end of harm with her old public if it became known that she had ever sung anything else but the top line."

Against such reasoning I was powerless, and I promptly released my leading lady from the awkward predicament in which I had innocently placed her.

The two native works included in my programme were the *Shamus O'Brien* of Stanford, a colourful, racy piece which had been produced some fifteen years earlier with much success, and *A Summer Night* by G. H. Clutsam, an able musician and the critic of *The Observer*. This little one-act opera, which was a novelty, proved to be bright and tuneful on its musical side, ingenious and effective in stage device, and pleasing to the more sophisticated portion of my audience. I do not think that it has been revived anywhere since that time, and I doubt if it ever achieved publication. Meanwhile we had been rehearsing the most important production of the season, the *Feuersnot* of Richard Strauss. The chief features of this gay and audacious work are the number and difficulty of the choruses and the indelicacy of the story. The music is best in its lighter moments and runs through the comedy scenes with a delightful swing and impulse. The hero, who has most of the serious stuff to sing, is a bore of the first order, but the other characters are attractively and amusingly drawn, and the whole opera is suffused with a spirit of youthful romance which provided a happy contrast to the gloom of the tragic masterpiece heard earlier in the year. The translation of *Feuersnot* bristled with thorny problems, and I sought once more the assistance of my scholarly and resourceful friend William Wallace. He produced a version that was a model of wit and scholarship, but for a short time balked at the awkward passage where the chorus outside the heroine's window strives to convert her to a richer conception of civic duty, so that the illumination of which it had been deprived by the magical arts of her disappointed suitor may be restored to the stricken town. An appropriate and at the same time decorous rendering of

> Da hilft nun kein Psallieren
> Noch auch die Klerisei:
> Das *Mädlein* muss verlieren
> Sein Lirum larum lei.

seemed beyond the power of any translator, but one day he burst triumphantly into the theatre with this hilarious quatrain:

> Now don't you shilly-shally,
> You know the only way,
> So honi soit qui mal y
> Pense, tol-fol-de-ray.

Those who saw the piece fully shared my partiality for it, but the larger public could not be induced to patronize it, possibly because it contained none of those barnstorming flights which had abounded in *Elektra*.

The only remaining actual novelty of the season was *Die Fledermaus* of Johann Strauss, and this lively piece, with the exception of *Hoffmann*, was our greatest triumph. This was not unexpected, as here at last we had nearly everything to present that was dear to the heart of the average English playgoer, including a large spice of that rowdy humour on the stage which he feels is out of place nowhere. As my regular company did not include a low comedian, I engaged Mr. Walter Passmore, the celebrated Savoyard, for the leading buffo part, and the audience, which had yawned over the anguished frenzies of *Werther* and the tender sentimentalities of *Muguette*, or had politely endured the sublime raptures of Mozart, demonstrated unmistakable joy at seeing this popular favourite trotting out all the time-honoured devices for securing a laugh, such as falling over sofas, squirting soda-water siphons in somebody's face, or being carried off to bed in a complete state of intoxication. By general consent it was agreed that here were the goods, and that the long-sought response which charm, beauty and delicacy had failed to evoke had been roused and sustained by slapstick horseplay.

On the whole this season in the opinion of most people was an artistic success. Under the most favourable conditions it could not have been anything more owing to the unusually large number of new productions. But the unexpected death of King Edward, which took place a few days before it began, cast a shadow over the whole of society and further reduced the chances of material prosperity. The musical public for opera in London is hardly one-half per cent of the population, and when national misfortune touches that part of it which is most constant in its support the prospects of any important enterprise are at once dimmed.

Yet I look back upon the few months I spent at His Majesty's with unusual pleasure, for apart from the fact that it is perhaps the most delightful theatre in the world, I was brought a good deal into touch with the late Sir Herbert Tree. From the moment I entered the building his staff was ordered to work for me as for himself. I never made a request that was not instantaneously granted, and the strenuous work during those three months would never have been half accomplished had it not been for the courtesy, ability and fine artistic sense of the subordinates whom he left behind him. There was never between the managerial office and myself any of that tiresome discussion or haggling over petty details which is the sordid side of so many theatrical transactions. The moment the main lines of our agreement were settled I heard no more about business, and on subsequent occasions my experiences there were invariably the same.

20

COVENT GARDEN AGAIN (1910)

WHILE THE SEASON OF WHICH I HAVE JUST WRITTEN WAS STILL RUNNING, I had begun to make preparations for another in the autumn at Covent Garden of similar duration. This, like my initial venture of the previous winter, was to be of international character, although I intended to make use in it of most of the British singers who were appearing at His Majesty's. The repertoire was to follow the lines laid down in my declared policy: famous works little or entirely unknown in England, unproduced pieces of merit from any source, and a healthy admixture of popular favourites to reassure that section of the public which is always disheartened by an excessive offer of novelty.

After the startling success of *Elektra* it was inevitable that my quest for an equal sensation should lead me at once to *Salome*, and I engaged a cast which was headed by Aino Akté, a slim and beautiful creature with an adequate voice and a remarkable understanding of her part. But one day I was unpleasantly surprised to learn that as the censor considered the work to be unfit for the British stage, we had been refused a licence for performance. As the fiat had come from the Lord Chamberlain's office, I was advised that if I were contemplating an appeal I should be wasting my time if I did not lodge it with someone in higher authority. There was only one such person in the State known personally to me, the Prime Minister, and he had just left for Gloucestershire, to spend a few weeks in the house of a relative. I communicated with Mrs. Asquith, who always interested herself in matters of this sort, and a few days later I received an invitation to join the party.

It has often been said that if anyone wants to see the English to advantage he had best turn his back on the town and hasten to the country. The average Briton is not genuinely urban in soul, although the evolution of industrial life has driven him from the countryside into cities; and the best evidence of this is the really shocking muddle he makes of the job when called upon to plan and lay out a new town. It is sometimes hard to believe that the men who built the churches or castles and designed the country towns and villages of Plantagenet days are of the same breed as those who created and tolerated the slum atrocities of the nineteenth century. With the wealthier class, it was never the house in London that was looked upon as the real home, but some fair haunt, Jacobean or Palladian, sufficiently remote from the capital, set off by gardens that would have satisfied the requirements of Bacon himself and half hidden in the trees of its girdling park. And I had already observed that the man one has been seeing for months at a time in town takes on a different aspect and undergoes an almost biological transformation when met a few weeks later in the country among horses, dogs, and dairymaids.

On first meeting Mr. Asquith at Downing Street I had been a little abashed by his magisterial demeanour, which was rather too obviously that of a personage accustomed to issue commands and wield authority. He treated us either to long flowing periods reminiscent of a college lecture-room or to a rapid series of staccato utterances not unlike those of the old Sergeant-major of the Engineer Corps in Lancashire, in which for a brief time I had held a commission. And although his wife had an easier and lighter hand in dealing with visitors or strangers, most of us remained rather more conscious than was quite necessary that here was the most influential lady of the land, with immense power in her grasp for good or ill. But in the freer air and more spacious accommodation of that charming house in the lovely Stroud Valley both of these essentially simple and warmhearted people became different beings. The giant's robes fell away from the shoulders of the Prime Minister, who made one forget in five minutes that he was what he was, save for his massively striking appearance and the intellectual quality of his conversation. He was learned, but deeply rather than widely. His acquaintance with Greek, Roman, and English literature was as comprehensive as any I have known, and he retained a clear memory of everything that he had read. But with that of foreign modern nations it was fragmentary, and for the other arts, architecture excepted, he did not seem to have much predilection. Of music he knew next to nothing; but unlike most people who, unattracted to the classics, take pleasure in popular jingles, he had no taste for anything that was vulgar or meretricious. In the presence of his wife, who had a wider general culture, he would display a statesmanlike caution in taking part in any discussion that touched on aesthetic subjects. But one evening when I found myself alone with him for a short while in a room where there was a piano, he asked me, with something of the expression in his eye with which a schoolboy makes a request that he is not quite sure should be granted, if I would play him the March from *Tannhäuser*. I did so twice, and having gathered from me that musicians did not think too disdainfully of this famous fragment; he repeated the demand for it the night before my departure, but this time boldly in the presence of the rest of his family. Of all the British politicians whom I have known from that time to this, Mr. Asquith, or the Earl of Oxford, as he afterwards became, always seemed to me the most satisfactorily representative. More human and less abstract than those two brilliant bachelors, Lords Balfour and Haldane, and of a solidity, reliability, and poise less conspicuous in the younger stars of the political firmament, his resignation of the Premiership in 1916 was not the unqualified advantage to the country that has been so often alleged.

I explained to him the nature of the *contretemps* over *Salome*. Strauss was the most famous and in common opinion the greatest of living composers; this was his most popular work; it was to be played for the first time to a few thousand enthusiasts who wanted to hear it; it did not concern, so far as I could see, those that did not want to hear it; being given in German, it would be comprehended by few; and lastly, I could not envisage the moral foundation of the Empire endangered by a handful of operatic performances. Would it not be more judicious to give the piece a chance? Otherwise we might run the risk of making ourselves slightly ridiculous in the eyes of the rest of the world by taking an exceptional attitude towards a celebrated work of art, as we had done so often in the past before the advent to power of the present enlightened government. The Prime Minister, more impressed, I think, by this last argument than the others, promised to speak to the Lord Chamberlain, and encouraged by this assurance I returned to town to complete my plans for the autumn.

There was not too much time as the new season was to start at the very beginning of October, but the organization which I had formed nine months before, and which had been functioning without a day's break since then, had reached a fair state of efficiency, each part of the theatre's machine working easily and harmoniously with the other. Yet our first month turned out to be full of little else than one anxiety and disappointment after another. I opened with a piece which I thought had a fair prospect of success, the *Tiefland* of D'Albert, which had won considerable favour abroad. Also D'Albert, in spite of his name, had been born an Englishman and had received his early musical training in London before leaving for the Continent, where he ultimately settled down permanently. But rarely have I had such a heap of trouble with any work. The principal lady, who at the request of the composer had been engaged for the part of Marta, found that she could not come, and we had to discover someone else who would competently fill her place. It was with some difficulty that we succeeded in procuring a likely substitute, only to be embarrassed by her disinclination to attend rehearsals and an unaccountable indisposition which broke out on the eve of the first performance, and prevented her taking part in it. I did not learn until some little time after that the lady was, or had been, the wife of one of my leading baritones, that the couple were in the throes of a vast and intricate matrimonial disagreement, that she had not known when accepting my engagement that the offending spouse was to be a member of the company, and that the mere possibility of meeting him under the same roof, although it was a pretty large one, had a devastating effect upon her emotional apparatus. The *première* had to be given with an understudy, and if intelligence, industry, and musicianship alone could have sufficed, the fate of *Tiefland* in London might have been happier. As it was, the want of the right female counterpart for the romantic and poetical interpretation of John Coates as Pedro deprived the piece of that essential measure of charm without which it suffered a severe handicap.

Then followed two French works, the *Hamlet* of Ambroise Thomas and *Le Chemineau* of Leroux. Of the former it is enough to say that it pleased no one, and of the latter that everyone who did come liked it and returned. But their failure, after that of *Werther* and *Muguette* during the summer, seemed to point to the inescapable conclusion that our public, outside a few familiar exceptions such as *Carmen* and *Louise,* did not want French opera. This was unfortunate for my plans, as the French repertoire is perhaps more extensive than any other, and if it includes but a limited number of absolute masterpieces, a deficiency it shares with its rivals of Germany and Italy, it can point to an exceptionally large mass of excellent achievement of the second rank. Also the continued indifference to almost anything off the thrice-beaten track was beginning to worry me, for I could not see how a permanent institution could ever be established while our potential audience, which had only a limited acquaintance with the world's operatic stock, steadily refrained from any effort to increase it. It certainly began to look as if the incessant clamour that had been filling the Press during recent years for longer and more varied seasons of opera had very little substance in it. Of the actual representations there was a minimum of criticism or complaint. Most of the leading British singers of the day were ini the casts: Agnes Nicholls, Zélie de Lussan, Mignon Nevada, Ruth Vincent, Maggie Teyte, John Coates, Walter Hyde, Frederick Austin, Robert Radford, and the foreign contingent included Akté, Litvinne, Urlus, Whitehill, and De Luca. De Luca, then in his prime and a brilliant success in all he undertook, except *Don Giovanni*, was comparatively unknown to Londoners, as were Litvinne and Urlus, who between them gave the most vocal rendering of *Tristan und Isolde* that any of us had heard since the famous performance some dozen years earlier of Jean de Reszke. Of the others, the most noteworthy perhaps were Whitehill among the foreigners and Ruth Vincent among the natives, who, with her beautiful voice and charming stage presence, was delightful as Antonia, Zerlina, and Gretel.

The immemorial privilege of the opposite sex to place the indulgence of its idiosyncrasies above the claims of art continued to pursue and jeopardize some of my later ventures. I had intended to give *Pique Dame* of Tchaikovsky, and as far back as the early summer had been introduced at one of the Embassies of a great East European country to a highly attractive personage, whose ambition I was assured was to sing the part of Lisa. As she had a capital and well-trained voice, a distinguished appearance and a thorough knowledge of the piece, I considered myself in luck and engaged her then and there. The only extra labour devolving upon her was to learn the French version, as I had no others of her nationality in my company and it was quite beyond the capacity of my chorus to sing an entire opera in a language of which they did not know a single word. Owing to the proficiency of my *prima donna* and the other artists taking part in it, the work was nearly ready about three weeks before the date set down for its production; and it was shortly after this that the lady asked my permission to go to Paris for nine or ten days, promising to be back well in time for the final rehearsals. I could offer no objection to this and off she went. But the days went by and there was no word of my soprano. The date of the first performance drew nearer and nearer; still she did not turn up and I began to be definitely troubled. Although, as in the instance of *Tiefland*, I had a capable understudy in case of emergencies, I knew that it would be hopeless to risk the introduction of another unknown work without the right sort of singer for this particular part. I waited until the eleventh hour, sent out messages and inquiries in a hundred different directions, but the missing stranger not only did not return but was never heard of again.

I applied as a matter of course to the Embassy of her country, but although the officials there were full of regret and apology, none of them seemed very disturbed about this extraordinary vanishing trick. Indeed, it was the obvious disinclination on their part to trace the erratic movements of the lady that deterred me from going to the police about the matter, and as I had not the courage to bring forward the work without the complete cast I had chosen, I withdrew it from the season's programme, and *Pique Dame* was not heard in London until five years later.* As this mysterious figure had made neither friends nor acquaintances in the house, visiting it only for her rehearsals and leaving immediately they were over, there was not so much curiosity and excitement over her flight as might have been expected; but naturally there were several rumours and conjectures floating around, all of them probably inaccurate. The one that obtained the most credence was that she was a person of exalted rank who some time before had quarrelled with her husband, and having a first-class musical education had decided to try her luck on the opera stage. While in Paris, the husband had reappeared upon the scene, solicitous friends had brought the couple together again, they became reconciled, and possibly lived happily ever afterwards. But the little flutter in theatrical life was something that had to be hushed up, and the only effective way of insuring this was that a veil of oblivion should descend and hide it from the memory of the outer world. Thie at least had the merit of plausibility in view of the caution and reticencs so unmistakably displayed by my diplomatic friends, but it was of small comfort to a young impresario who saw his carefully planned season staggering from one blow of Fate after another.

However, as the repertoire was by now fairly large I could partially replace our failures and semi-failures with successes or semi-successes, the latter including two fairly adequate productions of *Fidelio* and *Der Fliegende Holländer*. No general excellence of cast or spectacle has persuaded our public to look upon these works with more than moderate approval, at least in my time; but the appearance of a really great baritone such as Maurel or Van Rooy in the latter might induce it partly to change its mind. I had exhausted all my cards except one alone. This I had kept up my sleeve, until the last few weeks, and the time had now come for me to play it in the hope that it would turn out to be a winning ace.

---

* First given in London by Mr. Vladimir Rosing at the London Opera House during the summer of 1915.

21

THE EPISODE OF *SALOME* (1910)

TO THE FOREIGNER THE PRINCIPAL CHARM OF ENGLAND IS ITS ODD MIXTURE
of sprightly modern resource and stately mediaeval lumber. In most
countries when a custom outwears its use it is abolished; with us hardly
ever, even though it be quite obsolete or has long been crying out for
reform. But no one can do anything about it, for a mysterious force,
almost an occult influence, creeps insidiously through the body politic
and social to head us away from the folly and danger of change. We become ashamed of our seriousness and falter in our determination to make
wrong things right, nor does it matter in the least that our conservatism
is not only an inconvenience to ourselves but the object of ridicule to
others. We have a sneaking affection for the one and an open contempt for the other, and abuses or absurdities that would make some
nations blush for shame and others rush to the barricades we endure cheerfully for the sole reason they are our own, just as indulgent parents delight
to protect the weakly among their offspring.

A few years before the war a certain German envoy to our shores,
whose particular bee in the bonnet was Communism, fired off one evening
at a dinner-table a harangue in the best style of Third Reich oratory about
the activities of some of its British followers, who incidentally are a mere
fraction of our population. A well-known politician who was present
listened for a while in polite silence and then interrupted the stream of
eloquence by observing dryly, "I think, Herr X, you might remember
that they are, after all, *our* Communists."

One of our most characteristic institutions is the Censorship, which
functions as the watch-dog of decency over all that touches the drama,
literature, painting, or any other art, easily the most difficult and delicate
duty to fulfil in the world. I am no advocate either for or against it,
and I shrink from expressing an opinion on the theory of some of our
thinkers past and present that to the average Englishman there clings a
vestige of the old Adamic taint that stands in need of constant repression.
But that his rulers have a concern for his spiritual health as well as a rigid
belief in the perpetual adolescence of his mentality is sufficiently evi-
denced by their assumption of a paternal authority which none elsewhere
care or dare to exercise over their own citizens.

The history of the stage is full of episodes which illustrate the mani-
fold workings of the censorial mind but few, I think, have been more
closely linked with the true spirit of comedy, than that of *Salome*. Some
weeks after my conversation with the Prime Minister, in which he promised to look into the matter of the ban upon it, I received an invitation to
present myself at St. James's Palace, where I was received by the Lord
Chamberlain and his second in command, Sir Douglas Dawson. These
gentlemen informed me that their refusal to grant a licence was due in
no way to personal prejudice, but to the huge volume of letters they had
received from every corner of the country protesting against the appearance on the stage of a sacred character, Saint John the Baptist. I at
once pointed out that *Samson et Delilah* had been given now for many

years in London although it laboured under a similar disadvantage; but the Lord Chamberlain, who had undoubtedly been waiting for this obvious rejoinder, caught me up quickly with, "There is a difference—a very great difference; in one case it is the Old Testament and in the other the New."

Here followed a lengthy dissertation on this important distinction, punctuated by a wealth of doctrinal example of which I, although severely brought up in the bosom of the Church of England, had hitherto been ignorant; and the conversation, which had gradually taken on the tone of an elaborate theological debate, had to be diverted once more into the terrestrial channel of the theatre by the third member of the party.

"But we think we have found a way out," he interpolated. "There is no doubt that there are many people who want to see this work, and it is the view of the Prime Minister that subject to the proper safeguards we should do everything we can to enable you to give it. Now if you will consent to certain modifications of the text likely to disarm the scruples of the devout it would help us to reconsider our decision."

I could offer no objection to what seemed at first hearing a quite reasonable suggestion, and inquired how he proposed to get to work on the task. To this he replied that both he and the Lord Chamberlain were prepared to give their personal attention to it if I would do the same. I agreed without hesitation, and we arranged for an early conference at which *Salome* would be trimmed so as to make it palatable to the taste of that large army of objectors who would never see it.

The first thing we did was to eliminate the name of John, who was to be called simply The Prophet; and having invested him with this desirable anonymity, we went on to deprive every passage between him and Salome of the slightest force or meaning. The mundane and commonplace passion of the precocious princess was refined into a desire on her part for spiritual guidance, and the celebrated line at the end of the drama, "If you had looked upon me you would have loved me" was transformed into "If you had looked upon me you would have blessed me." It is only fair to say that my collaborators in this joyous piece of nonsense were, in spite of their outward gravity, as exhilarated as myself; for we all of us alike felt that we were making a solemn sacrifice on the altar of an unknown but truly national god.

The day arriving when our aim was accomplished and we had successfully metamorphosed a lurid tale of love and revenge into a comforting sermon that could have been safely preached from any country pulpit, I handed over the strange document to my friend Alfred Kalisch, who was to make an equivalently innocuous German version and send it along to the singers for study. I was neither surprised nor disappointed when there poured in one by one the liveliest communications from the unhappy creatures, who were asked to sing to some of the most vivid and dramatic music ever written words which not only had no discoverable association with it but were utterly devoid of any dramatic significance, the chief complainant being the leading lady, who did not see how it could be done at all. But I fixed an adamantine front, and, resolutely declining to discuss the matter with them for one moment, declared that everything must go through exactly as prescribed. England was not Germany, they should understand, but a country that took a pride in doing things in its own particular way, especially where the arts were involved; and here was an edifying example of it.   Before this unbending attitude the flood of remonstrance subsided, and with groans of resignation the artists submitted to the foreign yoke.   But it was hardly to be expected that they would observe a discreet reticence over the transaction, and for weeks those journals which were read mainly for their contribution to the lighter side of life enjoyed a large increase of circulation over the whole Continent.

In course of time the singers arrived, but rehearsals had hardly begun when a mild bombshell was exploded among us by St. James's Palace, which had just remembered that the decapitated head of John had to be handed to Salome on the stage, and that she was to sing to it in full view of the audience for about twenty minutes.   This would never do.   If it had been his arm or even leg it might have been different, but his head certainly not, and some substitute must be found for the offending member. We all went into close conclave, and it was settled that Salome be given a blood-stained sword.   But this time it was the *prima donna* who put her foot down, objecting that the gruesome weapon would ruin her beautiful gown and flatly refusing to handle it at all.   Despairingly I again made representations to headquarters and once more the official mind travailed and brought forth.   The best and final concession we could obtain was that Salome should have a large platter completely covered with a cloth, but that under no circumstances could any object, even the minutest, be placed beneath it that might suggest by its bulging protuberance the presence of the precious head.

The troubled voyage of rehearsals coming at last to an end, we reached the night of the first performance in which there was taken a much more than ordinary interest.   Not only had the story of our little difficulties got abroad, but, as always happens anywhere when there is the slightest hint of naughtiness in a piece, the whole town yearns to see it.   This in fact is the royal road to success, and if a young dramatist can only induce the bishops and clergy to denounce him with enough objurgation as a monster of impropriety his fortune is made.   At the last moment people appeared offering any price for a seat, and the performance began in a spirit of high tension on both sides of the proscenium.   For about half an hour all went just as had been planned, everyone singing their innocent phrases accurately, if somewhat frigidly.   But gradually I sensed by that telepathy which exists between the conductor of the orchestra and the artists on the stage, a growing restlessness and excitement of which the first exhibition was a slip on the part of Salome, who forgot two or three sentences of the bowdlerized version and lapsed into the viciousness of the lawful text.   The infection spread among the other performers, and by the time the second half of the work was well under way they were all living in and shamelessly restoring it to its integrity, as if no such things existed as British respectability and its legal custodians.

I was powerless to intervene, and visions of disaster crowded upon my agitated brain.   I saw Covent Garden, a theatre under the direct control of the Lord Chamberlain's office, losing its cherished Royal Charter; it was I who would be held responsible for this flagrant breach of good faith; I should never be able again to look my friends in the face, and I perspired in torrents.   I recalled an experience of Strauss himself at a rehearsal of the same opera, when, out of humour with vocal struggles on the stage, he had exhorted the orchestra to more strenuous efforts by calling out that he could still hear his singers; and I strove valiantly by the same methods to render my own even more inaudible. But I knew that in the end I should have to admit defeat, for looming like a spectre before me was that dreadful final scene where the orchestral accompaniment sinks to a dynamic level that the brutalest manipulation cannot lift above a gentle *piano*, and that every word of Salome would be heard in the last row in the gallery as she crooned away ecstatically to her empty platter.

After what seemed an age of purgatory to me, the performance came to an end, the public was enthusiastic, and the artists overflowed with delight at their success. I had not the heart to reproach them; I felt it was neither the time nor place. While I remained on the stage with them after the curtain had gone down I was horrified to see advancing towards me the party from the Lord Chamberlain's box. My first impulse was to fly, but as this would be a personal acknowledgment of the crime I decided to stay and fight it out. To my astonishment the magnate addressed me with beaming countenance: "It has been wonderful; we are all delighted, and I felt I could not leave the theatre without thanking you and your colleagues for the complete way in which you have met and gratified all our wishes." I think I must have effectively concealed my bewilderment at these unexpected felicitations, for the official group passed on radiating a benevolent satisfaction which I interpreted joyfully to my foreign contingent, who left the building in a greater state of stupefaction than ever at the unaccountable workings of the British mind. To this day I do not know whether we owed this happy finishing touch to the imperfect diction of the singers, an ignorance of the language on the part of my co-editors of the text, or their diplomatic decision to put the best possible face on a dénouement that was beyond either their or my power to foresee and control.

Although *Salome* served the useful purpose of filling the house every time it was played, it did not make the same overwhelming impression upon the public as *Elektra*. On the other hand, it provoked less controversy in aesthetic circles and adverse criticism was almost wholly absent, the only noteworthy instance being the not unexpected gibe of another celebrated musician that, while he reserved final judgment until further hearing, the overture appealed to him at once as a fine bit of writing as well as a perfect epitome of the whole work.*

22

THE COMING OF THE RUSSIAN BALLET (1911)

I ENDED THE YEAR 1910 IN A VERY DIFFERENT MOOD FROM THAT IN which I had begun it. I had plunged head foremost into the operatic arena under the cheerful conviction that I had only to present any work of fair renown in a tolerably adequate way for the public to crowd my theatre in gratitude and appreciation. The principal reason for the failure of other men's ventures, so I had been told, was that they had been too sporadic or limited in scope. But this could hardly be urged

---

* The point of this critical shaft will be appreciated only if an exhaustive study be made of the Prelude referred to!

against me, for during a period of twelve months I had given an almost uninterrupted sequence of about two hundred performances, had produced over a score of operas not heard before in London, revived many others that were hardly better known and had made use of nearly all the British singers qualified to appear on the stage, as well as a large contingent of front rankers from France, Germany, and Italy. A preliminary review of this trial trip only increased the suspicion that for the support of opera run on such a scale there was not nearly enough living interest in the existing state of London's musical culture. Out of something like fifty works there had been unqualified approval of four only: the short and sensational bloodcurdlers, *Salome* and *Elektra*, and the tuneful lightweights *Contes d'Hoffmann* and *Die Fledermaus*. Something was wrong somewhere, and I was not at all sure where the fault lay, with the public or myself. One thing, though, was clear enough: it would be courting disaster to continue along the same lines until my varied and comprehensive experiment had been submitted to a critical inquiry from which might be forthcoming some useful hints for the future.

Some months earlier I had been approached by the directorate of the Grand Opera Syndicate of Covent Garden, whose main enterprise was the summer season of three months, with a proposition to unite our rival forces and eliminate competition between us during this period. I had already made provisional plans for a season at Drury Lane Theatre during the summer of 1911, in which the Russian Ballet would make its first appearance in London, and the Syndicate had viewed with concern this intended encroachment on what had hitherto been its inviolate domain. The offer was not disadvantageous to my own organization, and I decided to accept it provided my contract with the Ballet was adopted by the new partnership. This was agreed, upon the condition that for the Ballet performances I would make a present of the services of my own orchestra, as the addition of a dozen or more unfamiliar pieces to the normal programme of work would be too much of a strain upon the regular body of players engaged for the opera itself.

During the spring I went over to Paris at the invitation of my friend André Messager to make preparation for the production of *Elektra* at the Grand Opera, for which I was to furnish my orchestra and the cast of singers that had made the success of the work in London. As there was much talk in circulation about the beauty and fitness of the Anglo-French Entente, it seemed to both Messager and myself that this pleasant little manifestation should be welcomed in the city of light. But we were mistaken. The musicians of the town, who were just then indulging in a particularly violent orgy of chauvinism, protested vigorously against this invasion of the sacred precincts of the Académie Nationale de Musique et de Danse by an alien mob under what one imaginative journalist dubbed "a Saxon chef". In the interests of public peace the Minister of Fine Arts felt bound to intervene, and I terminated a delicate situation by withdrawing from the scene before things became worse. I was less concerned over this fiasco than Messager, who was genuinely chagrined and rather ashamed of his countrymen. Several years previously he had been musical director of Covent Garden, his operettas were popular in London, and an exhibition of nationalistic prejudice such as this was as much against his interests as his taste and good sense.

During my stay there I took every opportunity that offered itself of inspecting the private musical life of Paris, particularly in the drawing-rooms of the great, as I was curious to see how they compared in this respect with those of London. There was very little difference between them so far as I could discover, Paris having a certain advantage over us in the perceptibly larger number of those well-intentioned persons who, professing to take an interest in art, sometimes carry it to a point where it bears more resemblance to interference than assistance. Most of these, naturally, were ladies who required very little encouragement to consti- tute themselves protectors of the whole family of Muses, and shortly after my arrival there was a vigorous movement to revive the glory of the ancient salon. Few of the enthusiasts had knowledge of the social con- ditions which gave birth to that institution in the seventeenth century and prolonged its existence until the close of the eighteenth, and small account was taken of the vast changes since that time which made any actual revival of it next to impossible. One and all were convinced that there was something hopelessly corrupt in all modern culture, which could be redeemed and regenerated only through the benignant wisdom of half a dozen new Egerias.

One noble dame had long been troubled by the obsession that what was lacking in all latter-day art was the imponderable element of style. She reflected often and seriously on the best way of recapturing this un- substantial sprite, which had somehow lost its way in the turmoil of our crowded life, and was at last seized with a remarkable inspiration. Sum- moning a choice company of her intimates, she addressed them as follows: "Each one of you knows at least one man of genius, a poet, a musician or anything else of the sort. Let us assemble them under this roof and set them in company to the task of creating a new style in each of their respective arts." This original proposition was received with joyful acclamation and the listeners departed to search the highways and by-ways of the capital for all the available genius that could be lured within the new sanctuary of Apollo. By one means and another a fairly large troop was brought together, and all intellectual Paris awaited with high expectation the results of the great experiment, regretting only that there was no Molière at hand to do it full justice.

Set in a large hall were thirty or forty little tables on which had been deposited pen, ink, paper and all other necessary materials. At each table a genius was invited to seat himself and remain for a couple of hours in complete silence, while he concentrated his faculties on the discovery of a new style. Whether it was imagined that the presence of so many first-class brains in close proximity would stimulate each one of them to heights of accomplishment hitherto unimagined, or that some large stream of mingled invention might be presently released and put into circula- tion, as is alleged to occur at other similar gatherings of the mystical sort, was never made clear to us. But the results were certainly not those which had been anticipated. For none among the painters or designers succeeded in turning out anything better than a recollection of the latest objects they had seen in some shop window which caught their eye while on the way to the assembly, and the poets and musicians appeared to be hypnotized by the haunting jingle of verses and tunes heard in the latest revues and cabaret shows. In spite of this setback the idea was considered too good to be abandoned without a further trial, which was duly held a little later. But the sacred flame of inspiration remained as dormant as before, and it had to be acknowledged with reluctance that the formula for creating a new style would have to be discovered by some other method.

The London season, which was now in full swing, was running its usually placid course when, like a visitation from another plane, there burst upon it the Russian Ballet. As rapidly as Byron won fame was the artistic section of the town taken by storm; people thought and talked of nothing but ballet, and extremists went so far as to assert that the downfall of opera was well in sight. All other branches of entertainment were thrown completely into the shade, and with some justice, for at long last London had the opportunity of witnessing a theatrical representation in which every constituent was of the highest beauty and splendour.

If I were asked who in my opinion was the greatest musician, painter, writer, or scientist I have known, I should have to think a long time before giving a decisive answer. But if the question were to include impresarios, I should not hesitate a moment, for Serge de Diaghileff was not only the greatest but the only one among them to realize my full conception of what this most ambiguous of all figures in public life ought to be. A Russian of the educated class, there was nothing that he did not know about dancing; he had a sympathetic understanding of modern painting, having organized several exhibitions of it in Paris, and he was a musician of estimable parts. This combination of abilities had enabled him to form a troupe of dancers second to none anywhere and to enrol under his banner a group of the most gifted composers and scenic artists of the day. Men like Bakst, Benois, Roerich, and Sert succeeded in lifting the whole craft of stage decoration out of the condition of dull decline into which it had fallen over a long period of years in England, France, Italy and Germany alike. There was a time when scenery for the theatre was the preoccupation of men of genius. A London museum contains the beautiful collection of drawings which Inigo Jones executed for the Jacobean theatre, while the France of the eighteenth century saw the labour of the exquisite Watteau and the elegant Boucher enlisted in the same cause. But in the nineteenth century all this somehow or other slipped from the hands of artists into those of artisans and sank gradually to the lowest level of an unimaginative mediocrity. Through those who had been praying long and fervently either for a return to an earlier tradition or a new vision of taste and charm the gorgeous spectacles of the Ballet sent a thrill of delight, stirred the slumbering consciences of all associated with the stage and sounded the death-knell of the existing system of organized incapacity.

Diaghileff was also the first to decree that no music but the best should be used by the Ballet, and that it must be executed with the same technical efficiency which the public until that time could count upon with certainty only in the concert room. There had been a venerable tradition that ballet music was smaller beer than operatic or symphonic, and entitled on that account to less consideration. But the presence of a large and first-rate orchestra, replacing the old moderate-sized and none too skilful body of players, brought the instrumental side of the performance well into line with the rest of it. Abandoning the employment of hack musicians to make orchestral versions of piano pieces such as the *Carnaval* of Schumann or the waltzes and mazurkas of Chopin, he delivered this sort of task to master-hands such as Stravinsky, Reynaldo Hahn, and Tcherepnin, and commissioned new ballets from every composer who, according to his own idea of it, revealed a feeling for the true spirit of the dance. Under his control the Ballet became and remained for over twenty years possibly the finest artistic institution of the day, and there was hardly a musician, a painter or dancer of note who did not at one time or another have some connection with it. To the dancers he was like a parent, but never an indulgent one; and a martinet of the first order, his discipline was rigid and his rule absolute. After the first night of a ballet which I had arranged for him I invited all those who had taken part in it together with a few friends to supper at the Savoy, and Diaghileff, rather to my surprise, took upon himself to make the seating arrangements. To the disappointment of some of my party, one of the principal dancers, an artist of international name, was not asked to join our table, and his explanation was that such an invitation would indicate a partiality likely to wound the susceptibilities of her colleagues and to diminish his own authority with them.

His musical predilections were individual and changing, and the cast of his mind cerebral rather than emotional. Nearly all romantic music of Teutonic origin was a bugbear to him, and most love scenes in opera he eyed with a cynical disapproval. When there was a question of making cuts in a piece which in his view erred on the side of length, it was generally those sections that dared to dally with the unsympathetic operations of the tender passion that produced groans from his heart and the immediate appearance of the blue pencil of excision from his pocket.

I think that during his later years his artistic judgment was largely under the influence of Stravinsky, for one day he broke into a long and extravagant eulogy of Gounod's *Faust*, which, bearing in mind something quite different I had heard him say not so long before about the same work, continued to surprise me until I learned that this was an opera for which the distinguished Russian composer had expressed a high regard. But I never entered into argument with him, for while he entertained a set of opinions, he clung to them with a fanatical tenacity which nothing could shake, and all one could do was to wait for time to replace them with another bunch, which in turn would be proclaimed with equal conviction.

Any scheme I might have hatched for continuing opera in the autumn and winter was halted by the unexpected appearance of another Richmond in the field. What it was that inspired Oscar Hammerstein to attempt the operatic conquest of London no one ever discovered. Perhaps he had been persuaded, like myself, into believing that the metropolis had a vast public thirsting for the sort of fare he had to offer. But whatever the reason, this gallant American was resolved to do the thing handsomely. In spite of the fact that London already possessed several theatres of grand opera dimensions, one of which I am sure he could have secured, he felt it necessary to build a brand new one in the Kingsway. I therefore deemed it more prudent to leave the newcomer in unopposed control of the ground, quit the stage for a while, and return to the calmer life of the concert room.

23

A VISIT TO BERLIN (1912)

ONE ADVANTAGE OF MY ALLIANCE WITH THE GRAND OPERA SYNDICATE
was that I became largely free from management responsibilities, as I
could leave to its own competent staff the supervision of my business
part in the joint undertaking.   This left me more time not only for concert
work with my orchestra but for the acceptance of outside engagements
with societies at Manchester, Liverpool and Birmingham, as well as the
Royal Philharmonic of London.   In Birmingham I conducted the whole
of the concert series during 1911–12 and 1913 and a gallant effort was
made to place musical affairs there on a more permanent basis, but
without success.   The old ghost of discord was still stalking the place and
it was not until some years afterwards that the various dissident parties
could be brought together to agree upon a scheme for a permanent
orchestra, in which I was privileged to take a part.

In my own concerts I continued the policy adopted four or five years
earlier, but with a little easing off in the practice of hurling at the public
such huge masses of modernity unrelieved by even a little of something
they had heard before.   These shock tactics are often useful and even
necessary as much to strike the eye as the ear with an appearance of
strangeness or singularity.   Wilde has said that nothing succeeds like
excess; but, though this is often correct in the opening moves of a campaign, it is not always so effective in its later stages.   For instance, in
one concert devoted to the work of a celebrated living composer I opened
with about two thousand persons in Queen's Hall and finished with less
than two hundred.   Having made sure that the Press, as well as the
public, was no longer in any danger of forgetting either the names or some
of the music of the composers I was endeavouring to advertise, I diluted
my programmes with a conciliating dash of the familiar, and soon found
that my listeners, who had overtly or covertly resented being asked to
swallow large doses of Delius, Sibelius, Mahler and others, became quite
placable on smaller allowances of the same fare.   Of course I am speaking
of ordinary everyday symphony concerts and not of festivals given up to
the work of a particular school or of one composer; of the latter kind there
is never likely to be a dangerous superfluity.

The reputation of Delius continued to grow, although it was not yet
rivalling that of Elgar, whom the British public had placed on a pedestal
higher than that occupied by any native composer since Purcell.   I did
not find this valuation shared by either our own or foreign musicians, and
on those occasions when in later years I played this composer's works in
continental countries, as well as in the United States, I observed that
time had failed to confirm it.   All the same, there is not the least doubt
that most of what Elgar wrote between 1895 and 1914 showed an undeniable advance over anything produced by his English predecessors or contemporaries in the more orthodox forms such as the symphony and the
oratorio.   The writing itself is clearer and more varied in style, the grasp
of the subject closer and keener, and the use of the orchestra is often, but
not always, admirable   The better side of him is to be found in miniature

movements, where he is generally fanciful and occasionally exquisite. His big periods and *tuttis* are less happy; bombast and rhetoric supplant too frequently real weight and poetical depth, and he strays with a dangerous ease to the borderline of a military rodomontade that is hardly distinguishable from the commonplace and the vulgar. Here and there are cadences of a charm that are quite his own, unlike anything else in music, evoking memories without being in themselves reminiscent, and breathing a sentiment to be found in much English literature written between 1830 and 1880, notably Tennyson. But whatever the quality of the invention, his is the work of a truly serious and honest craftsman.

According to Max Chop,* Delius belongs to the small group of wholly underivative composers. This is not to say that he is without musical ancestry of any sort, or that his is a greater genius than that of many who are less original in their aesthetic make-up. For instance, the actual musical accomplishment of Mozart is greater than that of Berlioz. But while nearly all that the former master wrote had a definitely pious kinship with the foreshadowing effort of the preceding generation, such extraordinary portents as the *Symphonie Fantastique* or *La Damnation de Faust* broke upon the world like some unaccountable effort of spontaneous generation which had dispensed with the machinery of normal parentage. Such human phenomena are invariably more complicated in their mental processes than their more simply constructed brethren of orthodox breed, and can rarely bring themselves to make use of the inheritance bequeathed to them by their predecessors. Theirs is no simple and primitive musical faculty like that of Schubert or Dvořák, each of whom was capable of pouring melody into any form of the art, without the least desire to vary or develop it. Wagner, as we know, saw clearly that Beethoven had said the last word in symphonic structure by stretching it to the furthest possible limits of expansion. But conventional minds thought otherwise and continued to hope for the coming of a successor who would open a new chapter in its evolution. It is now realized that nothing of the slightest consequence has been added to the architectural finality of the Third or Sixth, and that all those who have written symphonies during the past hundred years may have charmed but have not succeeded in surprising us.

Chopin, Wagner, and Debussy struck out on fresh lines, creating forms for themselves, and Delius is essentially of their kind and company. Although he had little or no aptitude for traffic with the sonata form, his efforts in this direction being his weakest, his capacity to create movements on a big scale which are shapely and logical, and which match the needs of his inspiration, is evident in such experiments as *Sea Drift*, *Paris*, and *Brigg Fair*. But the most underivative side of his genius, and that which separates him most sharply from all other modern composers, is undoubtedly his harmonic endowment. This is unique and peculiar in that it is present and audible in nearly every bar of any piece which he has written. I have often asked quite first-class musicians to play from memory some apparently easy-sounding passage of his that they have just been listening to, and while they have had no difficulty in getting the melody right, I cannot recall one occasion when they have been able

---

* An eminent German musicologist born in 1862, died in 1929. His best-known works are: *Liszt's Symphonic Poems*, *Wagner's Music Dramas*, and *Modern Musicians*.

to render the harmony correctly. And yet in performance all sounds simple and natural. Latter-day musicians have not yet given enough attention to this side of Delius, a genuine innovation for which the art is perceptibly the richer; and although his reputation during the past fifteen years has grown apace, the creator of *A Mass of Life* and *A Village Romeo and Juliet* has yet to receive that recognition which sooner or later will be his.

During the summer the Russian Ballet reappeared, repeating its spectacular success of the previous year and depreciating even further the already dubious credit of the operatic side of the season. Decidedly the stock of the music drama was on the decline and the position was in no way helped by the monumental failure of Mr. Hammerstein and his new opera house. With a repertoire drawn mainly from France, and with artists generally of the second rank who were better known in provincial theatres than in Paris, the American impresario encountered one reverse after another. After less than a year's trial of the artistic requirements of the British capital, he gave up altogether in sorrow and bewilderment, and his unsuccessful descent upon our shores will always be ranked among those of historic ill luck such as the Athenian expedition to Sicily and the French attempt on Russia.

The association between Serge de Diaghileff and myself had ripened into a friendship which bore happy fruit, when in the autumn he engaged my orchestra to go to Berlin and take part in a six-weeks' season of ballet at the Kroll Theatre. By this time the orchestra, thanks to its two years' experience at Covent Garden, had the repertoire of the company at its finger-ends, was at the top of its form, and promised to be, in Diaghileff's view, a distinct addition to the regular attraction of the Ballet. No English orchestra had yet visited Berlin, and probably as many people there as at home would be astonished that it could really play well at all. In any case, it was looked upon as an act of daring to present it to the critical ears of the German capital.

I thought I would take advantage of this Anglo-Russian invasion to go over at the end of it and give two or three concerts in which I would introduce some English works, as well as a few of my eighteenth-century trifles. I was also anxious to see Strauss again, who after the enormous success of his *Elektra* and *Salome* had been inquiring through his publishers if I had any intention of giving his *Rosenkavalier*, produced the previous year in Dresden and just as much of a triumph. I had already urged this work upon my colleagues of the Syndicate, but found them unsympathetically disposed, as indeed they were to most of my suggestions for the performance of novelties or revivals. Having a lively recollection of the public's apathy towards most of my own experiments, I had to admit the prudence of their attitude. But I had never seen any risk in *Rosenkavalier*, owing to the unquestioned popularity of its composer. Their argument, however, was that although our audiences might endure an hour and forty minutes of lyric melodrama, and even be thrilled or shocked by it, they would never sit quietly through four hours of German comedy, whether it were written by Strauss or Martin Luther himself. Nearly two years had gone by since a note of his operatic music had been heard in London, and it was beginning to look as if the chances of its being given in the next ten would be small unless I myself did something about it.

The concerts created a mild stir that was both pleasing and surprising to me. I had been a little apprehensive about the reception of my programmes, having been warned that Berlin musically was a stuffy sort of place, with a marked superiority complex *vis-à-vis* the rest of the continent. But everyone displayed the keenest interest in the new music, disputed warmly just as they were to do twenty years later over the authenticity of my classical readings (a certain venerable professor of the Hochschule said of my rendering of a Mozart symphony, "It sounds grand but it isn't Mozart") and wondered at the technical accomplishment of the orchestra, notably the wind and horns, which were without question superior to their own. One of the leading critics devoted an entire article to a close analysis of the style, tone, and method of my players, indicating in detail wherein they differed from those of the Austrian as well as German orchestras, and ended by saying, "These Englishmen play with a sovereign authority all too rare nowadays anywhere."

Strauss was deeply impressed just as he had been in 1910 at the time of *Elektra*, and was generous and penetrating in his remarks on the English composers. Of Delius he said charmingly and characteristically, "I had no idea that anyone except myself was writing such good music as this." Afterwards he went on to talk about the possibilities for *Rosenkavalier*, and before my departure I gave him an assurance that it would be given during the next few months. I had been turning over in my mind the plan of another winter season, and it seemed to me that the combination of a Strauss cycle, some later Wagner and the Russian Ballet in a few new productions ought to strike the public fancy. If this missed fire, then the position was practically hopeless. Accordingly upon my return to London I at once engaged Covent Garden for a season of about six weeks to take place in the early part of the coming year.

My orchestra, which quite rightly considered that it had covered itself with credit, was somewhat chagrined to find that its success was received rather coolly at home. In some quarters it was even minimized, one leading journal, now happily defunct, hinting that the reports sent over by correspondents on the spot had been inspired more by enthusiasm than judgment. I thought of the almost overwhelming fuss made by the people of every other country when one of their representative institutions ventured across the frontier for a week or even a few days. We had been in the stronghold, indeed in the inmost citadel, of the world's music for over two months, had conquered its prejudices, won its suffrages, and had been admitted to a status held only by two or three of its own organizations. This, however, in the England of 1912 passed almost unnoticed and, for some reason I was never able to understand, was even a little resented.

24

STRAUSS AND STRAVINSKY (1913)

DURING THIS TIME I HAD LOST TOUCH WITH MY FRIENDS OF THE CENSORship at St. James's Palace, but upon the announcement of a new Strauss opera they entered the scene again. As I had genuinely enjoyed my previous dealings with them I went in person to see what they had to say about it, and it appeared that they had discovered the presence of a bed in a remote part of the stage in the third act and were worried about some equivocal references to it in the text. Those who know the work will remember how Octavian, disguised as a girl, inquires the purpose of this object from the Baron Ochs, who replies, *"Das wird sie schon seh'n."* There was nothing more offensive in this than a hundred other things heard nightly on the lighter musical stage, but evidently the guardian angels of our national morality were haunted by the idea that what was harmless and innocent at Daly's or the Gaiety Theatre would be dangerous and reprehensible at Covent Garden. I was given the option of two courses. Either the bed could be exhibited without any reference being made to it, or it could be hidden away from sight and we could sing about it as much as we liked. As it was easier to move the furniture around than to tamper with the score of the work, I accepted the second alternative, and I have always regarded this as a nearly perfect example of our British love of compromise.

Der Rosenkavalier, much to the surprise of my colleagues of the Syndicate, obtained a success equal to that of *Elektra* and *Salome*, and the representation, at Strauss's request, followed closely the one given under his personal supervision at Dresden. In presenting a new work I always follow with complete fidelity the composer's wishes, even if I am often unable to agree with his choice of artists. The audience of Covent Garden is in my experience, and I have knowledge of nearly every important theatre of the world outside South America, the most critical as well as the best-informed on the subject of singing. For over two centuries it has been *facile princeps* the sanctuary of it, and scores of artists who are popular elsewhere fail to win approval there. It is inevitable in a house where all the operas are sung in their original tongues, and not in that of the locality, that purely vocal qualities such as tonal beauty, facility of execution and variety of colour should be regarded as the all-in-all of the art, with small concern for the niceties of diction and dramatic point, without which an opera sung in a language which everyone knows becomes an absurdity and an irritation. It is universally known and deplored that the endowments of a great vocalist do not often include those which we associate with charm and romance. But while the London public is as insistent as any other that in the ordinary theatre the claims of sight must be preferred above those of sound, there still remains a staunch minority which does not care a rap if the appearance of the performer fails to correspond with the character of the role, provided the music is rendered in accordance with its conception of what constitute the essentials of true or great singing.

For the representation of *Die Meistersinger* I had endeavoured to secure Hans Richter; but, as he declined my invitation, I conducted it myself, much to the discomfort of that small clique of Wagnerians who were convinced that the score was safe in no hands but those of its faithful transcriber and first custodian. It was generally asserted both publicly and privately that my *tempi* were too quick and that I hurried the singers, who had not time to breathe. Anticipating these judgments, I had taken steps to have the duration of each act checked by the stop-watch of one of the stage managers, and published the results, a little to the bewilderment of my critics.   The timing of my first act was within a quarter of a minute of Richter's, and that of the third half a minute, in each case longer and not shorter.   As for the middle act, the difference between the two timings was less than five seconds.   Further, the singers one and all declared that so far from being hustled and embarrassed, I had given them more latitude than they had known before for the easy vocalization of many of their passages.

If this were an isolated case of misunderstanding on the part of those listening to one of my interpretations, or a solitary instance of some queer aural illusion, it would not be worth while referring to it.   But throughout the whole of my career I have been looked upon as the protagonist of rapid *tempi*, in spite of the provable fact that in the majority of cases I have actually taken more time over performance than many of my contemporaries who enjoy the very opposite reputation.   And although I have frequently given explanations of the seeming mystery, I do not think that they have carried much conviction.   The truth is that the average ear confuses strong accent and the frequent use of *rubato* with *tempo* itself, especially if the accents are varied during the course of a single period, with the result that it has the uneasy sensation of being pricked or speeded against its will.*

Now the orchestra is a complicated instrument and patently more difficult to handle than any other.   A virtuoso can do exactly what he likes with his piano or fiddle; his own are the hands which fulfil the behest of his brain.   Anything approaching a similar freedom on the part of a conductor depends largely upon a long and close association between him and his players, who must be bent to his will as intimately as his instrument is to the virtuoso.   This is possible only here and there, for there are very few orchestras of accomplishment which play for a sufficient length of time under the same conductor, and incidentally there are not many conductors of natural talent who are also musicians of scholarship. Yet for the full revelation of all that is enshrined in a great orchestral or operatic score, the main essential is the same measure of ease and flexibility that we expect and receive from a solo performer.   At the moment there seems to be a struggle between those who favour a rigidly mechanical style of execution, which degrades music from an eloquent language to an inexpressive noise, and those who run to the opposite extremity of a licence that degenerates into anarchy.   Surely the truth, as is so often the case, may be found in the just mean (*auream mediocritatem*), and approximates to the style of perfect oratory, where a steady and unbroken line

---

* Connected remotely but perhaps interestingly with this vexed question is an incident which occurred about this time. Some of the musical organizations of London (including Covent Garden) united to give a musical festival in honour of the veteran Saint Saëns, and I conducted a concert at Queen's Hall in which his Third Symphony in C Minor was the principal item. With advancing years the distinguished French composer had imbibed a taste for somnolent *tempi* which was often a source of embarrassment to his interpreters. On this occasion his presence at rehearsals had an increasingly depressing influence on the players, and, convinced of a fiasco unless this could be counteracted, I did all I could at the performance to create an impression of life through purposely exaggerated accentuation without altering too perceptibly the prescribed directions as to speed. Later in the evening at supper I expressed the hope that the execution of the work had been to his satisfaction, and beaming benignantly he replied: "You mean, what do I think of your interpretation?" I assured him that nothing would please me so much as to hear his opinion, and he continued: "My dear young friend, I have lived a long while, and I have known all the *chefs d'orchestre*. There are two kinds: one takes the music too fast, and the other too slow. There is no third!"

of enunciation derives its vitality from a constant variation of inflection and speed which hardly any but the acutest ear is keen enough to follow. In other words, the secret of a persuasive manner is an elasticity of control, so exercised as to give the impression that the iron bonds of rhythm are never for a moment seriously loosened.

Many years ago a great musician said to me, "I judge a player mainly by his *rubato*," and it is upon the use of this device that most music depends for charm as well as clarity, and of which Chopin is reported to have given this definition: "Play a piece lasting so many minutes through in strict time: then repeat it with any number of variations of speed, but let its total duration remain the same." There is, of course, a great deal of music that depends for its supreme effect upon an implacably unchanging lilt, and no one with the smallest aesthetic sense would dream of directing the third movement of the Tschaikowsky Sixth Symphony or the finale of the Beethoven Seventh otherwise. And while it is true that there is infinitely more of this kind written for the orchestra owing to the composite nature of its structure than for any solo instrument, there is at the same time a great deal which is not, and it is of that of which I am speaking.

If *Der Rosenkavalier* was the star event of the operatic portion of this season, then certainly *Petrouchka*, seen for the first time in England, was that of the ballet. This remarkable piece is not only the most inspired work of its composer, but the high-water mark of the ballet's artistic achievement. Nothing before it had been so unquestionably a work of art. The bulk of the productions had been of a hybrid nature, the music and action not having been conceived simultaneously. Popular concert works, such as the *Invitation to the Waltz* of Weber or the *Scheherzade* of Rimsky-Korsakov had been transferred to the theatre, where choreography had been adapted to them as ably as possible. But however admirable the results were from the terpsichorean standpoint, they were not equally satisfactory from the musical. To meet the exigencies of the dance, it fell out that the time, the measure, and even the sentiment of the music had often to undergo transformations of which a ruthlessly mechanical style of execution was not the least disconcerting; so that in the new association the dance occupied the position of a senior partner who had pushed his junior into a background, where the outline of his genuine personality was obscured or distorted.

With the coming of Stravinsky the creative capacity of the Russian Ballet attained its full maturity. In *Petrouchka* the charm and poetry that peer out of nearly every page of his earlier *tour de force, L'Oiseau de Feu,* rarely make their appearance, the chief characteristics being a rhythm of extraordinary variety and vigour, a *bizarrerie* which, although entirely different from that of Strauss, is equally individual, and a fleeting hint of pathos that we find nowhere else in Stravinsky's work. It is, in fact, one of the musical landmarks of the past thirty years, and however interesting the later works of its composer may appear to that section of his followers which expects a fresh development of style from him every other season, I do not think that he has yet given birth to a second piece in which the most individual characteristics of his genius are so perfectly blended.

My association with the Russians had led me to a much wider study of the operatic output of their great composers, and I felt that the time had come for the introduction into England of at least a small portion of a large and completely unknown repertoire. But here once again I ran up against either the ignorance or the prejudice of my fellow-directors of the Syndicate, who not only had never heard the masterpieces of this school, but flatly refused to believe that anyone else could possibly want to do so; one of them going so far as to throw the coldest of cold water upon the engagement of Chaliapin, who had not yet been seen in London, on the ground that English audiences would not care for that style of singing. I began to feel that the alliance with an organization whose whole scheme of values as well as policy was so dissimilar to my own had outlived whatever utility it had at first contained, and I was becoming more convinced every day that nothing but the discovery of some new and vitalizing force could lift opera out of the deplorable stagnation in which it was languishing. It was impossible to overlook the undiminished popularity of the Ballet, and it was at least imaginable that another one hundred per cent Russian institution might be the key to the enigma. I accordingly resigned my position at Covent Garden, requested Diaghileff to negotiate the visit of a company from the Imperial Opera of St. Petersburg to include singers, chorus, new scenery and costumes—indeed, everything except the orchestra—and took a lease of Drury Lane Theatre. Thus I found myself for the summer of 1913 in the same position of rivalry to the house across the street that I should have occupied two years before had I carried out my old programme as first intended.

During the late spring, by way of an interlude, I gave the *Ariadne auf Naxos* of Strauss at His Majesty's Theatre in conjunction with Sir Herbert Tree, who himself played the part of Monsieur Jourdain in the comedy. The work was given in English, translated from the German through the French by Somerset Maugham, whose equanimity was on more than one occasion disturbed by the actor-manager's propensity to forget his lines and substitute an improvised patter for the polished prose of that distinguished master of the vernacular. Otherwise Tree, who in this line of broad and fantastic comedy had hardly a rival, was capital, and the whole production was adjudged superior to the original given at Stuttgart in the previous year. In this, the earlier version of *Ariadne*, I have always considered that the musical accomplishment of Strauss attained its highest reach, yielding a greater spontaneity and variety of invention, together with a subtler and riper style, than anything that his pen had yet given to the stage. The incidental music to the three acts of *le Bourgeois Gentilhomme* which form the first part of this unique work takes its place among other supreme examples of the kind, such as *L'Arlésienne* of Bizet and the *Peer Gynt* of Grieg; while the Bacchus section in the opera is one of the purple patches in the operatic literature of the twentieth century. It has to be admitted that it is neither an easy nor practicable sort of piece to give in an ordinary opera house, as it postulates the employment of a first-rate group of actors as well as singers: and for this reason, no doubt, the authors re-wrote it at a later period, making a full-blown opera of the old medley and thinking probably they were making a very good job of it. The result has been doubly unfortunate, for the later version has not only failed to hold the stage, but has dimmed the public recollection of the far superior and more attractive original. Our only consolation is that here we have a rare and refreshing instance of the inability of Commerce to read a lesson to Art, with a nice touch of Nemesis thrown in.

25

FIRST RUSSIAN OPERA SEASON (1913)

JUNE CAME ROUND, BRINGING WITH IT THE RUSSIAN OPERA COMPANY, and for the opening performances Drury Lane was by no means full, although this was the first appearance in England of Chaliapin. There is a belief, which must be general because of its constant reiteration, that the intelligent and enthusiastic music-lover is not to be found in the stalls and boxes but in the pit and gallery. Rich people, we are told, care little for opera as a musical entertainment; for them it is a social function only, and genuine appreciation must be sought among the less opulent classes. This comfortable article of faith has no foundation in fact, my own experience being in the contrary direction; for almost invariably when I have given master works with which the general public is unacquainted, there has been a conspicuous lack of support on the part of those to whom credit is usually given for superior taste and knowledge. And so in the case of our first Russian season it was only when it began to be known that the stalls and boxes were filled nightly with an audience of persons famous in politics, society and art that the man in the street also came to applaud and approve. When success did arrive, and it was not long delayed, it was total and fully equal to that of the Ballet two years before. Added to the anticipated spectacle of magnificent scenery and gorgeous costumery was the novel interest of a style of music unlike that of any other country and a standard of acting in all sections of the company superior to that which had yet been seen in an opera house. More of an advantage than a drawback was the pleasing vein of incomprehensibility in it all, hardly anyone in the audience knowing a word of the language, or having the slightest idea of what was taking place on the stage. For all we knew it might have been the most utter nonsense that was being sung; but the experts proclaimed that Russian was a very agreeable language to listen to, and that for most people was all that mattered.

It has always seemed to me that the surest guarantee of lasting fame for any work of art should be a spice of inscrutability. If its nature is susceptible of easy analysis, it is soon brought down to earth, examined microscopically and worried out of existence by criticism or ridicule, This melancholy fate can be avoided only if its meaning be shrouded in a reasonable obscurity, for the public may then go on wondering about it for generations, and, as no final solution of the mystery is ever likely to be forthcoming, will find itself after a few hundred years exactly where it was at the start. It looks as if this were the way, perhaps the only way, to make certain of immortality, and to it is due much of the lofty reputation of Greek drama and such works as *Hamlet*, *Die Zauberflöte*, and *Der Ring*, which are given credit for hidden significances when probably there are none there at all.

That the general credit of Russian opera not only stands no higher than in those days, but has undeniably gone down during the last fifteen or twenty years, is not easy to explain.   No one can urge that it has been overplayed, for the public is acquainted with a mere handful of works, and even these are given infrequently.   None the less, the Russian contribution to the repertoire of the lyric theatre, although less vigorous and revolutionary than the German, and inferior in architectonic skill to the French or in lyrical facility to the Italian, is perhaps the most noteworthy of the nineteenth century.   Of a consistently higher musical level than the first and of a more dignified order of utterance than the others, its two principal attributes are nobility of conception and the absence of cheapness and vulgarity, both evidences of a culture rooted soundly in simplicity and good taste.   Much has been written about the origins of the music itself, but hardly anything about its unmistakable affinity with the folk melody of Ireland.   That ever distressful country was occupied for four hundred years by the same irrepressible horde of Northern encroachers on other people's property who failed to obtain a permanent foothold in England, but succeeded under Rurik in planting itself solidly on the soil of Muscovy in the eighth century of our so-called Christian era. A salient example of their joint ancestry is to be found in the third act of *Prince Igor*, where the taking little tune associated with the spy Owlov is almost identical with that of a Celtic song of the Middle Ages.

But that which chiefly differentiates the Russian school from any other is its profoundly national character.   The masters of Western Europe, from Handel and Mozart down to Bizet and Verdi, have penetrated every known corner of the earth in their search for literary fuel to fire their inspiration, surveying all mankind operatically from China to Peru. But there is hardly one important Russian work that is not only in musical idiom, but in choice of subject, the product of the native soil.   The narrative operas of Moussorgsky, Borodin, and Rimsky-Korsakov are as much of a national possession as the historical plays of Shakespeare, and the sequence of *Ivan the Terrible*, *The Czar's Bride*, *Boris Godunof*, and *Khovantschina* as much a dramatic cycle as the *Oresteia* or *Richard the Second* and the three *Henrys*.

It is not surprising that in a people given so much to mass singing we should find the chorus playing a more prominent and interesting part than in the opera of other schools.   With few exceptions, such as *Lohengrin* and *Carmen*, its employment is casual and fragmentary, and more often than not it is brought on to the stage either to send up the curtain on a jolly opening or bring it down with an agreeable clatter.   Anyway, it is rarely an essential and vital element in the drama, while in a Russian opera it is a protagonist with a definite and independent role of its own to play, and its larger importance has the effect of adding tonal weight and visual splendour to all the scenes in which it takes part.

Socially the Russians are unlike any other European people, having a good deal of the Asiatic disregard for the meaning and use of the hour-glass.   Slow movement and time without limit for reflection and conversation are vital to them, and unless they can pass a substantial part of the day in discussions about the human soul they become ill at ease and unhappy.   For this reason, although they professed to like London, I do not think they were really at home there; for I often observed that they appeared astonished to find that other persons had something else to do and actually preferred going about doing it.   But although deliberate

enough in most ways, they had the capacity to blaze out almost volcanic-
ally if annoyed or affronted, and an entertaining instance of this occurred
towards the close of the season.

An extra performance of *Boris* had been arranged for the dual purpose
of enabling the Royal Family to see it and giving the chorus a Benefit;
and it was reported that Chaliapin intended to make a present to his
humbler colleagues of his salary for the evening. Of the rights and wrongs
of this matter I was never able to form any clear opinion; but undoubtedly there was a misunderstanding somewhere, for dissension and rebel-
lion broke out in the company with extraordinary results. On the fateful
night I did not go into the auditorium until the beginning of the third
tableau of the first act—"The Coronation of Boris"—and on looking at
the stage I was electrified to discover no sign of the Russian singers. It
was fortunate that for this occasion I had augmented the choral forces by
a fairly large English contingent, so that a complete disaster was avoided.
But as the adequate representation of this scene depended largely upon a
crowded stage and a mighty mass of sound, it missed more than half of its
intended effect. I hurried behind at the fall of the curtain and found
everything in a state of wild confusion—principals, chorus and ballet all
engaged in a fierce argument of which neither I nor my British assistants
understood a word. I sent in post haste for the manager of the Company,
but he was nowhere to be found; and I afterwards learned that, knowing
his countrymen better than we, he had sought safety in a remote corner
of the Savoy Hotel.

I contrived to disentangle from the crowd a few of the more responsible
members of the troupe, and with the aid of an interpreter gathered from
them that the cause of the disturbance was an acute disagreement between
Chaliapin and the choristers. Hard words had been exchanged between
the contending parties, tempers had run high; the only person who might
have put the matter right was the manager, and he had fled before the
storm. Eventually the indignant malcontents were persuaded to leave
the stage and retire to their dressing-rooms, as they did not take part in
the next act; but at the close of it, and just as Chaliapin was about to
leave, they reappeared. One of their leaders approached him, and a
brief altercation took place which ended dramatically with Chaliapin
knocking the man down. Like a pack of wolves the rest of the chorus
flung themselves upon him, brandishing the tall staves they were to use in
the next scene; the small English group rushed to his assistance and the
stage-door keeper telephoned for aid to the police station, which luckily
was hardly a stone's throw from the theatre. The struggle was still
raging when a few minutes later Drury Lane beheld the invasion of about
a dozen familiar figures in blue, and very soon something like order was
re-established, but not before my own manager had intercepted with his
head a blow intended for Chaliapin, which raised a lump as big as a fair-
sized plum. The latter departed for his dressing-room, passing through a
human corridor of protection in the shape of the British constabulary,
and by undertaking that their grievances should be investigated and
remedied I secured the presence of the chorus for the rest of the work.
So far from being upset by what had taken place, they went through the
great Revolution Scene with more than usual fire and enthusiasm; but
at the close of the performance nothing would induce them to leave the

stage, and they refused to budge a step until they had had it out with Chaliapin himself. The latter at first declined to emerge from his room, but, on being assured that he would be well guarded, finally came out with a loaded revolver in either pocket. By this time the warm reception given to the chorus for their magnificent singing had allayed somewhat their exasperation, and they seemed inclined to carry on the dispute in more orthodox fashion.

It was certainly a strange sight: the principal character still in his royal costume and fully armed for warfare; the choristers who had just played the part of an insurgent peasantry, wild and savage in appearance; the stolid English contingent in its everyday working dress; and the cohort of police silent but alert in the background. The proceedings began with a speech of immense length from one of the chorus leaders, and this was answered by Chaliapin in another of even greater length. A third speech followed from a female member of great eloquence and volubility, to which Chaliapin again replied in like manner. I began to wonder if this was how business was transacted in the Duma, for it seemed that this sort of thing might go on for ever. But all at once there was a huge shout of joy, and the next moment Chaliapin was being hugged and kissed by every member of the chorus, male and female. This little ceremony concluded, the general excitement subsided considerably, and the central figure embarked on another harangue in which I could distinguish frequent allusions to Drury Lane and myself. The eyes of the chorus turned in my direction and the terrifying suspicion crossed my mind that they were contemplating a similar affectionate handling of myself. Quite unable to face the prospect of being enthusiastically embraced by a hundred Russians of both sexes, I called out loudly to my native bodyguard, "Come along, boys, it's all over," and, making a precipitate dash for the doorway, left the field to the tranquillized foreigners. It was then about two o'clock in the morning, and I afterwards learned that they did not leave the building until well after five. Deciding that some kind of celebration of the happy ending of their troubles should take place, they had raided the refreshment rooms, lit the large tea and coffee urns, and made themselves wholly and delightfully at home. But the following morning they all turned up punctually for rehearsal, as blithe and unconcerned as if nothing unusual had happened, and as if wrath and violence had no part in the Slav temperament.

26

A PROVINCIAL ADVENTURE (1913)

FOR SOME YEARS PAST AN OPERA COMPANY HAD BEEN VISITING THE larger cities of the provinces under the direction of a Swiss-German whose headquarters were in Edinburgh, the tour taking place in the autumn and lasting usually thirteen or fourteen weeks. Most of the leading British singers took part in it, there was an adequate chorus and orchestra, and hitherto there had never been any lack of public support. I had accepted an offer to conduct some cycles of *Der Ring, Tristan, Die*

Meistersinger, and *Die Zauberflöte*, and the tour started with a two weeks' season at Birmingham. As I had nothing to do in the second week there I returned to London, where I had intended to remain about ten days before rejoining the troupe at Manchester, the next town in our itinerary. But towards the close of the first Manchester week I received an agitated telegram from one of the principal artists asking if I and my manager could go there at once. As the sender of the message was a serious and responsible sort of person it was evident that there must be some crisis in the organization, and up we went. There we found a pretty state of things. The audiences for the opening period of the season had proved unexpectedly meagre, especially in Manchester, which at that time looked upon itself as the true musical capital of England, the prospects elsewhere were not rosy, the impresario's resources had dried up, and the company, perhaps the largest ever sent on the road, was facing the unpleasant possibility of being thrown out of work for ten or eleven weeks. Was there anything that I could do about it? I called in a brace of auditors, procured the seating plans of all the theatres due to be visited, worked the telephone line in a score of directions, and after twenty-four hours discovered that if we could sell out every single seat for each remaining performance during the rest of the tour we had a sporting chance of getting through fairly well after all. How could this be done? Only through a hurricane campaign of publicity that would reach and wake up even the most lethargic and indifferent creature who had ever heard of the terms *music* and *opera*. But clearly there was no time to launch the kind of effort I had in mind over the week-end for the remaining portion of the Manchester visit. That must be abandoned, and perhaps the best possible thing too, as this self-styled metropolis of music would then enjoy the honour of having precipitated the breakdown of a great enterprise.

About ten days later we reopened the tour at Sheffield, carried it through to the end with results that did not fall too much below expectation, and even revisited Manchester at the end as a kind of epilogue to the drama. To me at the time the most noteworthy feature of this episode was the first use on a large scale of a method of public propaganda which I have found invaluable on numerous subsequent occasions. I have to admit that in the initial stage of its workings it rarely fails to arouse a storm of anger and disapproval; but when the text of the detested utterance has been re-read in calmer mood, the average person of ·judgment comes round to the view that there may be something in it after all. And indeed there is no reason why he should not, for it is no more than telling the plain and unflattering truth about the subject which at the moment happens to be under discussion. For instance, when I hear that one of our politicians dislikes music and refuses to hear it under any circumstances, while I feel sorry for his sake that he is so deficiently constructed as to be able to pass through life without desiring to savour one of its rarest pleasures, my respect for his character is not necessarily diminished. When, on the other hand, a community advertises a love for art, boasts about it, acquires and almost profits by a reputation for it, and yet fails to take the smallest interest in those institutions or enterprises without which it is no more than a fable or a dead letter, I then consider that anyone is justified in regarding such pretensions as rank hypocrisy.

So on this particular occasion I saw no reason why the public of those Cities, whose professions were so widely at variance with their performance, should not learn what one musician, also an impresario, had to say about it. I must do full justice to the Press for the handsomest co-operation conceivable, for they gave me almost unlimited space for a series of philippics upon the whole duty of society to art and the artist.

The first reaction on the part of those attacked and admonished was a fit of sudden fury, which relieved itself in epistolary warnings not to show my face anywhere near the place. The next was a rush to the box office of the theatre, prompted by a blind desire to retrieve, in the only way they knew how, the battered reputation of the town; and the result was that by the time I arrived to conduct the opening performance, the first week in Sheffield was almost sold out. Upon my appearance in the orchestral pit the house maintained a profound and deadly silence; but at the conclusion, when I went on the stage to join the other artists in acknowledging the applause, I was greeted with a shout, "Well, Tommy Beecham, are we musical?" Common courtesy obliged me to admit that so far as we had gone the answer was in the affirmative, but that I would defer my final judgment until the last night, when I should be coming before them again.

The opera I had just been conducting was *Die Meistersinger*, and during the rehearsal that same morning an incident had occurred which indicated that the mentality of these northerners had undergone no change since my departure from the district nearly fourteen years before. For the second scene of the last act, where a stage orchestra of some dozen players is required, my management had engaged the local theatre band; but when I arrived at the point where they had to play I observed that they were not on the stage but in the wings. I stopped and invited them by gestures to take their places on the little platform, but they shook their heads and remained where they were. Thinking that this attitude of passive resistance might be due to some dissatisfaction with their scale of remuneration, I invited their leader to descend into the house and adverted to it as delicately as possible. But the worthy man cut me short by saying with emphasis, "It's not the brass, mister, we've no complaint about that. But me and some of my mates have played in this theatre for sixteen years, and we are all respectable men; none of us have ever been in any sort of trouble, and we are not going to be bloomin' actors for you or anybody else." Nor did they; and I was reduced to the expedient of dressing up a body of supers, who pretended to blow into dummy instruments while the real players remained hidden from view behind the scenes.

It was not to Sheffield only that we were indebted for a grain of that comic relief which is as welcome to the artist as to anyone else working at top pressure. Another great city in the County of Broadacres furnished the pendant contribution to our gaiety, and Wagner was once more the happy medium of it. We had ploughed our way through a tolerable representation of the *Ring* cycle, and everything had gone without a hitch until the final scene, which as all the world knows is one of the grandest and most moving in opera. Brünnhilde was getting along in capital style with her farewell song, when to my dismay and astonishment the curtain came down. There was general consternation both on and off the stage; but continuing to conduct I pressed repeatedly the bell-button at my desk, and presently to my great relief the curtain rose and we went on as if nothing untoward had happened. But only for a minute or so: once more it descended. Again I renewed my attack on the button and again it went up, this time staying there until the end.

I hurried behind to discover the cause of this nerve-racking experience, and a sheepish and tired-looking individual was brought forward and introduced to me as the manipulator of the volatile piece of machinery. It appeared that, wearied by the length of the piece, he had gone off to sleep, and upon waking had found that it was well past eleven. As never before in the history of the theatre had any performance been known to continue beyond that hour, he had hastily concluded that it must be over and had rung down the curtain. On hearing my signal, he had hoisted it up, but, after a few moments of dazed reflection during which he remembered that his wife was expecting him for supper (also at eleven o'clock), and would be seriously put out if he were late, he could not help thinking there must be a mistake somewhere. So what with one thing and another he had thought it best to drop it again. I am quite sure that, if one of my own staff had not climbed to the lofty perch from where the dangerous contrivance was worked and relieved him of its charge, it would have remained down hiding the stage from the auditorium until the last note. I do not remember if we expected some little expression of regret from him for this unwelcome contribution to the evening's entertainment, but if so we were most certainly disappointed. Far from admitting that he could be in any way at fault, he declared emphatically that if people did not know enough to bring any piece, opera or play, to its termination by eleven o'clock at night, they had no right to be in the theatre business at all.

The general commotion caused by the early vicissitudes of our tour, and the unorthodox method of publicity employed to redeem it from disaster, excited a novel and lively interest among all classes in the general question of opera itself. Quite a number of persons who had never before given a minute's thought to it began to formulate theories and propound schemes for the establishment of opera houses all over the country. None of them was of the slightest practical value, but one or two of the propositions submitted to me were of that fantastically idyllic sort which can emerge only from the brain of a certain type of Englishman. The most fascinating of these was a project based upon the serious conviction of its author that opera could be made to flourish only in close association with agriculture. If I would consent to transfer the whole of my organization to the middle of some beautiful and fertile dale occupied by farms, which on an average were two miles distant one from another, I should find there the fulfilment of my dreams. The unromantic facts that the farming industry had not much spare cash at that moment to spend on such an expensive luxury as grand opera, that the total population of the district under consideration was less than ten thousand souls, that roads were difficult and sometimes impassable in bad weather, and that the local revenue likely to be forthcoming in one month would be hardly adequate to support the company for three days, were all ignored in favour of the beauty of the idea.

Ambitious musicians everywhere started writing operas with furious industry, generally on national subjects of inordinate length, the most promising of these being a cycle of six music-dramas on the life of Henry VIII. As I perused the sketch of this monumental offering to the shrine of wedded bliss, of which each section was devoted to one of the sextet of spouses, I tried vainly to expel from my brain the recurrent tum-tumming of that rapturous strain which some marriage-minded enthusiast chanted to a group of startled maidens in one of the Sullivan operettas.*

But undoubtedly the most original inspiration that reached me, although it went no further than the libretto, was one dealing with a psychological problem that should be of the deepest interest to everyone. The last day of the world had dawned and the whole of humanity save two persons had perished in the freezing temperature of a new Ice Age. These two survivors, a man and a woman, were thrown together in a certain spot with but one hour of life left to them. Although they had long loved one another, circumstances had thwarted any kind of union, and now a great moral question was posed to them. Should they maintain to the end their hitherto chaste relationship or, faced with impending extinction, surrender themselves to the joy of an unbridled orgy of passion? The dénouement was still uncertain in the mind of the inventor of this delightful situation, and he sought my advice about it. I could only answer that there was but one way to determine it beyond question, which was for him to go off somewhere where he could be frozen to the nearest point this side of death. Out of his own experience in passing through such an ordeal he would be admirably fitted to comprehend the emotional ecstasies of two other persons in a similar plight; and I felt sure that in the interests of science as well as art he would not shrink from undertaking the experiment without delay. But as I never heard anything more from him I was reluctantly obliged to conclude that he must have felt unequal to settling the question in the only way that seemed convincing and final to me, that of trial and (in this case, probably) error.

27

SECOND RUSSIAN OPERA SEASON (1914)

THE STRIKING SUCCESS OF THE FIRST RUSSIAN SEASON ENSURED THE return of the company for the summer of 1914, and it was the joint ambition of Diaghileff and myself to make of it something that London had never known before. On the first visit we had ventured to give three operas only, but we now drew up a programme of at least eight, and half a dozen new ballets, preluded by a short cycle of German works including *Der Rosenkavalier* and *Die Zauberflöte*. My father, whose name had been prominently associated with the 1913 enterprise, enthusiastically backed this imposing scheme, balking only at the idea of reviving *Die Zauberflöte*, which he claimed had never been anything better than an honourable failure in England for over a century. It was for this very reason, I contended, that the tide of fortune was due to turn in our favour. But to his solid business mind this long view sounded a bit metaphysical,

---

* " We'll indulge in the felicity
   Of unbounded domesticity."—*The Pirates of Penzance.*

and I took over the personal responsibility for this black sheep of the flock, much to his relief.

I was not without some reason for my confidence in this grand but at that time neglected masterpiece. I had recently conducted several performances of it and had had full opportunity to discover the weaknesses in the unwieldy and ponderous production which had been made for the provincial tour. There had been interminable waits between many of the numerous scenes when it was imperative that there should be either none at all or only those of the shortest duration. It should be quite possible to save from one half to three-quarters of an hour in the total length of the representation with as much gain to the musical and dramatic side of it as relief to a bored and impatient audience, and I remodelled the old scenery to square with this design, curtailed the dialogue, and engaged a cast which I hoped would interpret the music to my liking.

For some time I had been giving thought to the vocal style of Mozart and I was growing more and more doubtful whether some of the traditions of execution that for long had been associated with it could really be authentic. I fancied that I had already discovered in the symphonic works depths of poetry and passion which did not rise even to the surface in the average rendering, and which might be present in the operatic masterpieces also. Certainly I had never heard those transcendent airs *"Deh vieni"*, *"Dove sono"*, or *"Ach ich fühl's"* as I had dreamed that one day they should or might be sung. But in 1913 I had come across a young soprano at the Berlin Opera whom I had engaged for the parts of Sophie in *Der Rosenkavalier* and Eva in *Die Meistersinger*. I cannot say that in these she had been more than satisfactory if judged by an international standard, but the voice was remarkable for two qualities, a perfect *legato* and a phenomenal breath control, exactly what were indispensable for what I had in mind.

The appearance of Claire Dux as Pamina at Drury Lane in the spring of 1914 was one of those artistic events which are red-letter days in the annals of opera. In order to give her song in the second act the chance of making its fullest effect, I had manipulated the scene with curtains so that the singer appeared to be framed in a small space, thus focusing upon her more directly the attention of the audience. Over twenty recalls greeted the most exquisite exhibition of *bel canto* that London had heard for more than a generation, and even the old *habitués* who still crossed themselves when the names of Patti or Nilsson were mentioned had to admit that the days of great singing had not yet vanished. For the next performance the whole of the front row of stalls was occupied by vocalists, among whom were Melba, Destinn, Caruso, and Chaliapin, all genuinely curious to see just what it was that Claire Dux did with a piece that all of them must have heard many times without suspecting its full possibilities. Naturally it was the opinion of Melba, a soprano of world fame, that was most eagerly awaited, and I was almost as gratified as Claire herself when the formidable Nellie hailed her in my presence with the words: "You are my successor." The only person, perhaps, who failed to rejoice wholeheartedly over the unexpected success of the *Zauberflöte* was my father, who almost kicked himself with chagrin for his want of faith in it. After a few representations of *Der Rosenkavalier*, notable for a new Octavian, Charlotte Uhr, the best I have yet known, we came to the event which many were looking forward to as the climax of the social year, the return of the Russian Opera.

The preliminary interest in it had been immense and the theatre was almost sold out for the entire season before the arrival of the company; that is, so far as the purely operatic performances were concerned. Diaghileff had suggested *Prince Igor* for the opening occasion, doubtless for the reason that it gave singers, chorus, and ballet all the chance of appearing at their best, Chaliapin taking the two roles of Galitsky and Kontchak. I have figured both as actor and spectator in a goodly number of stirring episodes in the theatre, but can recall none to match the tumult among the audience that followed the fall of the curtain on the great scene in the Tartar Camp at the close of the third act. And yet the preparations for this triumph were as far from smooth sailing as any that can be imagined, and more than once I made up my mind that the production would never see the light of day.

Quite as interesting as the performance of any opera by an all-Russian company is the rehearsal of it, and it still remains a mystery to me not only how we ever reached that first night, but how everything during it went with such accuracy and swing. The few final days beforehand Drury Lane was more like a railway station than a theatre, with scenery arriving from three or four different quarters, and, when unpacked, disclosing frequently the awful fact that the artist had gone no further than indicate the design on some cloth sixty feet long without adding a stroke of paint. As Russians work on a flat floor instead of a vertical frame as we do in England, this meant finding at the shortest notice some horizontal space large enough to accommodate such huge areas of canvas, just the sort of thing that drives an overworked manager to despair or debauchery. The orchestral parts were full of blunders with most of the cuts marked wrongly, so that it took hours to establish any kind of correspondence between band and stage. The proceedings were interrupted every five minutes by the agitated appearance of a small legion of dressmakers, wigmakers, and bootmakers, all of them insisting that if immediate attention were not given to their needs, the fruits of their labour would never be ready in time. The leading singers quarrelled, the temperamental Chaliapin had a fisticuff encounter with the baritone who sang the title role, and the chorus took sides with as much ardour as if they had been Capulets and Montagues. The actual day before the production the final rehearsal began in the early afternoon, went on throughout the evening well into the morning hours, and came to an end only then because the conductor had an attack of hysteria, had to be taken off his chair, carried into a dressing-room, and put to bed on a sofa. It now seemed humanly impossible that the work could be ready in time; and yet such is the calibre of this remarkable people that fifteen hours later everything fell into place like the diverse pieces of a jigsaw puzzle and yielded a performance as flawless as exhilarating. It is true that while the first act was being played some of the scenery for the last was still in the hands of painters, but it was all finished with a good half-hour to spare and, when hoisted into position, looked none the worse for its neck-to-neck race with the clock.

Of the other operas that were wholly new to us *Le Coq d'Or* was in every way the most interesting. Rimsky-Korsakov is with Tchaikovsky the greatest of craftsmen among the Russian masters. Although inferior in the main to his rival in passion and rhetorical vigour, he frequently excels him in delicacy of imagination, and now and then, as in *The Czar's Bride*, in beauty and originality of melodic invention. As a writer for the stage he easily outdistances all his fellow countrymen in versatility and command of those technical resources that seem to be the happy possession of a bare handful of names in the history of the lyric drama. There are a dozen scenes in Russian opera more powerful, more moving, and more impressive than anything in *Le Coq d'Or*, but there is nothing more beautiful and exotic than its second act from the moment the Queen of Chemaka, one of the world's greatest dramatic creations, makes her appearance. For the first time in the theatre do we hear a cadence that convincingly links East and West. There are none of those over-familiar devices for creating local colour which sound so pathetically fatuous even in the hands of skilled musicians. Here is a character conceived and worked out from start to finish as a musical entity, with an idiom all its own, and we salute it with gratitude as a genuinely consistent as well as fragrantly lovely contribution to the world's stage. One has only to think of it in comparison with other attempts to reproduce the Orient, as, for example, the Flower Maiden's scene in *Parsifal*, to realize its immense superiority over anything else in this line. Of the remaining novelties in the operatic repertoire the most noteworthy were *May Night* of Rimsky-Korsakov, a charming and melodious light piece of work, and *Le Rossignol* of Stravinsky, which delighted the ultra-moderns of the town and was adorned by one of Bakst's most sumptuous scenic inventions.

It was now the turn of the Ballet, which during the first few weeks had remained a little in the background, to take the field, and worthily indeed it performed its task. There were many who regretted the absence of Nijinsky from the list of dancers this season, but there was some compensation in the return of Fokine, the choreographic creator of the Ballet, who had parted from it in 1912. These two events were not unconnected, and the choice between them was determined by the best friends of both Diaghileff and the Ballet, who placed the integrity of the finest ensemble in existence above the pretensions of even its greatest solo artist. The three star productions were the *Daphnis et Chloë* of Ravel, *La Légende de Joseph* of Strauss and *Le Sacre du Printemps* of Stravinsky. Of these decidedly the most attractive was *Daphnis et Chloë*, the most original *Le Sacre du Printemps*, and the least attractive and original *La Légende de Joseph*. The German master revealed no talent for this sort of thing; in spite of a few vivid and picturesque moments the piece went with a heavy and plodding gait which all the resource and ingenuity of the troupe could not relieve or accelerate, and perhaps the most memorable feature of the evening was the first appearance in the Ballet of Massine in the part of Joseph. *Le Sacre du Printemps* created more surprise than delight, although as there had been a good deal written and talked about it in advance, the public listened to it politely and attentively. I will express no other opinion on this striking and interesting work than to reiterate my mature view that *Petrouchka* remains its composer's masterpiece. *Daphnis et Chloë* has not only continued in the repertoire of most ballet companies until this day, but is familiar to every symphony concert audience. It is Ravel's finest achievement in instrumental writing and one of the treasures in the regalia of twentieth-century French music.

For variety's sake I interpolated an all-British effort, of which the music was by Holbrooke and the libretto by Lord Howard de Walden. *Dylan*, founded on an old Celtic legend, is less an opera than a series of scenes, with the frailest link of connection between them and the minimum amount of action, and it was not the easiest of jobs to put it on the stage at all. When the authors had completed their work they sat down to think of the right man to devise a production and supervise the *mise-en-scène*, which included a few doubtful innovations such as a chorus of wildfowl. They approached the most celebrated of English scenic designers, prolific in imaginative conceptions whose originality made them usually impossible of realization on any earthly stage. He asked for a copy of the libretto, kept it a few months, and then announced that if the authors would omit two of the scenes and condense the story and music into the two remaining, he might see his way to provide suitable pictures for them. Further than this he would not go, as the rest of the piece did not appeal to him. Naturally the authors were unable to accept this annihilating condition which reduced their work to insignificance as well as nonsense, but I have often thought that if the cinema should ever take it into its head to experiment with opera it should proceed in some such way as this, which for the ordinary theatre would be in the nature of putting the cart before the horse.

A producer would select a subject, design some twenty or thirty wonderful pictures to relate the outline of the story, and add words and music to fill an accompaniment of lyrical and dramatic illustration. The main reason why no opera written for the living stage bears adaptation to the film is that in it the music is of supreme and the rest only of negligible importance. On the screen it is the pictures that matter and absorb nine-tenths of the interest of the spectators. But in an opera the musical unit, be it a song, a duet, or concerted number, will last from five minutes to half an hour, and barring a very few exceptional instances it is quite impossible to change the scene during any one of them. In the cinema no one wants to look at a picture for as long as this, and as you cannot have a moving procession of sights while a soprano is struggling with the complexities of a coloratura aria as in *Lucia*, or a baritone is anathematizing those who have betrayed him, as in *Un Ballo*, the only alternative is to have musical units of much shorter length. As no operas exist where such are to be found, it will be necessary to write them: and when that is done, the "movie" industry will be enabled to bring forward a really novel artistic convention, the like of which it stands in evident need.

Holbrooke was (in those days, anyway) a musician of natural ability handicapped by a poor aesthetic endowment and a total want of critical faculty. No one with the united talents of Mozart, Wagner, and Verdi could have made an opera out of *Dylan*, and indeed not one of them would have tried for two minutes. I believe that much of the music was liked by those who heard it, but without question both the story and the text were wholly beyond the comprehension of the Drury Lane audience.

One of the drawbacks of opera in English, where everything that is sung or said can be instantly understood, is that our public, which has a lively sense of humour, never misses an opening for a laugh; and there were quite a number of these in *Dylan*, owing to the author's failure to remember that whatever else may take place in a wholly serious scene, not one word must be spoken to reduce it suddenly to comedy or farce. In the first act the hero signalizes his entry on the scene with the unfortunate line, "I sing, I have sung, I can sing better," and as that evening he was obviously in poor voice, the emotion of the audience can be easily imagined.

The London season was beginning to draw to its close, and my mind goes back to an evening in the latter part of July when a company of persons assembled to bid a temporary farewell to one another. It was in the garden of my house, an old-world dwelling in Hobart Place standing some way back from the street, in which a fountain playing day and night tempered the summer heat. There we gathered for supper, and to few of us came even a fleeting apprehension that the current of our lives would not remain unchanged for years to come. Plans for the future were made, hopes and promises of early reunion were exchanged, and the party broke up under the certain impression that the next year and the years after that were to be so many new links added to the existing chain of their comradeship in work.

Within ten days Europe was smitten with madness and the old world fell into ruins.

28

WAR TIME (1914)

SINCE MY FIRST VISIT TO GERMANY, I HAD FOLLOWED WITH KEEN INTEREST the progress of its imperialistic ambitions. At that time it possessed no navy; a few years later it had a formidable one and the earlier balance of power in Europe was a thing of the past. Public opinion was divided into two opposing sections: a minority which saw the country in danger and clamoured not only for a large shipbuilding programme but the creation of a powerful army, and a majority that had complete trust in the friendly intentions of Germany and looked upon war in the twentieth century as unthinkable under any circumstances. In these pious beliefs it was greatly fortified by the appearance of Norman Angell's *The Great Illusion*. This remarkable work, whose main argument was that since war was no longer a paying proposition for any nation it had become meaningless and obsolete, made a deep impression upon that large mass of people who were incapable of understanding that men may sometimes labour for ends other than those of pecuniary advantage. They refused therefore to see any sinister motive behind the rapidly growing forces of Germany on land and sea.

With the public generally in this mood, the prophets of action did not make much headway. To create a minimum army of one million men some measure of conscription would have been necessary, but this would never do. Every free-born Briton would resist it as a gross infringement of his personal liberty, as well as an insult to the very spirit of democracy. There were many inconveniences that a man was legally obliged to stomach, whether he liked them or not, such as paying taxes, serving on juries and keeping the peace. But military training for the defence of his country was quite another matter, and not to be contemplated seriously for a moment. Such was the doctrine not only preached to but accepted by the average citizen of the day, and if his war-inured descendant of 1943 may be inclined to look upon this picture as overdrawn, I venture to recall that as late as the summer of 1915, after the war had been raging for ten months, a prominent Labour leader declared at a public meeting in the Midlands that if the Government attempted to introduce any measure of compulsory service there would be revolution in the land. Six months later the dreadful deed was done without a protesting voice raised anywhere, and for this sublime effort of prescience its author was not long afterwards rewarded by a seat in the Cabinet, where he continued presumably to serve the nation's interests by prophesying calamities that never eventuated.

But that which lulled the public into a torpor of indifference more completely than anything else was the proclaimed conviction of eminent bankers and actuaries that, even if war did take place, it could not last longer than six weeks, owing to the closely interwoven relations of international finance. The money machine would run down quickly with sand well in all its inwards, and how would men go on fighting after that? In England, if it is a writer or artist who utters a serious opinion, he is at once suspected of trying to be funny; if a scientist, then he is a crank or faddist; if a politician or even a mere Member of Parliament, he is listened to with respect if not always with credence. But when a banker speaks, an awe-inspiring silence descends on the land and every word is received as a revelation from on high. This invocation to Mammon settled the question, for surely the Germans, who were a clever people, must recognize these lofty truths as clearly as ourselves.

When accordingly the fateful fourth of August did arrive, and the Government, much against its will, was forced to declare war on Germany, the only European people to be surprised was the English; and how it was possible for it to have continued all the while in this happy state was hard for anyone to imagine who had spent much of his time on the Continent. In Italy during the summers of 1912 and 1913 I met statesmen, journalists, and industrialists, who one and all discussed the coming conflict as a certainty; and as for Germany, it had been regarded there as inevitable for the past ten years. The rival pretensions of Austria and Russia in South-Eastern Europe were impossible of reconciliation, the overblown bubble of concord might burst at any moment, probably just about the time when the new Palace of Peace at The Hague would be opened, and both France and Germany would be drawn in to the aid of their allies. The only unknown quantity was Great Britain and her conception of her obligations to France under the Entente; and this was the question which agitated the whole country during the few final days when it was at last realized that hostilities of some sort were unavoidable.

It is a fact that on Thursday, August 1, no one knew the answer to it, not even the Cabinet. On the late afternoon of that day I went to the French Embassy with the Princess Alice of Monaco to see the Ambassador, M. Paul Cambon, who had just returned from the Foreign Office. He was in a state of considerable perturbation, having failed to obtain from Sir Edward Grey definite assurances of aid in the event of France being attacked by Germany. ·The peace *bloc* in the Cabinet was powerful, almost overwhelmingly so, and was backed up vigorously by the influential Press of the Liberal Party such as the *Daily Chronicle*, the *Manchester Guardian*, and the *Daily News*, one of them cheerfully advocating non-intervention for the reason that neutrality would give us an unprecedented opportunity of making money out of all the belligerents in turn. Fortunately for the Entente, the hand of the Prime Minister was strengthened by the support of the leaders of the Conservative Party, so that the following day Germany received the ultimatum which expired at midnight, August 3.

I do not think there were anywhere two persons more distressed at the catastrophe than the German Ambassador Prince Lichnowsky and his wife Mechtilde. Only a few weeks before I had given a private concert in the Embassy with my orchestra, and the couple were devoted to music, being constantly seen at the Opera and Ballet. Of an amiable South-German stock, they were both of them heartbroken at the breach between their own country and one to which they had become attached, and felt that in some way they had made a pitiable failure of their diplomatic mission. Strictly speaking, this was true, for Potsdam had been guided less by the Ambassador's advices than those of his first lieutenant von Kühlmann, who, exaggerating the embarrassment of Great Britain over the Ulster imbroglio, was convinced that she would not intervene in the struggle.

The first reaction to the declared state of war was that all public entertainment should cease. It would not do to fiddle while Rome was burning, a pompous precept trotted out invariably by those who have done the least to prevent the conflagration. Concert societies all over the country were closing down, and it soon began to be clear that unless some countermove were made quickly, England would find itself without music of any sort. It appeared to me that the first thing to do was to ensure the continuance of some of the older and more indispensable of the big institutions, and as I happened to be staying at the time with my father in Lancashire, I went to see the manager of the Hallé Concerts Society in Manchester, which at the moment was without either conductor or policy. The venerable Richter, having retreated two or three years earlier to the tranquil refuge of Bayreuth, had appointed in his place another German, one of those solid and painstaking hacks whose insensibility to every finer shade of music was (and still is) accepted in most quarters as the eighteen-carat hallmark of a true orthodoxy. The crisis cutting short his labours, the Committee of the Society, to whom the future of their concerts appeared dark and dismal without the guiding hand of a true-blue Teuton, was in a pathetic state of helplessness and vacillation.

Here was a situation that should be met without delay. The organization was the centre and chief of an imposing number of lesser or satellite bodies who looked to it for example and guidance; and its excellent orchestra travelled far and wide, not only giving its own concerts but taking part in those of choral societies whose work would be hampered or curtailed without its co-operation. Any infirmity of purpose at this critical moment, or, worse still, abnegation of leadership, would depreciate morale, diminish zeal and undermine the outer defences of the gallant stronghold of culture which Charles Hallé had toiled so laboriously to consolidate over a period of thirty years. I entered into a partnership with the Society under which I would work for it as an unsalaried musical director, conduct the concerts when on the spot and engage a fitting substitute when absent.

I lost no time in reversing what had been its artistic policy for the past fifteen years, filling the programmes with French, Russian, English and Italian works, hardly any of which the public had yet heard. It is doubtful whether this could have been done in such a wholesale fashion in pre-war days, but with anti-German feeling increasing daily, the audiences soon developed a temper which made them ready to listen to anything written by the composer of an allied nation. Manchester having been successfully planted on what appeared to be the solid ground of security, I turned my attention to London and the Royal Philharmonic Society, which was also in a mood of hesitation. With the support of two stalwart directors, Stanley Hawley and Mewburn Levien, I concluded an arrangement which enabled it to carry on the series which had been running uninterruptedly for over a hundred years, even during the Napoleonic Wars. It would never have done to permit the Kaiser to succeed where the great French Emperor had failed.

The more I observed the general situation of music arising out of the war, the more I was appalled by the disorganization caused in its professional ranks. Artists of name and ability, singers, pianists and others who a few weeks earlier had been making a comfortable and in some cases a handsome living, now found themselves without a single engagement. The only regular event which survived intact was the annual performance of *Messiah*, which every choral society with a spark of vitality left pulled itself together to hold. Isidore de Lara, who had lately arrived in London from France, where he had been living for the past twenty years, started at Claridge's Hotel a set of wartime concerts confessedly for the relief of those in difficulties. This was an enterprise of high merit which was not treated at the time with the respect it deserved. It ran throughout the war, provided work for hundreds of musicians and was the medium by which a large mass of British compositions was introduced to a section of society which so far had been unaware of its existence. For the audiences were largely composed of women of fashion and of those who liked to be seen in their proximity, all of them a little curious to inspect at close quarters a man who had become a shadowy figure of romance.

Some twenty-five or thirty years earlier de Lara had been a popular young composer of whom much was expected. He had written a few songs of the ballad type that were sung in every drawing-room of the Kingdom and even an opera on Edwin Arnold's poem, "The Light of Asia". Realizing that there was next to no opportunity at home for anyone who wanted to devote his career to the lyric theatre, he had transplanted himself to Paris, where he remained until the beginning of the war, and during the intervening period had written some half-dozen operas of which the most popular was *Messaline*. Both as man and musician he was adroit and knowledgeable; with a shrewd eye for the sort of subject likely to make a good libretto and the sense to invoke the aid of a practised hand at the game.   Thanks to these useful qualities his operas were a plausibly attractive entertainment when heard for the first time, the ingredients making up the dish served to us being blended with cunning enough to disarm the critical part of our musical attention.   But further familiarity soon made it evident that here was another talented writer who had succumbed to the lure of the stage without the possession of those gifts which alone have the power to create a work containing the nerve and sinew of true drama.   De Lara's bent was purely lyrical and devoid of the capacity to construct big movements, build up climaxes, or endow his puppets with the breath of individual life.   The listener must have a sluggish ear indeed who fails to discern that the songs sung by the Countess, Susanna, and Cherubino in *Figaro* are utterances of three clearly differentiated personalities, and this investiture of stage figures with variety of portraiture through the medium of the music itself is the prime essential of any opera which asks that it be accepted as a genuine work of art.   For it can never be emphasized too often that it is the music alone that matters, and if it be of the right sort, no one troubles about anything else.

There were at that time half a dozen composers of de Lara's stamp who were unable to comprehend the distinction between the two entities, drama and theatre, and who imagined that so long as they made full use of the devices and paraphernalia of the melodramatic spectacle or the pageant play such as thrilling tale, troops of dancing ladies and houris, Roman amphitheatres and mirages in the African desert, all would be well with the music.   If we accept this formula as canonical, we shall probably have to reject that employed in *Pelléas et Mélisande*; and I have more than once heard apostles of the former declare that neither Debussy nor Delius knew how to write for the theatre.   Possibly not, but they could write for the opera house; and although they show next to an desire to dazzle or "upset" us, we do remain interested even after a dozen hearings, for the reason that these men are fundamentally musicians who are able to satisfy our ears with a line and volume of sound that makes all else going on of secondary importance.

In disposition, de Lara was a simple, kindly, and manly fellow who almost to the end of his life boxed and rode daily on a bicycle in the Park. But through his long association with the stagier sort of people he had developed a slightly theatrical air with which his British colleagues did not always find themselves in sympathy.   The idol of his earlier years had been that great master of posture Maurel, some of whose tricks of manner and speech he had unconsciously absorbed; and these rarely failed to come to the surface with amusing fidelity at the rehearsals of his operas, or during discussions of those artistic problems on which his proto-type had never wearied of holding forth, so long as there was someone at hand to listen.   By reason of his long absence from England he was inclined to overlook the considerable changes that had taken place during that period in public taste, and to present us with diversions that might have met with keener appreciation in the 'eighties or 'nineties.   On one occasion we were electrified by a stirring address on the subject of Passion, delivered with immense gusto to an audience mainly composed of aged dowagers and their great-grandchildren; and on another by a concert of his own songs, most of them dating back to his salad and ballad days. This latter event attracted enthusiasts from all parts of the country, and I sat next to two ladies of extremely advanced years who had travelled the whole way from Cornwall to listen to his own rendering of his famous ditty *The Garden of Sleep*. As the moment drew near for the performance of this favourite gem their excitement was almost painful to witness, and at its conclusion one of the pair murmured to the other: "Thank heaven, my dear, I have heard him sing it again before I die."

More than one musician of commanding stature has been known to envy the authorship of some of the Johann Strauss waltzes, and I dare say there are many others of larger accomplishment than de Lara who have journeyed through long and honourable careers without ever evoking such a pious tribute of devotion.

29

MUSICAL TRAINING AND A TOURNAMENT OF SONG (1915)

ABOUT THE BEGINNING OF 1915, DELIUS AND HIS WIFE, WHO HAD BEEN forced to make a hasty flight from Grez when the German armies were advancing in the Marne district, arrived suddenly in England. They had buried their stock of wine in the garden, left their beloved jackdaw Koanga in charge of the parish priest, climbed on to a manure-cart and, after a painfully long and circuitous journey, contrived to reach one of the Channel ports, from which the steamers were still making their daily crossings. I had a house a few miles out of Watford where I thought the wandering couple might care to take up their residence. A pretty little place, formerly the dower house of a large estate, with a millwheel to provide soothing music day and night and well away from main roads, it seemed to me just the sort of a retreat where a hunted composer could repair his ravaged nervous system and continue his work in peace. And settle there they did, but not with full content until they had succeeded in bringing over their own French cook from Grez and relegating my homely English help to duties of a strictly non-culinary kind.

As my occupations were increasing rapidly I could pay him only occasional visits, usually at a week-end when other visitors would look in to pay homage to genius in exile, and among them was a young man just down from Cambridge who surprised us all by his sympathy for and understanding of modern music. His ambition was to edit a journal which should be progressive and aggressive in tone, and as the idea had the enthusiastic backing of Delius, whose chief delight in life next to composing was to stir up any kind of public controversy provided it was acrimonious enough, we drew up a scheme for launching it under the title of *The Sackbut*, or *The Anti-Ass*. But nothing much came of this promising venture, for although the paper did make its appearance some months later, it remained but a short time under the control of Philip Heseltine, or Peter Warlock, as he afterwards became known. Passing into the hands of a safe commercial house which shore the title of its provocative and better half, it ran with success according to the most unimpeachable rules of good journalistic conduct. This strange and gifted youth was born out of his time and suffered from a duality of nature whose two divisions were opposing and irreconcilable.   One half of him looked wistfully back to the healthy naturalism of the sixteenth century while the other faced boldly the dawn of an age whose music shall have parted company with every element which for centuries we have believed to be the essence and justification of its existence.   Such types have small part in the present; they "look before and after and pine for what is not", and either consciously or subconsciously are in perpetual conflict with it. Their spiritual isolation makes it hard to say whether they are the remnant of a biological experiment which Nature in a capricious mood has already tried and abandoned, or the premonitory symptom of one that is in an embryonic stage of gestation.   But Peter Warlock, if he was a lost soul, was a brilliant and lovable character, a man among other men, and an intellect that never wholly lost touch with a past without which there cannot be a future.   In this he stood apart from some of his contemporaries and most of his successors, who were not only an innovation in European music but the negation and denial of it, and can be viewed with equanimity on the one condition that they are the close and not the beginning of an era.

For some time I had been more and more interested in a problem which no one heavily involved in the business of public performance could afford to ignore, the failure of our leading colleges to produce an adequate output of superior talent.   Something like five thousand students were assembled in the London institutions alone, and while it was our custom to hold regular and frequent auditions of those singers who were represented to be the prize specimens of the year's crop, we were hardly ever able to make use of any of them in the condition they were sent to us.   The bulk of the English singers who had taken part in my seasons had received their training either abroad or at home privately, and those who had actually passed through one of the colleges were obliged almost invariably to seek out some additional instruction to supplement the scanty measure they had obtained there.   Hardly more satisfactory was the state of advanced instrumental playing, for although it had earned our gratitude by raising the standard of style and execution in the orchestral player, the existing system seemed incapable of producing the class of performer who could pass beyond that stage to one of higher individual excellence. I once escorted Maurel on a tour of inspection through one of the largest of the great teaching establishments, and the Principal, thinking to make a telling impression, told us how many thousands of pupils were working under his roof.

"*Étonnant,*" commented the distinguished relic of an older and leaner day, "*mais combien d'artistes avez-vous?*"

Perhaps this was asking too much, and any academy is justified in protesting that it is not within its power to guarantee the creation of lofty natural ability.   But this would have been no answer to or explanation of the undeniable fact that much the greater part of it as did exist had passed through hands other than its own.   Remembering what Charles Wood had once said to me about the knowledge of orchestration, I began to wonder if these great nurseries of the art possessed either the will or the insight to employ pedagogic skill of a sufficiently expert order, for I knew quite a few instances of posts held by men who in the spheres of singing and playing had been anything but shining lights in their profession.   As I have said before, the supreme artist has always a difficulty in handing on his own peculiar method, but if it were true that the bulk of the youth on the Continent that ultimately found its way into its two hundred opera houses had been sent out by the conservatories of Paris, Vienna, Milan, Berlin and a dozen other centres it was inevitable that someone sooner or later should ask why our own could not do the same.

My interest in this question, which is as much alive today as then, has been resented and misunderstood on nearly every occasion I have expressed it, sometimes in those quarters where I had the right to expect a more attentive hearing as well as a more thoughtful reply.   For it is not as the conductor of an orchestra that I have spoken but as an employer of musical labour, and by no means the least active in my own country. As I cannot run opera seasons without singers, or give certain works at all without some of a specific class or kind, it should follow that it is I as much as anyone else who am concerned that they should be forthcoming.   In another sphere of discovery the same responsibility extends to the concert room, in which during the half dozen years before the present war it was my task to draw up or assist in drawing up something like a hundred different programmes of music annually.   As my appetite for genuine novelty has in no wise abated I am constantly on the lookout for it, but hardly once a year do I come across an indubitable example.   If some unprejudiced inquirer would take the trouble to make one list of the admittedly great orchestral works written between 1890–1910 and another of those written between 1920–1940, a cool comparison of the two might start him on a line of salutary reflection.   And if he cared to go on to a brief examination of the true state of opera, his surprise would be increased by the disconcerting revelation that, while in the earlier period we were blessed with a score of masterpieces or quasi-masterpieces, one piece only during the later has managed to maintain its place in the international repertoire.

This none too sound condition in the kingdom of music is familiar enough to those whose preoccupation is to search for first-rate work and bring it to the light of day.   But if any one of them is moved from time to time to issue a word of warning about it, he is informed with the minimum of polite consideration that he is guilty of an unworthy pessimism and an action of gross disservice to an art which is still flourishing with undiminished vitality.   The depressing truth is that the capacity for self-delusion seems to be as great in the aesthetic world as in the political, and that little short of a series of catastrophes will bring enlightenment to those who continue to ignore the writing upon the wall.

Being present in Manchester for a few days during the spring of 1915 in company with Delius, I found myself dining one evening at the house of the principal patron of the College of Music there.   The conversation turning to the subject of academic training in general, Delius, who had enjoyed about as little of it as any musician living, entertained the party with a magnificent effort of abusive condemnation.   Our host, sensibly alert to the possibility of a little fun, asked him if he would address the College on the following evening, when, as there was an annual celebration of some sort, professors, students and everyone else connected with it would be present.   This Delius declined to do on the plea that he was no public speaker, which was true. Like several other brilliant conversationalists I have known, he was fragmentary and incidental rather than comprehensive and sequential, and disdained the humbler faculty of marshalling ideas with that semblance of logical order necessary to the mental comfort of any audience that is asked to bear with patience the ordeal of a lengthy delivery on a single subject.

As it was known that I had done a good bit of this sort of thing for many years past the invitation was passed on to me, and, thinking that here might be a chance of venting a few of the doubts and misgivings which for some time had been troubling me, I accepted it. But since I knew that to create a lively interest and provoke any useful reaction over a wide area I should have to employ the tactics of an out-and-out offensive, I thought that I should first ask our local Maecenas if they would be likely to injure the interests of the especial object of his protection. He answered that the more outspoken my criticism the better, as there was far too much self-satisfaction in the place for his own liking.

Encouraged by this admirable objectivity of outlook, I took for my text Dante's famous line, *"Lasciate ogni speranza voi ch'entrate"*, which I suggested should be written over the entrance door of every academy in the land, and challenged the particular one I was addressing to point to a single musician of outstanding distinction produced by it during the twenty-odd years of its existence. The result was equal to any I had expected, and for weeks the Manchester papers were full of indignant letters citing the names of singers and instrumentalists who, in the opinion of the various writers, gave the living lie to my insult. Presently there came an opportunity to put the issue to a practical test. I had advertised in one of the Hallé Society programmes, Delius's *Sea Drift*, which requires a solo baritone with gifts not only of voice but of diction and poetic insight. As I had not yet engaged a singer, I issued an invitation to the College to bring forward one among its students, past or present, who could interpret the part adequately. The composer, who was on the scene, would act as judge; and as he was likely to want a performance of his work as much as anyone, the conditions of trial would be favourable to the competitors. There was intense excitement in the whole county: its artistic prestige had been not only questioned but derided; it was determined to wipe out the affront convincingly, and it looked as if we were going to have a tournament of song that would rival in importance that historic contest on the Wartburg.

I knew that eventually I should have to choose someone to sing the work, but I hoped that the argument would drag on long enough for me to extend it to a much wider domain of debate, to create a pleasantly dramatic tension, and that by spinning out the trials I would be enabled to make the ultimate verdict all the more gratifying to local pride. But I had reckoned without the incalculable element of Frederick Delius, who, at the opening audition, forgetting entirely the real purpose of the whole adventure, approved the first singer who presented himself. It availed nothing that in aesthetic endowment the fortunate vocalist was far from being a fitting selection for this particular piece; the decision was given, and the triumph of the College complete. For if the very first candidate who appeared had proved acceptable, then it followed as a matter of course that there must be many more of equal eligibility. My discomfiture was as total as the elation of the other side, and I vowed that never again would I entrust the casting vote of decision in any other of my carefully calculated projects to the unaccountable impulse of a composer, however eminent.

Shortly after, on my return to London, I was dining by myself at Pagani's and was joined by Landon Ronald, who was also alone. My acquaintance with him was of the slightest, and by the turn of circumstances we had generally been in opposite camps of public activity. For when I severed my connection with the New Symphony Orchestra at the end of 1908, he had been appointed its conductor and had shared a little of that emotion of rivalry which the players had felt upon the unwelcome appearance of a new body of competitors. He had meanwhile succeeded to the Directorship of the Guildhall School of Music, an organization which had been a special object of attack in my Manchester address, and he now wanted to know what he had done to deserve it. I explained to him that there was nothing in the least personal in my action, that it had been taken for the sole purpose of arousing public interest in the whole educational system, and to assure him further on this score I proposed that he assist me as conductor both in the Hallé Concert series and elsewhere during the coming autumn. To this he willingly agreed, but suggested that we might begin our co-operation earlier by doing something together during the summer in London, which otherwise would be entirely without music for months to come; and we there and then planned and subsequently gave a short season of Promenade Concerts at the Albert Hall which the pair of us conducted on alternate nights.

Landon Ronald was a man of integrity, scrupulous in all his dealings with his fellows, and an affectionate and constant friend. He had unquestionably a great and natural talent for conducting, and his bearing and movements in action carried an ease and grace that I have never seen rivalled. His sympathies, however, did not equal his endowment, and this limitation of taste, combined with an inborn inertia, placed a check upon the growth of his repertoire which I often deplored. I judged from the answers to my remonstrances that he was not fully aware of his own unusual ability; and this self-depreciation, highly uncommon in an artist, deprived him of that extra ounce of incentive which is the impelling force behind any sustained endeavour or successful accomplishment.

My only other effort of consequence that summer in London was the organization of a public meeting at Queen's Hall, to demand that the Government should place cotton on the list of contraband goods. For some reason wholly inexplicable to the entire country, this had not been done, although we were well in the eleventh month of the struggle and the dangerous stuff was pouring into Germany through every available opening. The war had come just in time to prevent the adoption by half a dozen great Powers of the "Declaration of London", an extraordinary document which seemed to have been designed for the main purpose of crippling the power of the British Navy. Anyway, at the head of a long list of articles to be made non-contraband in the event of a conflict stood cotton, the most vital of all the materials used in the manufacture of explosives. The only conclusion one could form was that, although the declaration had never been signed, the Government which had fathered it was striving to abide by its terms; for in spite of much protest in the Press, the Foreign Office, preserving an unbroken silence, offered no explanation of its cryptic attitude. Many of us in Lancashire, the home of the commodity, considered that the time had come for a series of public meetings far and wide, and that at Queen's Hall was the opening event, with Sir Charles Macara, President of the Cotton Spinners' Federation in the chair and a group of scientific and industrial celebrities on the platform. During the course of the day the Foreign Office made an unsuccessful attempt through my father to discover my whereabouts, though for what reason I never knew. It could hardly have been to request the cancellation at the last hour of a public gathering that had been advertised for weeks, but as Government departments in those days moved in every way as mysteriously as they do now, such an impromptu step would have been no surprise to us. Whatever its purpose, that evening was the beginning and end of our campaign, for a few days later appeared the welcome proclamation that, so far as was within the nation's control, the enemy would receive no more cotton. It is probable that the Government had been on the eve of taking this belatedly necessary action, but it pleased us all to imagine that our little effort had done something to accelerate its decision.

30

A GREAT JOURNALIST (1915)

DURING THE SUMMER OF 1915 THERE HAD BEEN A GROWING DISSATISFACTION not only with the conduct of the war, but with the inadequate control of business firms suspected of profiteering on a large scale, as well as the lax supervision of provisions supplied to the armies in France. It was in connection with this that I became involved in the fortunes of a paper which enjoyed some reputation as an upholder of straight dealing in public affairs, *The New Witness*.

Most readers of books know something of the late G. K. Chesterton, essayist, playwright, verse-maker, and creator of Father Brown. Not many probably have heard of his younger brother Cecil, who was in some ways an equally remarkable personality. He first attracted public attention a few years before the war as the centre of a libel action brought by the British Government against a weekly journal, the *Eye-Witness*, of which he was the editor and guiding spirit; and it was shortly after the trial that the paper changed its name to the *New Witness* and I became acquainted with Cecil.

I must confess that the first sight of him was a distinct shock. I had pictured to myself a dashing and romantic knight of the pen, a champion of dangerous but righteous causes, and here was one of the most ill-favoured and unprepossessing individuals I had ever looked on. His method of speech—or, rather, delivery of it—was hardly better, for he stammered, stuttered, and spluttered and seemed to swallow his tongue as well as his words when he became carried away by enthusiasm or indignation. But it very soon became evident to me, as to everyone else, that here was a fine and fearless spirit, a born fighter filled with a sacred zeal for honest living and a burning hatred of humbug and crooked ways. As I too was very much in the crusading vein just then, my heart warmed quickly to this doughty little figure, and when the *New Witness* shortly afterwards began to enter a period of difficulty I offered my collaboration. This was accepted, and enabled the paper not only to get firmly on its feet, but to expand in the way of bringing in as regular contributors some of the most famous names in English letters and journalism: Hilaire Belloc, Bernard Shaw, G. K. Chesterton, Ernest Newman, Alice Meynell, and a few distinguished foreigners such as the Abbé Dimnet with a weekly article on French affairs. Although I never used or attempted to use the paper as a vehicle for any of my own opinions, I kept in fairly close touch with Cecil and made many appearances at his Friday board meetings, which were held in a dingy room in Essex Street just off the Strand.

The meetings began at five, and for about half an hour were conducted in an atmosphere of torpid lassitude. A boy would then enter with a large tray on which were glasses and several bottles of Burgundy, one being placed before each member present. This agreeable indulgence, so I learned, owed its adoption to Hilaire Belloc, one of the most renowned wine-drinkers of the day, and it certainly seemed to have a miraculous effect upon the proceedings. During the next half-hour tongues were unloosed, ideas floated in the air, epigrams were coined, and at times I could almost fancy myself in the old Mermaid Tavern of three hundred years ago. At the end of another half-hour the next week's issue was wholly planned and partly written, and we went our different ways contentedly. But among this brilliant gathering of wit, fancy, and solid learning it was always Cecil who was the centrepiece of the show. Without any of the subtlety and paradoxical charm of G.K., or the massive knowledge of Belloc, he had a direct and powerful intelligence backed by a pungent and telling prose-style that were vital to the conduct of an organ such as the *New Witness*. The paper existed and was read mainly for its belligerent and critical policy; it was he who undertook the lion's share in maintaining its reputation as a courageous revealer of malodorous misdeeds, and no influence or argument could ever turn him from a course which he had definitely made up his mind to follow.

One day he wrote to tell me that he was going into the Army; there lay his duty and he would not seek to avoid it; and a little while after he announced his forthcoming marriage to Miss Prothero, a gifted contributor to the paper. Their wedding breakfast was given at the Cheshire Cheese Tavern in Fleet Street, the favourite rendezvous of Dr. Johnson; practically all literary London attended, and a few days later Cecil left for the front. The sequel was pathetic. The hero of a hundred public controversies succumbed after a few months, not to the rage of battle but to an attack of influenza, and the paper did not long survive his loss. It might have managed for a while to carry on in some shape or other; yet without that sledge-hammer stroke of his in attack and that unrelenting persistence in argument, like a good bulldog gripping its antagonist, it would not have been the same. Thus came into and passed out of my life the man who to my mind was the finest journalist of his day in England; and as a memorial to him London can point to the Cecil Houses, of which there are now about a dozen in existence, every other year seeing one more added to the number. These are institutions where women who are strangers to the city or depressed in means can obtain accommodation for a nominal sum, and were almost unknown when Cecil and his wife began a journalistic campaign for their foundation. Always the friend of the poor, the unfortunate and the down-at-heel, he would rejoice if he could see how the executive ability of his widow and the appreciation of the public have realized one of his most cherished projects.

I spent a portion of the summer with my father in Lancashire, who had begun to worry a good deal over a venture he had embarked on just before the outbreak of war and which was not going at all to his liking. Some time about the close of 1913 he had met James White, generally known as Jimmy White, one of that group of financial wizards who appeared and vanished like comets in the sky of the business world during the period 1910–1930. White had persuaded him to enter into a contract to purchase the Covent Garden Estate at a price well exceeding two millions, and it was then intended, in co-operation with a well-known Northern firm of brokers, to float a public company to deal with the estate as a commercial proposition, when my father would receive back the considerable sum he had paid as deposit money together with a bonus for his services as financier. The scheme, the sort of thing done a hundred times a week in the City during normal conditions, was sound and workable enough, for whatever were the abilities of James White in other walks of business he was a first-rate authority on anything to do with real estate. But before this public flotation could take place, the war supervened, the Treasury refused permission for any further issues of capital other than those for war purposes, and my father found himself saddled with a contract to buy a vast property he did not want, and which, without the co-operation either of the public or other private individuals, he could pay for only by making very heavy sacrifices. For a man approaching seventy, who had never known a day's financial worry of a serious nature, this was a trying predicament, and one from which the habitual ingenuity of the City seemed unable to extricate him. Failing a modification of official restrictions, the only alternative was to obtain some revision of the terms of purchase from the vendors of the estate, and he asked me if I would take an interest in the matter and assist him and White to that end. As this was the first commercial transaction of magnitude with which I had been brought into touch since my departure from the North fifteen years earlier, I felt at some disadvantage beside White, who had not only been handling it for the past twelve months but was one of those fortunate creatures who have the answer to everything. He declared himself to be full of optimism, to which I replied that my father was equally lacking in it and viewed the whole position with justifiable anxiety. Something must be done about it, and as the whole deal was the child of his brain, he was the man to take action. He said he already had the figment of a plan floating around the back of his head, that he would discuss it with his associates of the broking firm together with some private bankers, and lay it before me in a few weeks' time. I then went down to Watford for a short stay with Delius, watched the progress of two growing compositions, *Eventyr* and *Arabesque*, and made preparations for a new enterprise that was to start in the autumn.

The deplorable condition in which the musical profession was plunged worried me considerably, and during the past six months I had been examining it from every angle of approach. It seemed to me that the best contribution a single individual could make to the necessity of the moment was to form an opera company which, running for the greater part of the year, would give regular employment to a substantial number of singers, orchestral players and stage technicians. The new organization opened in October at the Shaftesbury Theatre and played without a break until Christmas, meeting with a fair measure of public support. As I had taken upon myself the direction of so many concerts there was very little time for work in the theatre, and I looked around for promising recruits not only to the conductor's desk but to the field of scenic design, as the public taste, completely spoiled by the wonders of the Russian seasons, was in no mood to tolerate a return to the old hum-drum settings of pre-Muscovite days. Although I had already a stalwart adjutant in Percy Pitt, who through his ten years' experience at Covent Garden had a complete knowledge of the routine of a theatre as well as a full familiarity with the scores of a hundred operas, the work of musical direction was too much for a single hand, and competent assistants must be found.

I had recently engaged as general secretary a young man of about twenty-two who had come to my notice through the de Lara concerts, where one of his compositions had been played. Issuing from a musical family, both his father and grandfather having been conductors of the Carl Rosa Opera Company, Eugene Goossens had plenty of background and example for an operatic career, and the only question was whether he could conduct. I entrusted to him the charge of two new operas, and as I did not expect to be on the scene at the probable time of their produc-tion, he would be left alone to manage for himself, on the principle of sink or swim. These novelties were *The Critic* of Stanford and *The Boatswain's Mate* of Ethel Smyth, and from the start the resourceful youth comported himself with the baton as if he had been a veteran with a life's experience behind him. His coolness and facility were phenomenal, and he had good need of both, as I do not think any man of his age was ever subjected to such ordeals as those I imposed on him. It was my frequent practice to produce and conduct the opening performances of an opera and then hand it over to my young coadjutor, who had to step into my shoes at any moment and take over without a rehearsal; and many were the times I sent him here and there to conduct a symphony concert, carrying a bundle of scores with which he would make his first acquaint-ance during the train journey. All this may seem to the orderly soul a little haphazard, but the situation at the time was both trying and complicated: train travel was unreliable and in the interests of several institutions I had taken on more work than I should have done had I foreseen more clearly the troubled course of events. Goossens remained with me over five years—indeed, throughout my association with the company—and was an indispensable stand-by, as well as a loyal and devoted colleague.

An equally fortunate discovery was Hugo Rumbold, a scenic artist of genuine invention, impeccable taste and unfailing resource. Although I had known him socially for some time prior to this, I had seen nothing of his work, and so far had been under the impression that he was a clever amateur with ideas that might be attractive enough on paper but of little practical use in the theatre. But there was nothing of the dilettante about Hugo Rumbold; on the contrary, he was the most absolute professional in his line that I have ever known. While he rarely painted with his own hand, he supervised every square foot of the execution of a scene, took an infinite amount of pains over every detail of the costumery, bootery and wiggery, and in no theatre anywhere, the Comédie Française not excepted, have I seen such perfection in head-dress as his. He would experiment laboriously with the lighting plant until he got exactly the effects he wanted, and heavy was his wrath if some careless mechanic ventured at any later performance to vary his plot by the substitution of a single unauthorized shade of colour. Such was the personality who arrived just at the right moment to give the decorative side of the new company a touch of distinction and originality that was badly wanted, for a contingent of the singers, although not wanting in talent, was painfully inexperienced and would require many months of arduous work before beginning to settle down as good usable material. A certain young man, who later on became one of the best actors of the lyric theatre, startled us all at his début by solemnly scratching his wig during a delicately poetic passage addressed to him by another artist on the stage. But the stamp and character which Rumbold introduced to the pictorial side of the company's work only placed on me the necessity of finding others of like accomplishment to back him up.

31

A STRANGE MISSION (1916)

IN SPITE OF MY ARTISTIC ACTIVITIES I HAD KEPT IN TOUCH WITH JAMES White over the Covent Garden position and stimulated his energies whenever they showed any sign of slowing down. The plan which his fertile brain had conceived was taking longer to work out in detail than he had foreseen, and it would not be until the close of the year that it could assume workable shape. But it was sound and practical enough in embryo to let in a little light on what had become an unpleasantly obscure situation, and as it relieved considerably my father's mind I felt free to shelve the problem for a while and to undertake a task of a rather singular nature in Italy.

Suggested by a member of the Government, it was a composite affair, an odd mixture of the social, political, and artistic in one. The aristocratic class in Rome was none too sympathetic towards Great Britain; indeed, a fair proportion of it favoured the Central Powers. A good many Romans had married Austrians and Hungarians, and these alliances were thought to be something of a danger to our cause. It might therefore help at this juncture if some Englishman would go out there, make himself as agreeable as possible, give parties and throw in a few orchestral concerts as well. The idea seemed fantastic to me and I should certainly have never put it forward on my own account; but as it emanated from a responsible politician I listened politely, if incredulously, and set out for the Eternal City.

My arrival was inauspicious, for while in Paris on my way through

I had caught a touch of influenza which kept me indoors for several days. But the enforced inactivity enabled me to obtain an advance idea of how the land lay, for my old friends and acquaintances turned up in force, all overflowing with information and advice. One of my most frequent callers was Oscar Browning, whose chief delight on earth was Mozart, and each time he came to see me he insisted upon my playing him one of his favourite pieces. But as he had a perverse affection for little-known specimens such as the concerti for horn and bassoon or the opera *Zaide*, it was not always easy to oblige him. Afflicted by a delightful vein of snobbery of the historico-social kind, he was inspired with a profound veneration for the antiquity of the noble Roman houses. One day he was positively shocked when I caused a certain lady who had been announced to wait below for a few minutes, asking in a tone of gentle rebuke if I was aware that she could trace back her lineage to our Saxon times. The most adequate excuse I could make for delaying her admission was the truthful one that I first wanted to finish the Mozart movement I was strumming for his sole benefit, but while this may have flattered his vanity I could see that his outraged sense of propriety was only half tranquillized.

For my first symphony concert I selected a programme of ancient and modern music in more or less equal parts. I knew very little of the state of local musical culture, and had I been better informed about it I should have proceeded even more conservatively, for Rome is not really a musical city if compared with other great European centres. But things went smoothly enough until we reached the *Paris* of Delius, a piece of musical impressionism *pur sang*, mysterious and poetic for the most part, with here and there wild outbursts of hilarious gaiety. The public of the Augusteo, dumbfounded by the tone-picture of a city of which their acquaintance probably did not extend much beyond the Avenue des Champs Elysées, the Ritz tea-room and the cabarets of Montmartre, endured it in silence for about ten minutes, and then began to shuffle their feet and break into conversation. A few serious listeners endeavoured to silence the chatter but succeeded only in increasing it. Presently a few bolder spirits began to whistle; the opposition responded with furious cries and gestures of protest, and from that moment on the rest of the work was inaudible. I did not attempt to finish it, but waited for a likely place to stop and walked off the platform. The unexpected cessation of the music had the instant effect of quieting the uproar, and I returned to play the little overture of Paisiello's *Nina o la pazza d'amore*, whose artful simplicity enchanted both sides of the house and saved the situation.

After the concert I was accosted by a stranger of great age, who introduced himself to me as Cotogni.* I strove to manifest recognition and delight. All the while my brain was working furiously to remember who it might be. Then suddenly I recalled having seen the name on an old programme and in accounts of opera performances half a century or more earlier, and decided that a heaven-sent opportunity had been

---

* One of the most popular operatic baritones of the second half of the last century, and a frequent visitor to Covent Garden. British admirers of the late Nellie Melba may be interested to know that at her London début in *Lucia di Lammermoor*, during the season of 1888, Cotogni sang the part of Ashton.

offered me to elucidate dozens of doubtful points in the production of certain works which had been puzzling me for years. For here was one who had sung constantly under the eye of Il Vecchio himself, had been an actor in and spectator of great events, and might be a witness to the truth almost as impressive as the voice of the oracle. I invited the old gentleman to dinner and posed the hundred and one questions to which I longed to receive replies. What did Verdi mean by this or Ponchielli by that; how did Mariani take such a section or Faccio another; and what did the chorus do here and there? To none of these interrogations did I obtain a satisfactory answer, and I began to think that the mind of my venerable companion had failed to retain any clear impressions of the past. But here I was wrong, for with perfect lucidity he explained that why he could not answer my questions was that hardly any of them were concerned with scenes in which he had a share. In his time a singer was expected to learn nothing but his own part and to devote his energies to executing it to the best of his ability. What his fellow artists were doing was no business of his, and I could see that he was inclined to regard any suggestion of mine to the contrary as an amusing flight of Anglo-Saxon eccentricity. I doubt if he knew the stories of half the works in which he had sung, for while perfectly reminiscent of his own share he had only occasional memory of the names of other characters in them. I have often wondered whether this method is inferior to that of many modern singers who have an intelligent knowledge of an entire work, but do not seem able to make much of their own roles.

For my second symphony concert at the Augusteo I eschewed anything in the way of dangerous novelty, relying upon pieces which had the maximum of *cantilena* and the minimum of polyphonic complexity. About the most advanced item in the programme was Balakiref's *Thamar*, and the performance threw a flood of light on the ways of Roman orchestral musicians, and their attitude to the obligations of public appearance. In this work there is a third clarinet part of some importance, as it contains a small solo passage, and the player of it who had attended all the rehearsals was missing at the concert. No satisfactory explanation was forthcoming from the management, every other member of the orchestra professed total ignorance of the cause of this defection from duty, and I had nearly forgotten all about it when ten days later I ran into the absentee at a street corner and inquired what had happened to him. He looked distinctly embarrassed for a moment, but, deciding to make a full and frank confession, said with the most engaging simplicity, "You see, Signor, it was like this. My wife reminded me on the morning of the concert that I had promised to take her to a Fiesta, and I couldn't disappoint her, could I?" With this burst of confidence he looked at me with such anxious entreaty that I hadn't the heart to do more than compliment him on this touching sacrifice of art upon the altar of conjugal devotion, which I felt must be unique in the annals of modern Italy.

In the intervals between public performances I had plenty of time to probe the state of feeling in the various social circles of Rome on the subject of the war, but I failed to discover any strong prejudice one way or the other, the prevailing sentiment being a mild indifference, with

here and there a gently expressed regret that Italy had been dragged
into it at all.   There was a wholesale fear of the might of the Central
Powers and little confidence in the capacity of their own forces to cope
with the Austrians should an invasion take place.   A few super-pessimists
declared that such a disaster would be the end of all things, and, one
among them, the son of a former Prime Minister, vowed that on the day
it happened he would blow his brains out.   The dreaded event did take
place and he kept his word.

While I could discover little danger to the Allied cause from anything
the Romans might or might not do, I did learn much about the tenacious
hold which the Germans had over large masses of the agricultural population through a widespread system of purchase by instalment.   This
was operated through the big business banks of the country, the travellers
granting the easiest terms to the rural client, who, never before having
been treated so liberally, blessed and revered the name of the kindly
Fatherland.   One large commercial house was financed almost entirely
by German capital, which concealed its existence behind a façade of
Italian nomination.   Before long, however, there was an exposure of
this ingenious deception, Teutonic influence was eradicated, and a British
bank took over control until the end of the war.

Shortly after the turn of the 'thirties German economic influence,
which with our help had been extirpated from one end of the peninsula
to the other, began to lift its head again, and, allying itself with a powerful
industrial group in the North, made such rapid headway that a few
patriots, who had poignant memories of what had happened before,
travelled to France and England with the object of once more enlisting
aid to resist the new incursion.   In neither country were they received
with anything but languid indifference, and the ultimate result was that
a few years later Italy passed under the alien commercial yoke more
completely even than twenty-five years earlier.   In the spring of 1940
the Anglophile editor of one of the leading Roman newspapers told me
that the Italo-German combines headed by Count Volpi were more
powerful than either the King or Mussolini, who were now almost figure-
heads without actual power.

For a great capital there was very little public entertainment in
Rome, not even the opera being open, although at any time one could
view the manager (a lady) sitting all day on the steps of the front entrance
and indulging in the unusual pastime of watching funerals go by.   The
most interesting theatrical show was Il Teatro Dei Piccoli, where
marionettes gave delightful performances of some old operas never seen
on the living stage.   Among these was *Il Barbiere* of Paisiello, a charming
work and worthy to be remembered, if for nothing else, for having
suggested to Mozart the key, the time, and the mood of *Voi she capete*.
Once I had acquired a little knowledge of the habits of the noble Romans,
I adapted myself to them to the best of my capacity.   My new circle of
friends liked music a little, but dinners and suppers much more, especially
if there was no stint of champagne.   I therefore gave some concert-
dinners, where the provision for the carnal man exceeded in length and
importance that for the spiritual, and this concession raised my stock
appreciably in the eyes of my guests, who began to look upon me as
"gentile", *"amabile"* and almost un-English.   It was at one of these

that the celebrated artist Gemma Bellincioni appeared, she who in the early 'nineties had created the part of Santuzza in *Cavalleria Rusticana*; and although the freshness and purity of the voice were no longer there, she sang with charm and understanding and was still a very handsome woman.   Two other distinguished singers were in Rome about this time, Titta Ruffo and Edouardo di Giovanni, better known to Anglo-Saxons as Edward Johnson.   This excellent tenor, the best yet born and bred on the American continent (he is actually a Canadian), was enjoying an unquestionable success, notably in the *Manon Lescaut* of Puccini, in which as Des Grieux he surpassed all other interpreters of the role in romantic grace and delicacy of emotion.   If it had been foretold to us two in the year of grace 1916 that after the passing of another generation we should be in the grip of a second world war, that he would be in command of the Metropolitan Opera House of New York and that I should be conducting there, I think that we should have given the prophecy as little credence as Caesar gave to the warning against the Ides of March.

32

ENGLISH OPERA (1916)

I RETURNED TO ENGLAND WITH MY STATUS ADVANCED FROM PLAIN "Esquire" to "Knight", for what precise reason I never knew.   It is related of the great Coquelin that after a season in London, where he had been handled rather unkindly throughout by the critic of *The Times*, he called on the latter to say good-bye and tender thanks; and upon the slightly astonished scribe asking why, answered, *"Oh généralement."* I did not know whether this honour which was conferred on me during my absence had any connection with my mission, or, like Coquelin's appreciation   of   well-meant   if   unwelcome   criticism,   was   merely *"généralement"*.   But I was well aware that there is a heap of solid advantage appreciated by all men of sense in the possession of a title in England.   I had once asked an elderly friend why, after many years of refusal, he had unexpectedly accepted one, and his answer was that in his observation all those of his acquaintance who had some distinction of the kind invariably obtained better and quicker attention on trains and boats.   As he himself travelled a good deal, he had at last made up his mind to join their company and bask equally in the approving smiles of railway conductors and liner stewards.   Of course, one is expected to tip on a more generous scale, but then we just murmur *"noblesse oblige"*, and try to look as if we had been doing it all our lives.

Also in my absence the two operatic novelties, *The Critic* and *The Boatswain's Mate*, had been produced and with considerable success. Of the latter work I have already written, and of *The Critic*, while there is little to be said of the music than that it is an able but pedestrian setting of Sheridan's brilliant text, Rumbold's scenery and costumes were a triumph of comic art and made the piece worth seeing for their sake alone.   As it now seemed likely that the new company had arrived to stay, I suggested to my father that we establish it permanently in the Aldwych Theatre, of which he was the proprietor and which at the moment was untenanted; and he agreeing with me that it was better to have the house occupied than empty, we moved there in the early spring. Prior to this I had spent some time in Manchester with the Hallé Society and had discussed with its directors the chances of success of an opera season there in which their orchestra could be employed. The important question was the choice of theatre, and here opinions were divided. The largest and most suitable building was the New Queen's Theatre, which held over three thousand persons, many hundreds more than any other, but it had one fatal disadvantage in the eyes of most Mancumians. It was fifty yards on the wrong side of the street, Deansgate, which divided the sheep of the town from the goats. The right sort of people, my advisers alleged, would never cross the historic line of demarcation, and the wrong were without the means to pay the price of an opera ticket. I was unconvinced by either argument, for already in the concert room the public had shown a willingness to throw overboard the traditions and loyalties of a bygone age, and in a very large building I could afford to have a greater number of seats at a price which almost anyone could afford to pay. So with much shaking of the head on the part of my associates I decided in favour of the house in the unhallowed area and took a lease of it.

The Manchester season of opera was the turning-point in the career of the company. Overnight it evolved from the chrysalis state of a smallish troupe of Opéra Comique dimensions into the full growth of a Grand Opera organization, with an enlarged quota of principals and an augmented chorus and orchestra. I opened with *Boris Godunof* sung in French, the title role being taken by Auguste Bouillez, the Belgian bass-baritone, who had been already heard in London; and as there had been formed for the occasion a special choir of about 120 voices to augment the regular professional chorus of the company, we had a fine choral display on the stage for the big scenes. This amateur body of singers, selected from the best voices in the district, gradually developed a remarkable proficiency which enabled it to take part in several operas on its own with assurance and success. The fine voice of Bouillez, the splendid scenery of Benois (it was the first time that Manchester had seen a Russian opera), and the vitality and pathos of the music combined to make a deep impression on those who had heard nothing more ambitious than the limited efforts of the moderate-sized touring companies. Lukewarmness and curiosity grew apace into keenness and enthusiasm and opera became one of the more important subjects of the hour.

If I were asked to look back over the years and to say in which of them I considered the British people was to be seen at its best, I should choose the period 1915–16, with perhaps the first half of 1917. At the outbreak of war it was for a short time too startled to take in fully just what had happened and to find its bearings in a new order of things that had come into being overnight. A hundred years had passed since it had been involved in a conflict with a great West European Power; it had been ignorant of the huge field of military operations and had failed to realize why its tiny expeditionary force counted for so little alongside armies totalling fifteen to twenty millions. The trumpet-blast of reality,

blowing away forever into the air the theories and arguments of
economists, politicians, philosophers and novelists, was the appeal by
Kitchener for a mighty army of volunteers to serve for three years or
the duration of the war. Here was talking, as they say in my county of
Lancashire; this was real war with a vengeance. The most popular and
successful of English soldiers was at the War Office, and was he or was
he not likely to know more of the true position than the mob of dreamers
who had already been proved to be wrong on every count? Anyway,
the whole country woke up, rubbed its eyes, and stared into the abyss.
Not that it yet knew the full depth and terror of it, for that the issue
of the campaign could possibly be in doubt never crossed its mind for a
moment. Clinging to the purely legalistic *casus belli*, the violation of
Belgian neutrality, it flattered its soul to appear before the world as the
champion of the weaker side and the sanctity of the written pledge. The
greater part of it knew nothing of the fundamental causes of the continental struggle, of the far-reaching ambitions of the German rulers or
even of the true nature of its own Empire. Forgetful of how it had been
founded and maintained by commercial enterprise, often during its
earlier and heroic stages in painfully fierce competition with other nations,
it had grown to look upon it as a gift, bestowed by an approving Providence upon *his* favourite people as the reward of superior virtue and
valour, and preferred to believe that out of the store of its abundance
it was taking part in a great conflict from motives of conscience. This
romantic interpretation of all its actions assorts well with the character
of the British people, at all events the English part of it, which still
retains in its secret consciousness something of the chivalrous sentiment
that runs like a thin streak throughout its history. As Mr. Shaw pointed
out long ago, it is the Celt who is the hardheaded and practical fellow,
not the sentimental and visionary Englishman.

The only person of importance in Europe ever to understand the
true nature of the French Revolution was the simple realist, Bismarck,
who saw in it a racial rather than a social or political upheaval. The
conquering caste which had ruled the country for a thousand years had
degenerated in vigour and authority, and the older submerged and
conquered races roused themselves from their long sleep to step into its
place. One has only to compare the portraits of prominent Frenchmen
down to the end of the seventeenth or even the eighteenth century with
those of a group of modern politicians to realize that here are two wholly
different breeds of men. Similarly in England the grand amalgamation
of two peoples, beginning in the eleventh and ending in the fourteenth
century, found little room for the ancient and isolated races of Celtic
origin; and until well on in the eighteenth century that portion of the
nation that counted for much was a Franco-Anglo-Saxon-Scandinavian
fusion. Only with the industrial revolution did a critical change take
place in its structure, and the centre of it was Lancashire, which had
been the most backward of the counties, with its Celt-Iberian stock of
antiquity, and which in its new-found importance drew to itself a large
recruitment from Wales and Ireland. The influence of the Celt has
grown stage by stage in England so imperceptibly that the English
themselves have failed to realize the meaning and consequence of it.
Consider for a moment that great organ of opinion and communication,

the Press of London. How many of the leading journals are in English hands and reflect the temper and psychology of the English people itself? We find one powerful group possessing a dozen or more papers to be Irish. Another of equal influence is Welsh, a third Scotch-Canadian. Smaller groups or single publications reveal a like alien ownership, and even the greatest and most representative of all British newspapers is only partly under English control. The voice of that part of Britain which is essentially and characteristically English is silent today in the capital of the Empire, and this strange revolution has taken place almost entirely during the past sixty years.

Is it possible that there may be some connection between this phenomenon of the resurgence of the Celt and the steady decline visible in every part of the Empire during that period, similar to that which has overtaken France? For a decline there has been unmistakably, not so much moral as intellectual, and manifested most conspicuously in the decrease of the capacity to govern wisely and well. In no quarter is there satisfactory evidence that we retain undebilitated that instinctive gift for successful administration which in former years extorted the unwilling admiration of most other nations. In Canada there is the spectacle of a disunited people that local statesmanship has signally failed to adjust. In Australia we view the unpleasing predicament of a small community in a large continent, retarding its development, discouraging immigration and resenting any effort from outside to relieve its statically backward condition. In India, although we have made a prolonged, honest, and gallant attempt to lighten the imbroglio of its racial tangle, which is understood and appreciated by no one, the plain fact remains that we have so far failed. Lastly, but worst of all, we stand convicted before the civilized world of want of will to prevent the recovery of a beaten and powerless Germany as a stronger menace than ever yet to the peace of the world. What is the cause of it all? There is only one answer: the want of will to govern firmly and the absence of the ability to make clear decisions. The time spirit will overlook mistakes but it never pardons inactivity, and the Empire will have to breed a different class of ruler if it is to survive. The so-called professional politician is the dismallest failure of the ages in all countries; he is not only dead but damned, and until the people fully realize it there will be no hope of a saner, wiser, and stronger system of government.

If any of my readers should begin to wonder what all this has to do with the occupation of an artist, I might remind them of the title of this work, which suggests a selection of topics without limit. But why should an artist be talking about politics and statecraft? Precisely for the same reason that vitally concerns the fishmonger, the cab-driver, and the railway porter. Not less than these is he interested in how his country is run, and his opinions are not inevitably of less consequence.

I have frequently been struck by the singular attitude adopted towards persons of my profession, or indeed of any other artistic profession, by so-called business men, members of parliament and journalists. For instance, when in 1940 I was in Australia, a Sydney newspaper asked me for an interview, and under the mistaken impression that it was interested in the war, I spoke at some length about my experiences in Germany, which I had visited annually between 1929-38. I recounted

how my numerous appearances at some of their great festivals such as
Cologne, Salzburg and Munich had brought me into touch with all
classes of the people, how on one occasion I had spent two months
working in the Berlin State Opera, how I had met Hitler personally
as well as nearly all the other leaders of the Nazi party, and I made
special reference to my meeting with Rudolf Hess at Munich in 1936.
In the published account of the interview next day there was not a
single reference to any of these matters. All that the reporter had
thought fit to relate for the edification of his readers was a description of
my buttoned boots and the particular brand of cigar I was smoking.
Had I been a politician who had never been to Germany in his life and
who betrayed an obvious ignorance of everything that had to do with
its public and private life, my windy platitudes would have found a
welcome in about three columns of the front page. I am uttering
no grievance, for it was not I but the newspaper which had sought the
interview, and it was a matter of total indifference to me whether it
printed my remarks or not.

But, returning to the spiritual condition of England in 1916 and the
progress of opera in particular, the combination of a high mood of
idealism in the public and of economic stringency in the musical profession was effective in enabling me to create and develop the finest
English singing company yet heard among us. In war time the temper
of a section of the people for a while becomes graver, simpler, and more
concentrated. The opportunities for recreation and amusement are
more restricted, transport is limited, and the thoughtful intelligence
craves and seeks those antidotes to a troubled consciousness of which
great music is perhaps the most potent. But whatever the reason may
have been, the public for opera during war time was everywhere greater
than it had been before 1914 or than it became after 1919. Although
it is true that there was a good deal of new money being made through
war industries, that, I like to think, was a collateral cause only. The
artist, for his or her part, owing to the paucity of work occasioned by
the closing down of so many concert societies, was happy to remain
in one organization, where a satisfactory if not handsome remuneration
for the greater part of the year could be gained. Had the musical machine
of the country been running at pre-war speed I could never have retained
the almost exclusive services of such a fine group of vocalists, for half a
hundred towns would, in competition with me, have been offering fees
that would often have been beyond my capacity to pay.

The importance of the Manchester venture in my plan of operations
was that it functioned as a kind of pointer for the other great provincial
cities. London I knew would support only so much opera in the year,
and if I were to maintain the company for most of the twelve months
I could do so only by a series of seasons elsewhere. The performance of
Boris had proved to be an auspicious opening, and I followed it up
shortly afterwards with a new production of Verdi's *Otello* executed by
the Russian painter Polunin. It was sung in its original tongue with
Frank Mullings in the title role, Bouillez as Iago, and Mignon Nevada
as Desdemona. Of these three artists Bouillez was the least successful,
his downright delivery and robust deportment being less suited to the
sinuous line of Iago than to Boris. The Otello of Mullings was a remark-

able study in drama, and the vocal part of it improved fifty per cent when later on the work was sung in English, in the use of which his accomplishment matched that of John Coates. The Desdemona of Mignon Nevada was the best I have seen on any stage. The gentle helplessness of the character and its simple pathos were rendered with perfect judgment and art, and the quality of the voice in the middle and upper middle registers suggested a tender melancholy admirably in keeping with the nature of this part. As compared with most other sopranos, its colour was as ivory is to white, and what it lacked in brightness and edge was more than set off by the charm of its subdued and creamy tone. Both of these highly gifted artists suffered from the same serious weakness, an unsound vocal method. In the case of Mullings I do not think he ever had one at all, and when he tackled, or rather stormed certain high passages in *Otello*, *Aïda*, or *Tristan*, I used to hold my breath in apprehension of some dire physical disaster, averted only by the possession of an iron frame that permitted him to play tricks which would have sent any other tenor into the hospital for weeks. But in the centre his voice had ease and uncommon beauty, and his singing of quiet passages had a poetry, spirituality, and intelligence which I have never heard in any other native artist and in very few elsewhere. Like most large men he was also a first-rate comedian, and his fooling in *Phoebus and Pan* as Midas was a joy to all who saw it and has come down as a legend to the present generation.

The case of Mignon Nevada was wholly different. She had been trained exhaustively and exquisitely, but along the wrong lines. Her mother, Emma Nevada, had been the happy possessor of a light voice of beautiful timbre with a natural coloratura equal to that of any of her contemporaries. But on taking up teaching she had contracted the dangerous belief that every other soprano, without exception, should be a model of herself, and she strove with zest and ardour to make them into such. This worked out all right in the case of those who had been created and dedicated by Providence to this end, for within these limits Emma Nevada really knew how to teach. For those, however, who were otherwise endowed, this employment of the mechanism of the Procrustean bed was less successful. Her daughter was naturally a lyric soprano of a character as far removed from the usual specimen of light coloratura as is possible to conceive; and upon this foundation the zealous Emma had striven to superimpose a top that would enable Mignon to sing all those parts dear to her own heart, like *Sonnambula*, *Linda di Chamounix* or *La Perle du Brésil*. This maternal ambition to see her daughter go one better than herself was frustrated by the stubborn refusal of Nature to submit to such an arbitrary experiment, and the unlucky subject of it eventually found herself just one more sacrificial victim on the altar of misguided enthusiasm.

33

AN UNEXPECTED LOSS (1916)

IT WAS DURING THE SAME SUMMER THAT I RECEIVED AN INVITATION to attend a meeting in Birmingham summoned to consider the best way of forming a municipal orchestra. It was surprising that what had proved impossible in peace time should be regarded as feasible in the middle of a world war; but so many unexpected things had happened since 1914 that this perhaps was but one more to be added to the list. So there I went and duly attended several gatherings, at which all the trite sentiments ever uttered upon such a subject anywhere since life began were rolled out by one speaker after another. How necessary it was for Birmingham to have an orchestra, what a valuable contribution to the city's culture it would be, how the plan ought to be supported by everyone, and what a wonderful thing music was with its power to inspire and uplift! But of any idea how to put it into practical operation there was little evidence; certainly no one seemed ready to spend any of his own money on it, and the Lord Mayor, Mr. Neville Chamberlain, was very clear that the present was not the time to add one farthing to the rates in the interests of the fine arts.

This negative kind of zeal was as usual getting us nowhere, but I did discover among the representatives of about half a dozen leading societies a much greater willingness to co-operate than formerly, and I told Mr. Chamberlain that if the scheme under discussion did not materialize he might let me know, as I had the skeleton of another in my head which might result in something tangible. A little while after I did hear from him that he saw no immediate chance of any civic project being carried into effect, and that I was free to work out something on my own lines if I wished to do so. As soon therefore as I could go to Birmingham again I called into consultation two or three energetic spirits whom I had known in earlier days, obtained a list of the concerts given during the past season by all the societies operating within a radius of thirty miles, and finding it to be larger than I expected, invited their managers to come and see me.

They all attended and I told them that I was willing to engage an orchestra on a permanent basis for six or seven months in the year, if I could rely on their co-operation; which meant simply an undertaking from them to use it for the whole of their concerts. The cost so far as they were concerned would be no more than in previous seasons; indeed, if they cared to lengthen their respective series it would be less, in view of the conditions under which the new body of players would be working. On satisfying themselves that there was no catch or snag in the proposal they unanimously consented, and my next step was to ask the principal supporters of the seasons I had conducted in 1911-12-13 if they would join with me in reviving them, as it would hardly do to have a resident orchestra in the town playing only for choral societies. This too was agreed, and I set about the task of founding yet another institution, which I maintained in this fashion for two years without incurring more than a reasonable loss. I was preparing to continue for a third when my representative in the town notified me that the Government had taken possession of every building where music could be given and asked what was to be done about it. I replied that the proposition was transparently clear: no hall, no music; no music, no orchestra; and that it was for Birmingham to decide if this was what it wanted. As none of the local authorities took enough interest in the matter to intervene and preserve the existence of the young organization, I had no alternative but to abandon it, and once again the adverse fate which frowned upon every serious enterprise in Birmingham had got the better of us. But the effort was not entirely in vain. I had demonstrated that the thing could be done in a practical and fairly economical way, and a few years later the city council came forward with a grant which brought about the establishment of an actual municipal orchestra.

The opera company returned from Manchester to the Aldwych Theatre, and I made several additions to its repertoire, which by this time included about fifteen operas. The most important of these was *Il Seraglio* of Mozart, which I had not given since 1910. I have never understood why this beautiful piece has failed nearly everywhere to win the full favour of the public. Even as late as 1938, when the popularity of Mozart had reached its zenith and I gave it with a superb cast at Covent Garden, it was received coolly. According to Weber, its author never again brought forth a large work so thoroughly imbued with the spirit of youth and happiness, and as it coincided with the time of his marriage to Costanze it may be looked upon as an epithalamium for that event. Its artistic consequence eclipses even its domestic, for here at last we find the full-grown and mature Mozart, emancipated from the traditions and conventions of a style of operatic composition that had held the stage for eighty years and of which his *Idomeneo* is a first-rate example. In *Il Seraglio* we are introduced to a new and living world. Gone from the scene are the pallid heroes and heroines of antiquity, the unconvincing wizards and enchantresses of the Middle Ages and all the other artificial creatures dear to the whole tribe of eighteenth century librettists. In their unlamented place we have ordinary human beings of recognizable mould, singing their joy and sorrows to melody that rings as freshly in our ears today as in those of the Viennese one hundred and sixty years ago.

In songs of the highest excellence the score is exceptionally rich. Instances are the '*O wie ängstlich*', with its wonderful accompaniment expressing more perfectly than any other music known to me the tremulous expectation of the anxious lover; the three arias of Costanze, of which the second is the most haunting idyll in all opera; and lastly those of that grand old rascal Osmin, for whom the composer confesses an obvious affection by the gift of the finest explosion of triumphant malice in vocal sound. But astonishing as is this exhibition of solo virtuosity, it is outrivalled by the ensemble pieces, of which the finale to the second act is the crown. Here we have the first instance on a large scale of that matchless skill with which Mozart could weave together a succession of movements, each representing a different mood or stage in the action, into a complete unity that is entirely satisfying to the musical sense. And as the absolute fitness of the music to the dramatic situation is never in question for a moment, all flows on with a natural ease beyond which human art cannot go. In the last number of all, the Vaudeville, we have a specimen of that haunting strain peculiar to this master, half gay, half sad, like the smile on the face of a departing friend. These tender adieux abound in the later Mozart, notably in the slow movements of the greater instrumental works, such as the piano concertos in D minor, in A major, and in C minor.

I had succeeded in finding another scenic artist of talent, Adrian Allinson, and it was in *Il Seraglio* that he first gave the public a taste of what he could do. Allinson had hardly the same unerring flair for stage design as Rumbold; his effort was more unequal and he required some guidance in all that he attempted. But he had a larger fund of poetry and imagination which enabled him now and then to create pictures of the highest charm, and the second act of *Il Seraglio* was quite one of the loveliest I have seen anywhere. Another branch of our work to which we gave particular attention was translation. For general purposes we had an experienced collaborator in Paul England, who invariably provided us with a scholarly first version. Afterwards I would summon together the principal artists who were to appear in the opera, go over each phrase with them and ascertain what words they could the most easily vocalize on certain notes. Our two leading baritones, Frederic Austin and Frederick Ranalow, had a high degree of ability in this sort of thing and were often able to find in English the vowel sounds which corresponded exactly to those of the original text, a valuable alleviation of a notorious thorn in the flesh of every conscientious singer.

Among the other operas which continued to swell the repertoire were *Die Zauberflöte* and *Tristan und Isolde*, both in English. The former proved to be more popular than any other piece I gave with this company, and the latter was a near rival to it, due mainly to the strikingly individual impersonation of Frank Mullings. I have often (especially during the last twenty years) been baffled as well as amused by the attitude towards Richard Wagner on the part of a large number of apparently intelligent persons. Although it finds its origin in a dislike for or want of sympathy with the sentiment and style of the music itself, it claims to discern in the man and his work all sorts of sinister significances which so far have been hidden from me. One of the fruits of this antagonism is a strange theory which made a tentative appearance in the first World War and has cropped up again with greater persistence in the present one. It is, that while the pantheist Beethoven represents a spirit completely in accordance with that of the struggle to preserve the religious ideals of the past nineteen hundred years, the Christian Wagner is as much of an opposing element to him as Beelzebub was to Jehovah. How the creator of *Der Fliegende Holländer*, *Tannhäuser*, *Lohengrin* and *Parsifal*, all quasi-religious dramas in praise of the creed, the traditions and virtues of the ancient faith, could ever be regarded as other than the most stalwart and persuasive champion it has produced for centuries passes my comprehension. Even the pagan *Ring*, considered didactically, is a weighty sermon on the anti-Christian vices of lust of power, fraud, the arbitrary exercise of force and the tragic consequences that proceed from them. But what of *Tristan*, which it has become the fashion to refer to as an indelicate exhibition of shameless eroticism? Even if this were true, it would not be surprising in the case of a man who devoted most of his time to the preachment of the doctrine of renunciation and the eulogy of Venus Urania. Such reactions are a commonplace of the world's dramatic history, and contrariwise the gayest of all English playwrights turns without effort or embarrassment from the unabashed naturalism of *The Custom of the Country* to the delicate and lofty spirituality of *The Knight of Malta*.

Everyone is privileged to read into music that which dogs his own private thoughts and emotions. But if anyone can find in the great love drama a single sign that Wagner did not look upon the passion of its protagonists as a dream outside all practical fulfilment in a world dominated by the claims of duty and honour it must be someone with a telescopic vision denied to ordinary creatures like myself. The plain fact is that music *per se* means nothing; it is sheer sound, and the interpreter can do no more with it than his own capacities, mental and spiritual, will allow, and the same applies to the listener.

The value of Mullings's interpretation was that while the music was sung with greater alternate vitality and tenderness than by any other artist I have heard, the whole part was endued with a high nobility, an almost priestly exaltation of mood and a complete absence of any wallowing in the sty of mere fleshly obsession. The general effect was one of rapt absorption in an other-world phantasy, hopeless of realization on this earth, and this I believe to have been Wagner's own conception.

All this time I had kept my eye on the progress of the scheme for placing the Covent Garden contract on something like a manageable basis. There was no question of my father being relieved of any of his personal responsibility to the vendors; indeed, an essential part of the new deal was the provision by him of another large cash payment which would increase the amount advanced by him on account of the purchase to upwards of half a million pounds. On the other hand, James White had secured the offer of some fresh financial backing as well as an agreement between the contracting parties that everything else would stand over until the conclusion of war. There was no doubt that the unsettled state of this affair had weighed heavily on my father's mind during the past two years, and he had aged visibly. I made a point of seeing him more frequently and on most occasions we were alone. All through his life he had been a man of unusual reticence and could rarely bring himself to discuss subjects of an intimate nature with anyone. The antithesis of my grandfather, a personality of vigorous utterance and changing impulse, who did not hesitate to let everyone for a mile around know what he was thinking about, he always tried to avoid giving a definite answer to any question. Because of this inability to meet others halfway or open his mind freely, he was something of a trial even to those friends who were sincerely attached to him; and occasionally some old crony who had known him for forty or fifty years would seek my aid under the mistaken impression that I could tell him what my father's thoughts were about some question on which he himself had been unable to extract any expression of opinion.

But during the late summer months and early autumn of 1916 he, for the first time in our association, unburdened himself to me as much as I believe it was in his nature to do. His had not been a very satisfactory life. He had married against the inclination of his family; his wife had been an invalid during the greater period of their union; he did not seem to understand his children very well, nor they him; and the reserve which had afflicted him since boyhood was due to an incurable shyness and a fear of being misunderstood if he talked on any conversational plane save the most prosaic. The greatest of his misfortunes had been the break with myself, which occurred at a time when he needed most the friendship and companionship of a member of his own family. This was something he had been looking forward to during the years I was at school and Oxford, and the loss of it had the effect of causing him to withdraw still further into his shell. For books he cared little; for pictures rather more. But music, after his business, was the main interest of his life, and the operas and symphonies that he loved he would hear over and over again without tiring of them. *Lohengrin* was his favourite, and he must have seen it a hundred times in nearly every opera house of the world.

It was about the beginning of October that I went up to Lancashire to stay with him. The signing and sealing of the document which was to free his mind from further anxiety about Covent Garden was to take place some time during the latter part of the month, and there were final details to be discussed and settled before the date of completion. As I had to make preparations for the Hallé Concert Season which was to open in about two weeks' time, the intervening days were spent between Liverpool and Manchester. He attended the first concert, which was on a Thursday; and as it was over at a comparatively early hour, he decided that he would return that night to his home. As I saw him into the train, he reminded me that the appointment at the lawyer's office to approve finally the various agreements under the revised deal had been made for ten o'clock on Monday and asked me not to be late for it. The next day I went South and spent the week-end in the country, going up to London early on the eventful morning, and arriving at the Aldwych Theatre about half past nine.

My manager was waiting for me with the gravest face and the most unwelcome news. My father had died in his sleep some time during the previous night.

34

MUSIC VERSUS NATIONALITY (1917)

THE UNEXPECTED DEATH OF MY FATHER, DUE TO HEART WEAKNESS, deeply affected me. Our relationship had been a strange one; outwardly there was an apparent formality, but inwardly an actual sympathy, almost an affinity, between us. He was, I think, inclined to be a little afraid of me; and I, for some reason I could never explain to myself, generally felt rather sorry for him. Even in the years when I never saw him he had been a vivid personality in my mind, and it took me quite a time to realize that I should never meet him again. Although I knew that without his all-important participation the scheme which had taken nearly a year to bring to fruition was definitely at an end I could not yet measure the contingencies hanging upon his disappear,

ance from the scene; and what further consequences of the disaster
might be in store for us no one could foretell until the true position of
his estate was known. But several weeks would have to elapse before
this point was reached, and for some time after that no business outside
the preliminary duties of administration could be undertaken.

James White had acted as general business adviser to my father over
his London interests, and he now proposed, and I and my brother agreed,
that he should look after ours in the same way. Impressed by his conviction that he could handle successfully the problem of the Covent
Garden Estate, this seemed a satisfactory arrangement at the time, and
for a while it worked well and pleasantly enough. But his was not the
sort of intelligence to guide us safely through the complications of the
intricate tangle in which we were involved. He was dashing and
effective in the opening stages of a financial adventure, but later on, and
especially if there were occasion to make a wise retreat, he was apt to
become apprehensive, sometimes to the point of panic. Such dispositions
in business are akin to those who in military tactics are invaluable when
on the advance, but of small use if forced to take the defensive or play a
waiting game. He had the minimum of education but a considerable
charm of manner; an easy capacity for making money, and one still
easier for spending it. He once confessed to me that life without £100,000
a year was not worth living, but how he could ever have got through
such an income I do not know, for he lived in a very modest way. For a
brief period he owned a steam yacht which was intended to serve as a
retreat from the bustle and flurry of city life, but the first thing he did
when arriving on board was to have a radio apparatus fitted up so that he
could be in continual touch with his office. Later on he acquired and ran
personally a theatre, about the least unexciting diversion to be imagined.
His office in the Strand had become a rendezvous for all sorts and conditions of Londoners, politicians, newspaper proprietors, actors, jockeys,
and prize-fighters, and through this variety of acquaintanceship he
sometimes acquired information on current events of importance before
the outside world had any inkling of them.

It was during the late autumn that he one day startled me by saying:
"Your friend, Mr. Asquith, won't be long where he is." I asked him
what he meant, but he affected a casual air and said it was just a rumour.
I knew his manner too well to be put off like this, and at last wormed
out of him a story so extraordinary that, had it not been for the names
of his informants with whom I knew he was on intimate terms, I should
have looked upon it as a fairy-tale. Satisfying myself that he was perfectly
serious about it, I sought out a member of the Cabinet, a close friend
of the Prime Minister, told him in detail of the existence of an intrigue to
oust his leader in favour of Mr. Lloyd George, and that this and that
person were in it up to the neck. He said that he would make inquiries
from his end and would see me about it again. The days went by and
White one evening confided to me that the bomb was shortly due for
bursting, and that if any counter-move were intended the time had
come to make it. As I had heard nothing from the Minister, I passed
on to him the further facts which had come into my possession, but he
replied cheerfully that he was convinced that there was nothing really
to worry about and that Mr. Asquith was never in a stronger position.

Just previously I had caused the whole story to be communicated through an influential friend who might succeed in making a more serious impression to Mrs. Asquith, whose only comment was: "Nothing but death can remove Henry." Within a week Mr. Asquith was forced to resign the premiership and Mr. Lloyd George stepped into his shoes.

In Manchester the affairs of the orchestra were flourishing, for in addition to the usual six months' series of concerts, it now had several weeks of opera, and I had recently inaugurated a season of "Promenades" in the building of ill-fame, which had now been rechristened the Opera House. The cotton and mining industries were booming throughout Lancashire and money was flowing plentifully. In London the Royal Philharmonic Society was on a sound footing, and I had extended my interest to the London Symphony Orchestra, which had been making a gallant fight all this time to keep its head above water. The opera company had increased its popularity and enlarged its audience so widely that I decided to move for the summer season from the Aldwych to the much larger Drury Lane, where I had spent such pleasant days in 1913–14. As shortly before this we had increased our provincial connection by taking in Birmingham, Glasgow, and Edinburgh, the barometer for the future seemed to be set at "Fair", and I saw no reason why it should not remain there. For the migration to Drury Lane it was essential to provide something in the nature of a *coup* that would place the reputation of the company on a pinnacle higher than any it had yet reached. I again called to my aid Hugo Rumbold and requested him to prepare designs for a new production of *Figaro* that would surpass all that he had hitherto done for me. A fresh translation was made of the text to include the whole of the trial scene in the third act, which is usually curtailed and sometimes omitted, and then came the all-important question of *mise-en-scène*, for I had in mind to reproduce as far as possible the style and gesture of the Théâtre Français with singers who could also act. We approached Nigel Playfair, who agreed to co-operate on the condition that I would let him have the artists selected for the performance every day for at least three months. But I had to tell him that their necessary appearances in other operas prevented such an exclusive absorption in one work, and that he must be content with having them some of the time for five. And throughout this period, two and often three times weekly the chosen band turned up for rehearsals and worked away enthusiastically to fulfil every direction of the first authority in England on the comedy of the eighteenth century.

It was generally allowed that this production topped a peak so far unscaled in the annals of any native organization. Outside the Russian seasons nothing like it had been seen before, and certainly nothing has appeared since to excel it. And yet the cast, which had been selected more for appearance than voice, contained hardly one of the better vocalists of the company, although the singing was both adequate and stylish. But no one felt poignantly the lack of a higher level of vocalism in an entertainment replete with charm and elegance and providing an object lesson in what can be done with a piece like *Figaro* or *Così Fan Tutte*, given a bold and novel approach to a fitting method of presentation. There was, however, a distinction of the highest merit common to every member of the cast, a first-rate diction. One evening I went up to the top gallery and stood right at the back to listen, and from there I could hear not only every syllable of the songs, but of the ensemble pieces as well, all as clearly enunciated as if it had been spoken instead of sung.

A quasi-novelty was an English version of *Ivan the Terrible*, which is by way of being a companion piece to the beautiful *The Tsar's Bride*, which I gave many years later. Both of them are unduly neglected, but it may be that performed by a company other than Russian they fail to make their full effect. As I have already said, the bulk of the Russian repertoire is intensely national and liable to lose much of its potential appeal if dependent upon an alien interpretation. An actual novelty was a charming little opera which won an instant success everywhere and remained in our repertoire for years—*The Fair Maid of Perth*, by Bizet. When first given in London the Press took up a hostile attitude towards it, one newspaper asserting that there were half a dozen British composers at hand to write something much better. I at once offered a prize of £500 for a work which, in the opinion of three competent judges, should equal it in merit, and guaranteed its production as well as the publication of the score; but not a single competitor came forward to answer the challenge. It was an interesting symptom of the broadening public interest in opera everywhere that this piece, which is a typical specimen of French *opéra comique*, should have been so quickly and generally accepted when six or seven years earlier it would have been an almost certain failure. It was also the means of converting a Philistine friend of mine in Manchester to the appreciation of serious music; for, dining with him one night, I asked if he had yet been to the opera, and he replied that nothing on earth would induce him to go anywhere near it. Years before someone had taken him to a later Wagner music-drama, given very indifferently; he had been bored to death, and had no intention of repeating the awful experience. I bet him a box of cigars that he would not find the *Fair Maid* a bore, won over the sympathies of his wife, and finally prevailed on him to make the trial. The next day he rang up to say that he had found it almost as good as a musical comedy and asked if there were any more like it. I thought for a moment of recommending *Tristan*, but repented and proposed *Il Seraglio*. This he found equally to his taste, no doubt for the reason that it is itself nothing more than a musical comedy, differing only from the popular type in that, while the comedy is in no way inferior, the music is vastly superior to any other of its kind in the world.

The addition of *Tannhäuser* and *Die Walküre* to the repertoire provoked the ire of a certain newspaper magnate, who liked to think of himself as the real ruler of England and the keeper of all men's consciences. In his view German music was an integral part of the German soul, and as that especial entity was a very unpleasant freak of nature, it was unfit and improper to foist on the public anything born of it. I really ought, he urged, to banish it from my theatre; otherwise he would have to launch the thunderbolt of disapproval against me in his columns. I pointed out that Wagner was the favourite composer of that section of the audience which was in khaki, and that it was because of its insistent demand for these two operas that I was playing them at all. This shook him a bit, but not enough; for he went on to suggest that if members of His Majesty's Forces had such perverted tendencies, their erring steps should be guided into the right path. I thought it was time to resort to the use of the *argumentum ad hominem*, and made him a sporting offer. I knew he had some fine old German pictures in his house of which he was justifiably proud, and I undertook, if he would bring them into Trafalgar Square (having well advertised the event a week ahead in all his journals) and burn them in full view of the public as a protest against the abysmal iniquity of the Teutonic spirit, that the very next day I would withdraw everything of Wagner from my programme. But until he was prepared to make some personal sacrifice of the kind he could hardly expect me to do so. He was so bowled out by the proposition that for quite half a minute he was silent. Then the suspicion of a smile appeared on his face which by and by broadened into a grin, and he at last said: "It is rather silly, isn't it?" And there we left the matter.

I have often been baffled and disconcerted by the phenomenon, in an era which vaunts itself to be progressive, of the big newspaper owner. That he is occasionally a problem to Government also was to be recognized some ten years later when the Prime Minister of the day had to remind two of the more presumptuous specimens of the breed that the alliance of great power and small responsibility was not one to be tolerated indefinitely in an orderly State. Most of those whom I have met have been men of moderate education, less culture, repelling manners, and victims of the most offensive kind of megalomania. One of them, perhaps the most grotesque of the whole set, having attended an opera performance for the first time in his life, telephoned the next day a friend of mine to say how much he liked it, but wanted to know more about this fellow Wagner, who he understood had written the piece. On being told that Wagner was a tolerably well-known composer, whose works were quite popular, his comment was, "Not half enough, I am going to give him a boost in my papers." The gist of this interesting conversation was communicated to me without loss of time, and I rang up one of the great man's more knowledgeable editors to warn him that his chief had just discovered Wagner and was preparing to introduce him to the notice of the public. "Good Lord," he groaned, "this must be stopped at once," and stopped it was, rather to my regret, as there must have been hundreds besides myself who would have appreciated this announcement of Richard's existence from the latest of his converts.

It is only just to add that here and there were others of a different denomination, a few survivals of a journalistic age on which had not yet been showered the blessings of the Yellow Press, and one or two who combined the liveliest modern technique with some respect for past tradition. Standing head and shoulders above any rival, not only in this latter group but in all others, was the brilliant and dynamic Alfred Harmsworth, Lord Northcliffe. Patriotic, far-seeing and receptive, of him alone can it be said that the forces and influence of the new school were on the whole employed beneficially as well as audaciously. As in the case of nearly all men who have risen from a modest position to one of authority over so many of their fellows, he both received and welcomed any amount of adulation. But I think that however large may have been his capacity for absorbing it, he must have felt a twinge of embarrassment at some of the tributes offered him. Among these the most picturesquely strained was that of a popular versifier who, struck by the coincidence in Christian names, proclaimed to an astonished public that during its thousand years of troubled history the three out-standing heroes among the company of England's saviours in time of peril were Alfred the Great, Alfred Tennyson, and Alfred Harmsworth. It is no disparagement of the sanity of his views on most matters to say that some of his utterances and prognostications have a slightly comical ring in the light of political developments both at home and abroad during the past twenty-five years. Among the formidable crowd who have been preaching and prophesying to us all this time, all but one or two have been proved to be hopelessly at fault, and incidentally some of them, now of advanced years, are still at the game, probably with equal fatuity and credulity. Evidently once a seer always a seer, and the itch for looking into the future appears to be as irresistible as any other form of speculation, the only difference being that it is practised at other people's expense instead of one's own. But one instance of Lord Northcliffe's more uncalculated pronouncements I cannot help recalling, for the double reason that it was, I think, the last occasion I saw him, and a perfect example of the way in which the whirligig of time brings in its revenge. It occurred at a public lunch at which he was the guest of honour, and on being called upon for the usual speech, delivered a fiery onslaught on Mr. Winston Churchill, who not long before had left the Government. In his opinion the present Prime Minister of England was a man unfit to hold any important office of the Crown, it was unthinkable that he should ever do so again, and he (Northcliffe) would see to it that he never would!

35

A UNIVERSAL PROBLEM (1917)

NOT SO LONG AGO AN INGENIOUS AND LEARNED AUTHOR BROUGHT OUT a book entitled *The Age of Fable*. The purpose of the book, which is moderate in tone and franked by a wealth of instance, is to show that for the last generation or longer the public has never known the real truth about anything, has existed in a thick fog of error, ignorance and delusion, and that for this appalling condition of things the Press, rein-forced in the later years by the Radio, has been mainly responsible. In my country it is next to impossible to run successfully a newspaper that has not a party label of some sort, with the result that in addition to general policy, the presentation of opinions and the juggling of news are influenced and dictated by its political trend. Every time a great national question is raised in our so-called democratic States, instead of an immediate agreement between the various party machines to treat it as something that vitally affects the health or prosperity of the com-munity as a whole, it is made a football to be kicked about for their private amusement.

One would think that the adequate defence of the nation was a self-evident proposition; we protect our private lives and property from accident by insurance, so why not provide for the safety of the realm so that it shall not suddenly be endangered by attack from outside? But in my day not only has this never been accepted as the first axiom of national preservation, but has been the constant subject of irreconcilable dissension among the various political groups.

The foreign policy of a country like England is not determined by what is best for the interests of the people as an indivisible unit, but by the sympathy of one party or the other with those States whose systems of government or ideological creeds bear some resemblance to their own. It is true that the average man likes to take sides; existence would be intolerable without the clash of opposing ideas. But equally he does not want to wrangle the whole day long or see applied the meretricious methods of the forum or the political tub to the management of national affairs, any more than to the running of his own business or home. Also he sometimes likes to hear the other side of the question stated with lucidity (*audire alteram partem*), and above all he wants to know the truth. But this is precisely what he never does get. He is talked at, lectured, and admonished from morning to night, but enlightened never. I have just been reading a book by an American author on England, and it is hard for me to understand how such a piece of work came to be written, unless for reasons directly antagonistic to the interests of plain veracity; for the picture drawn of it is unrecognizable by anyone whose eyes are not blinded by illogical prejudice or emotional antipathy. The career of an artist in Great Britain is not one to beget a fanatical worship of everything there, and I have passed a fair portion of my life in other lands where I have seen much to admire and respect. But there are certain aspects of English life which remain pre-eminent, and only a total inability or disinclination to acknowledge their existence can account for denying or ignoring them. For example, the protection of life and property, two not inconsiderable interests, is greater than in any other state of importance. In comparison with another great democratic community, the statistics of crimes of violence are in a proportion of one to eighteen hundred, or, allowing for the difference of the two populations, one to six hundred, and no one but a thug or gangster will deny that here we have a slight advantage. Although much of our legal system is cumbersome or obsolete, the actual administration of justice is admirable, notably in the criminal courts, whose simplicity, dignity, and celerity are a model to all others.

The personal liberty of the poor man is greater than elsewhere, for he can be oppressed by neither employer nor fellow employee. Recently in a Canadian province a talented musician was fined by his union for giving his services gratis to a war charity, a species of tyranny surpassing anything known to the Middle Ages and out of the question in England, where freedom still means the privilege of the individual to do all those things that seem right in his own eyes, provided he do no wrong to his neighbour. If my country could for a few years rid its collective mind of all the political and social shibboleths, "isms", and "ologies" that have been crammed down its throat and dinned into its ears, compose its domestic differences, which after all are very few and trivial, and above everything reject decisively all nostrums and specifics (mostly of foreign origin and completely out of date) for the improvement of human nature, there might be still a chance of its playing a leading part in the affairs of the new world which is now being born.

Our failures during the past twenty years may be attributed to one overriding cause, stagnation. We have marked time, maintained a negative attitude to every critical event that has taken place elsewhere, and we have not made one practical contribution of the slightest value to the preservation of peace and sanity in the world. On numerous occasions our leadership and counsel have been sought and our decision or action implored, but we have responded with mere words. Less than a year before the outbreak of the present war the distinguished leader of the Conservative Party in the House of Lords indicated in a letter to *The Times* the danger to the entire world of an empire like ours which seemed incapable of ever making up its mind or coming to the point. The evil must be fairly deep-rooted when a political mandarin, usually the last person to acknowledge any deficiency in the existing system, can bring himself to issue such a warning.

The general mist of misrepresentation which envelops nearly all public transactions covers those of private persons also, especially if the latter are of the kind that journalists call "news". It may have been observed that in my foregoing chapters I have made the scantiest references to my personal or intimate life. I cherish the old-fashioned prejudice that every man must have a sanctuary to which he can retire, close the door, pull down the blinds and exclude the world outside. This was the substance of the old doctrine that an Englishman's house is his castle, once a reality but now a fiction owing to the monstrous ubiquity of the modern Press reporter and his accomplice in persecution, the camera pest. Any genuine privacy and seclusion, unless one goes into the heart of the desert, has been rendered impossible by the malign industry of that basest creation of the age, the gossip-writer. This slinking, sneaking, worming and reptilian creature passes his time listening at doors, peeping through keyholes, corrupting the servants, and all to discover and retail in print an illiterate jumble of incoherent rubbish about something which no one with the self-respect of a baboon would dream of concerning himself. I once asked the editor of a leading London daily how he came to allow the publication of some nauseating piece of twaddle that had just appeared, and he answered: "We live on garbage." But if the slightest protest is ever made in any quarter the cry at once goes up to heaven: "The freedom of the Press!" Until a few years back a considerable amount of space in certain London papers was given up to long, lurid, and salacious reports of divorce cases, and the kind of stuff that we used to read every day would, if forming part of a novel or even a scientific treatise, have been banned by the police magistracy. When the incongruity of this preposterous situation at last penetrated the intelligence of the public there was a demand for the compression of such accounts, which after a while was conceded by a rule of the courts. But the resentment of the journals that lived on "garbage" was so loud and strong that if a stranger from another sphere had descended among us he would have concluded that the foundations of justice, society, and the State itself would totter dangerously if the champions of free speech were deprived of their scavenger's cart.

All of which brings me to the point where I propose to throw a ray of truth upon certain affairs of mine which have received a good deal of notice in the Press of most countries and about which I have preferred to remain silent during twenty years and more. Everywhere I have found the impression that I inherited from my father a large fortune, the greater part of which I have spent on artistic enterprises, and that generally I am thriftless, prodigal, and without understanding of money. One part of this opinion at least is as far removed from the truth as anything can be. It may be that I have expended very large sums on music and other artistic ventures, but not out of my inheritance, for the simple reason that I was powerless to touch the capital of it. How has this misconception come about? Mainly through the indefinite character of much of our legal system and the casual methods of reporting in the Press, as will be seen hereafter.

My father's executors, having completed the preliminary examination of his affairs, called me into consultation. The disposition of his estate was simple enough in outline, his Lancashire business being left almost wholly to my brother and myself and the residue mainly to four of my sisters. But upon the whole property lay the burden of the Covent Garden contract, on which two million pounds were still owing. There was no possible chance of finding this sum out of the assets at our disposal, for even if the business could be sold in war time, which was highly doubtful, it would not bring in enough to discharge the obligation. Although its yearly profits were considerable, its capital value was moderate, consisting as it did mostly of goodwill, with few tangible possessions such as land and buildings to back it up. A larger portion of the residue than expected would have to go in paying debts and overdrafts, and it looked as if my sisters' share would be considerably below anticipation. It would help the situation, argued the executors' advisers, for the whole estate to be in the hands of my brother and myself alone, and if we would purchase the residuary part of it, we should be left in undivided control and in a better position to deal with Covent Garden.

James White was well on the side of such a transaction, being just as anxious as the executors to get the estate out of their hands and into ours; and as he was quite confident that we could find the money to carry it through, my brother and I entered into a contract under which we undertook to pay for the residue about twice as much as it eventually proved to be worth, and sat down to observe the operations of the financial wizard.

My father, in full anticipation of many more years of life as well as the imminent settlement of the Estate problem, had only a few weeks before his death made a fresh will, and if he had survived a year or two longer its terms would have presented no difficulty to his successors. But having been drawn with an eye to the big deal which was awaiting early completion, his unexpected demise made it almost unadministrable. The portion of the business bequeathed to me was left in trust, which proved to be a constant stumbling-block in the path of White's schemes for handling the property in the broad, bold fashion with which he was familiar; and as the months went by it became increasingly evident that here was a puzzle beyond his capacity to solve. He could raise the money neither to complete the residuary estate contract nor to finance

Covent Garden, and he was not helped by the war situation, which had deteriorated rather than improved. Air raids had become more frequent, the U-boat menace was the constant nightmare of the Government, and the public was beginning to realize that it was involved no longer in a chivalrous crusade but a war of life and death. Official restrictions continued to remain unrelaxed, the City was unresponsive, financial wizardry had bitten off more than it could chew, and its magic wand was waving in vain. We had no alternative but to go to the executors and confess our impotence. If only the war would stop and the wicked Germans admit defeat, all might be well; the wheels of company flotation now at a standstill would revolve again merrily and our troubles would be over. The executors sympathized with these pious hopes for the future but were naturally more interested in the present. They had a contract with us for a very large sum of money, and where was it? The only answer to this question was, nowhere, and there appeared small chance of an improvement in our unlucky position.

There happened to be in Liverpool at that time an accountant with a talent for figures nearly akin to genius. He had been called in by the executors on taking over their duties, had advised them throughout, had been half anticipating the present impasse, and now produced overnight a scheme for the reconciliation of the conflicting interests in the estate and the unravelling of the Covent Garden tangle. It was necessary, however, in view of the numerous trust shares in the will and the ambiguous position of the executors, for the estate to be administered under an order of the Court of Chancery; and the essentials of the scheme were that a large sum be borrowed from the bank to reduce the unpaid balance of the Covent Garden purchase money, that the property be nursed over a period of years, that my brother and I agree to accept a much reduced income from the business and that the balance of such income be accumulated to pay off the bank and ultimately the residuary contract.

When the suggestion of Chancery was first mooted, my thoughts reverted to a disclosure which my father had made to me during that summer of 1916 in Lancashire. An old friend of his and a man of great ability had died leaving a will which he had innocently imagined to be crystal-clear and fool-proof. It had proved to be so difficult of interpretation that his estate had to be thrown into Chancery, where it remained for over five years. While deploring this disaster my father had been a little critical of the carelessness of its author and declared with a certain complacency that, profiting by this experience, he had caused a will to be drawn up which under no circumstances could give the slightest trouble to those appointed to carry out its provisions. I was filled with disquiet and foreboding at the prospect before us, but there appeared no other way out. The vendors of Covent Garden were getting restless and something had to be done about it. So off to the Court we went and obtained an order of administration which took six full years and more to run its appointed course.

This critical step brought me up sharply against an unpleasant reality. My father during his lifetime had stood solidly behind my numerous enterprises, sometimes shouldering a part of the burden himself, at others loaning me amounts which would be debited to my eventual share in the estate. At his death therefore I had several overdrafts which could have been discharged or reduced without difficulty had I been receiving all the dividends due to me from the St. Helens business under ordinary conditions, but not with a materially reduced income. Undoubtedly the wise thing from the prudential point of view would have been to part company with those organizations which I had been assisting to keep alive since the outbreak of war, or at all events to cut down substantially my contribution to their support. But I shrank from the immediate application of the axe of economy to the root of the dilemma. Hundreds of worthy people were for the moment dependent on the continuance of my efforts; I had created the finest native opera company ever seen in England, my audiences were increasing all over the Kingdom, and although my outlay was heavy I was hopeful that after a while it would diminish. Only in the last extremity did I feel like throwing up the sponge, for after all the war might end before long and the situation change for the better. I therefore threw caution out of the window and determined to go on as long as it was within my power.

36

THE RETURN OF PEACE (1918)

WE HAD NOW REACHED THE SPRING OF 1918, AND OUR OPERATIC performances began to be disturbed more and more by air raids. During one week a bomb killed the stage-door keeper of the Aldwych Theatre, another wrecked the premises of a publishing firm just up the street, and a third shattered the sixteen thousand panes of glass of the Covent Garden flower market, the most stupendous clatter I have ever heard anywhere. The shrapnel from our anti-aircraft guns occasionally came through the roof of the stage, to the discomfort of the singers on it, and one night when I was conducting *Figaro* and the second act had just begun, a terrific bombardment opened all about us, and for minutes at a time the music was hardly audible. There was a momentary nervousness in the audience which was at once relieved by a courageous lady in a box rising and exhorting it to follow the example of the artists, who were singing away gaily and confidently as if there was no such thing as a world war going on outside. But these raids and a few in the summer were the last attempt of the enemy on London; the Zeppelin attack was singularly futile, almost every one that came over being brought down in flames, and I myself saw two or three destroyed, in each case by a single airman who climbed up within easy firing range and punctured the huge mass with gunfire.

An interesting interpolation in our summer season at Drury Lane was a production in conjunction with the Stage Society of Byron's *Manfred*, the opera company providing the orchestra and choir for Schumann's music. This fine but gloomy drama is very much of a monologue, and I saw it falling flat unless cheered up in some way indicated neither in the play nor the score. I introduced a part song or two as well as some short orchestral fragments into what seemed to be fitting places, but the tedium of the piece remained unrelieved, and it finally occurred to me that what might save the situation was a little dancing, recalling that whenever George Edwardes of Daly's and the Gaiety Theatres saw his piece lagging and failing to catch fire he would invariably call for a fancy-dress ball to be brought on the stage. But as Schumann had never written any ballet music it was necessary to invent some, and I selected about a dozen of his short piano pieces and handed them to my two lieutenants, Eugene Goossens and Julius Harrison, for orchestration. As there were only a few days to go before the first performance, these invaluable young men sat up for three nights with wet towels round their heads, turning over the ballet as it was scored, page by page, to the copyists who were to make the orchestral parts. The dances were inserted in the scene of the Hall of Ahrimanes, the décor of which was borrowed from Boïto's *Mefistofele*, and did something to enliven a work which perhaps was never seriously intended for public hearing.

During the winter and spring the nation, realizing that the supreme moment of the war had arrived, had been following with strained concentration the final effort of the Germans to break through to Paris. But as the year advanced there came a gradual relaxation of the tension, due to a conviction based more on instinct than knowledge that the enemy's attack had failed and victory was in sight. Both Turkey and Austria were out of the struggle; only Germany remained in the field. The end came suddenly and unexpectedly and the Armistice was signed almost before we were aware that fighting had ceased. Excitement was intense, and the whole country gave itself up to a spell of riotous enjoyment. During the past eighteen months I had noticed a growing change in the attitude of most people towards the war and each other, and the sacrificial spirit of the early days that we see mirrored in the verse of Laurence Binyon and Rupert Brooke had given way to a harder and coarser condition of mind, generated I think by the brutalizing monotony of trench warfare.

The employment of women on a large scale in war work had brought the sexes closer together, with results that appeared to be as little attractive aesthetically as ethically. The few years that followed the Armistice were a frank return to the outward freedom of Restoration days, and an erudite historian said to me one day during 1920 that he did not think anything quite like it had been seen in England for hundreds of years. But of this one can never judge with certainty, for almost the same thing was said to me by an elderly friend in 1913. So far as I can read between the lines of history, men and women have been much the same in all ages, the only apparent difference between well- and ill-behaved periods being that in the latter they care less for the opinions and judgments of others. But what undoubtedly was, and remained for years, the universal obsession was dancing; not dancing in the free-limbed bouncing style of twenty years earlier, when a few couples scampered vigorously up and down a spacious room, but a funereal assemblage of creatures, tightly packed together in an exiguous space, bumping and banging into one another, hardly moving the while and all looking as if they were practising some painfully penitential exercise. The comment of a distinguished French diplomat on his first sight of this singular species of amusement deserves, I think, to be remembered: *"Les visages sont si tristes, mais les derrières sont si gais."*

About this time I was fortunate in being able to form a small syndicate to take over the opera company, for I had come nearly to the end of my resources and should not have been able to continue unassisted much longer. As it was I was heavily in debt, but for the moment was not greatly concerned about it, as, like most others, I was expecting, now the war was over, a rapid return to the economic ease of 1914. A part of the recent estate transactions had been the formation of a Covent Garden Estate Company, which, upon the payment of a further sum of £500,000 to the vendors, who granted a mortgage for the balance, became the proprietors of the Opera House in addition to Drury Lane and several other theatres. But the possession of the Opera House was more honourable than profitable, as the Grand Opera Syndicate had an old lease of the building which still had twenty years to run and for which they paid the modest sum of £750 a year. During the war it had been used as a storehouse, so that a good deal of refurnishing and redecorating was required to restore it to its former condition, and while this was being done I renewed my former association with the lessees for the purpose of a Victory season in the summer.

It was a few weeks before its opening that an angry figure stormed into my office and asked what the deuce I meant by painting her room green. It was Nellie Melba, and very upset she seemed to be. I had never before come into working contact with this imposing personality, although I had heard something of her autocratic ways; and considering the best method of defence here to be attack, I pretended not to remember who she was, and asked what the deuce she meant by entering my office unannounced, adding that I knew nothing of private ownership of rooms in the building. This produced a fresh explosion of wrath which, as I remained grimly silent, gradually subsided and was eventually succeeded by an aspect of resignation and the mild complaint that she would not have minded so much if the green had been of a cheerfully light instead of a depressingly dismal hue. I thought of the gentleman in *Patience* who suffered from a similar prejudice—

> I do not care for dirty greens
> By any means,

and as she was going to sing on the opening night under my direction, I decided to be magnanimous as well as diplomatic to the extent of offering to repaint "her" room any colour she liked. This little concession delighted her more than the most costly present could have done and we soon became excellent friends. Melba was a singer who had nearly all the attributes inseparable from great artistry. The voice was beautiful and bright, of uncommon evenness throughout; and she handled the whole range of it with absolute mastery except in measured coloratura passages such as those at the end of the Waltz Song of *Romeo and Juliet*. She was extremely accurate, insisted on her fellow-artists being equally so, was punctual to the tick at rehearsals and while at work was a shining example in discipline to everyone else. But there was always some element lacking in nearly everything she did, and it is not easy to say just what it was. It was hardly absence of warmth, because many an artist has had the same deficiency without one being made uncomfortably aware of it. Of the mysterious quality known as temperament she had certainly a little, and her accent and rhythm were both admirable. I am inclined to think that she was wanting in a genuine spiritual refinement, which deprived the music she was singing of some virtue essential to our pleasure; and perhaps it was for this reason that in the maturer musical culture of the Continent she had comparatively little success, her popularity being confined to England and those other Anglo-Saxon communities where the subtler and rarer sides of vocal talent are less valued.

This season was in every way a pleasant and successful affair, notable chiefly for the appearance of four unknown tenors, all of them good, Burke, Hislop, Dolci, and Ansseau. The old Covent Garden favourites reappeared from various corners of the earth, few of them the better for the lapse of time, although the graceful Edvina gave admirable performances of *Manon* and *Thaïs*. The *Thérèse* of Massenet was among the novelties, of which the more interesting were the *Iris* of Mascagni and *L'Heure Espagnole* of Ravel, and for the latter work Hugo Rumbold furnished a setting of the greatest brilliance and charm, perhaps his *chef d'œuvre*. *Iris* contains so much beautiful and poetical music that its incapacity to maintain a regular place in the repertoire must arouse some of our sympathy. But it convincingly points the old maxim that metaphysics and the theatre, especially the lyric theatre, hardly ever go comfortably hand in hand, as Strauss also discovered in the case of his *Die Frau ohne Schatten*. The English section of the company distinguished itself in a translated version of *Prince Igor* conducted by Albert Coates, who had not been seen in England since 1914, and in a new production, with magnificent scenery and costumes by Charles Ricketts, of Isidore de Lara's *Naïl*.

A holiday spirit was everywhere in the land, and those portions of the community which during the war had been making a good deal of money for the first time in their lives were spending it with a fine freedom. The high wages earned by many of the cotton operatives and miners in the North produced some interesting manifestations of the use of it. One day I was in the principal music shop of Manchester when a couple entered, the lady wearing a shawl on her head and a fur wrap round her shoulders, and asked to see a piano. On being asked what sort of piano, the man replied that they were not particular, but it must be upright and have a green marble top. The director of the establishment, who was also the manager of the Hallé concerts, was about to say that they had nothing in stock answering to that description, when I whispered to him that it was quite easy to have it painted to resemble marble and they might never know the difference. He then assured the intending buyer that although there was not at that moment in the showroom anything exactly like the article he wanted, one would be produced for him within a few days. My curiosity aroused by this unusual preference, I inquired the reason for it, and learned that having recently taken a house in the parlour of which there was a fireplace with a green marble top, they must have a piano of similar colour to match it perfectly.

There was a diverting sequel to this event, although I was unfortunately unable to take part in it. Some weeks later the pair visited the shop again and ordered a second piano to correspond with the first in every particular. In the course of conversation they volunteered the surprising information that it was going in the same room on the other side of the fireplace. They had spent most of the intervening time in looking for a piece of furniture that would suitably fill the vacant space, but finding nothing to their liking had decided that the only satisfactory alternative was a replica of their original purchase!

37

THE BRITISH LEGAL SYSTEM (1919)

DURING AUGUST THE ENGLISH OPERA COMPANY BROKE FRESH GROUND by putting in a month at Blackpool, the Margate of the North, and this was a fortunate addition to the year's work, as it had given fewer performances during the season at Covent Garden than in any previous summer, owing to the return of the Internationals. I went there myself for a few days, stayed at a country hotel halfway between Blackpool and Fleetwood, and before leaving, walked once more along the well-remembered road to Rossall. Since I left to go to Oxford in 1897 I had revisited the school once only, when I took the Hallé Orchestra and gave a concert in the hall where as a boy I used to play the piano. To my eye the place was beginning to lose much of its old attraction, quiet isolation: buildings were springing up where formerly there were fields, and the ancient landmarks had vanished or were hard to trace. I rarely contemplate returning to scenes after long absence from them without a nervous apprehension that I shall find a difference too great for my happiness; and it is the same with people whom I have not seen for many years. If I find serious alteration in their appearance I am so uncomfortably embarrassed that I half wish I had not met them again. It is otherwise with those with whom we are in touch almost daily: they too alter, but imperceptibly, and preserve for us much of the semblance they wore when first we knew them. But where music is concerned, the passage of time has been powerless to change or modify my first attachments, and that which I loved as a youth still holds the foremost place in my regard. No matter if a generation go by without my hearing some strain of which I have affectionate memories, I always find undiminished the brightness of its early spell.

Towards other arts, particularly painting and architecture, I have been unable to maintain this constancy of mood. Nearly every time I find myself after a lengthy interval in a great gallery like the Louvre or the Vatican, I am startled by the entirely different appearance of pictures which I have been carrying clearly in my mind's eye the while, and I have the same disconcerting experience with buildings, although here it is less a question of individual examples than of whole styles. In my earlier days, and I believe most young people share a like obsession, I was wholly wrapped up in Gothic: neither Romanesque nor Renaissance had any but the slightest interest for me, and as for Baroque I fled at the sight of it. Then gradually I began to see these other periods one by one with a new vision, and to find in them points I was incapable of appreciating before. Reflecting on this experience, I have often conjectured whether the ear be an organ that retains its sensory faculties longer than the eye: or if it is that the pictorial and monumental arts are tangibly bound up with scenes, peoples, creeds and philosophies of which our personal ideas and evaluations are continually changing, while music is after all in the last analysis devoid of association with any other definite thing in our consciousness.

A well-known British statesman has told us that the only man alive who ever inspired him with awe was his former schoolmaster. At the height of his career and fame he never went down to his old school and into the presence of the Head without feeling that he was in for a severe "jaw" or something worse. Similarly there was at Rossall one whom I had equally dreaded, and his pedagogic austerity had not diminished with the passing of time. He still addressed me in the style of twenty years back, only now and then pulling himself up for a moment to apologize for what he thought was a lapse into undue familiarity; but in ten seconds he had reassumed his wonted manner and was the terrifying old Dominie once again. This continuing consciousness of a pupillary state extending into mature manhood is characteristic of the public school, and I sometimes wonder if, despite the many admirable features of its system, this particular one does not carry some disadvantage. Its conservation of the boyish element in the British character to which I have alluded, although questionable, is less baneful than the perpetuation of those numerous prejudices and inhibitions that separate the bulk of our ruling class from every other community of men. A member of the Government that was in office when the present war broke out had been visiting Rossall while in the North, and to his surprise had seen my name on boards as both the captain of my house and a member of the cricket eleven. A little while afterwards he met and said to a friend of mine: "You know, he can't be a bad sort of fellow after all." This attitude to music and musicians is peculiar to England; it exists nowhere else and is an abnormality of nineteenth-century growth. Its possessors are under the melancholy impression that it is the mark of a sterner manhood, as if the Germans were any the less virile for the possession of over eighty permanent opera houses. If they could be persuaded to give a backward glance at their Elizabethan and Georgian ancestors, who were busy creating that Empire which they themselves appear to have been almost equally absorbed in disrupting, they would discover that music then played a part nearly as important as in ancient Greece, also an historical epoch not wanting in heroic character. The simple truth is that the want of the musical sense is just as much of a deformity as the non-existence of an eye or any other organ, and means that the one truly international link between a hundred different peoples, separated by the differences of language, customs and institutions, has no place in their understanding. Furthermore, they are cut off from their fellow creatures in other lands in a way that no musician or musical person can ever be, either of whom feels completely at home in any circle whose culture joins his own on this common meeting-ground.

In no quarter is this disdain of music and this ignorance of the part it plays in the life and estimation of other peoples so profound as among the otherwise worthy men who adorn the judicial benches of our Law Courts. That they administer the law, when they happen to know it, with scrupulous rectitude and clear-sighted ability is not to be denied. But in England very few persons do know the law, including all solicitors, who can rarely advise their clients on any question of importance without rushing off to obtain the opinion of Counsel. This opinion is not based upon any fixed code approved by either the legislature or a college of lawyers after the fashion of the Pandects of Justinian or the Code Napoleon, but upon the latest decision of some individual judge, usually made on the spur of the moment. This is admirable from the standpoint of the fraternity itself, for the law becomes an obscurity and a mystery like the climate or fortune-telling. The consequence is that no man knows where he is, sometimes not even the judges, for in recent years quite a few of them have demonstrated their incapacity to draw up their own wills correctly. It is less satisfactory to the laity, for if there is one thing in a well-ordered society that ought to be as clear as day and free from the least ambiguity it should be the legal position of every man and his possessions *vis-à-vis* the State and his neighbour. Unfortunately, the learned practitioners of the craft have not yet realized that the dubiety and uncertainty surrounding it have tended to bring them into almost as much contempt and ridicule as the modern politician; and the old-time respect and esteem for the judiciary has not been increased by the deplorable garrulity of that portion of it which never loses a chance of airing its views and exposing its intellectual limitations at the expense of those who are seeking from it only the administration of justice.

Years ago I heard a judge of notorious indiscretion declare his inability to trust the word of a witness on the ground that he was a Roman Catholic. I am no member of that community, and I was very young at the time, but I still recall vividly the shocked astonishment I felt at hearing from an occupant of the Bench an insult levelled at a large number of His Majesty's subjects throughout the Empire, not to speak of something like two hundred millions of the same creed in Europe. In another instance, during a matrimonial case, a woman who conducted a business independently and with high success was branded as a worthless person. I have not the same respect for money as the ethereally-minded Ruskin, who somewhere described it as character. But it did seem to me that anyone who on her own could run a concern which made a large annual profit and employed a substantial number of people could not be wholly without qualities of one sort or another. Anyway, the question involved was a purely moral one on which no lawyer is any better fitted or more entitled to have and express judgment than any of the other twenty million adult citizens of the kingdom.

I have not been able myself to escape this offensive tendency. Quite early in the course of our Chancery proceedings it was disclosed that I had spent a considerable amount of money in the cause of music, and the wise judge's instant comment was: "What is the good of that?" It was nothing to his childlike intelligence that through the use of this sum, wisely or unwisely, a goodly part of the war-time music of the country had been kept alive. Had the objects of my outlay been a group of racing stables, a shooting-box, and a steam yacht, things in his eyes that were the proper indulgence of the manly Englishman, he would probably have expressed his approval. But music, never.

On a later occasion, another legal luminary, hearing my counsel refer to the musical profession, interpolated this stupendous comment: "What's that? You don't call music a profession, do you?" A third instance where a young man I knew happened to be a party to a suit and it was mentioned that he was studying to be a musician, the arbiter of equity raised his eyebrows, shifted his wig, and snorted, "Why doesn't he go into some honest trade?"

Of course these pathetic revelations of eccentricity and ill-breeding, which in most other countries would procure the early retirement of their authors, are hailed with delight by that section of the Press and public which still clings to the conviction that knocking little balls into holes or hitting other little balls about a green field is almost the only acceptable evidence of virility in a great nation. And so the disabilities of continued immaturity handicap fatally a large mass of my countrymen, and while this anachronistic condition remains there will be no return to that commanding position we once occupied in the esteem of others. For over twenty years I made a point of reading the reports of annual congresses and other junketings of the Labour Party, and I cannot recall one occasion when the subject of the higher education of the people was brought forward for discussion. The time of the meetings was taken up with infantile complaints about one alleged grievance or another, fulminations against this system or that, and declarations of faith in some ology or other unshared by the mass of their fellow countrymen. Not a word about the most vital business of all, the mental advancement and spiritual enlightenment of the classes whom they professed to represent, and no wonder an intellectual darkness hangs over the land when the better part of man is treated as something of little account. Blazoned on the entrance to half our public buildings should be the admonitory verse from the Epistle to the Corinthians, which begins with the words: "When I was a child I spake as a child."

The autumn and winter seasons of opera in London were both given at Covent Garden and separated by one of two months at Manchester. For the first of these the main additions to our repertoire, which now included some fifty operas, were *Parsifal*, *Khovantschina*, and *Die Meistersinger*, all in English, of which I conducted only the last. The decline in health of my able and devoted second-in-command, Donald Baylis, had thrown upon me much of his administrative work, and, combined with the necessity of giving more of my time to private business, was reducing rapidly my public appearances as conductor. Baylis had been with me since 1910 and had started his career as a correspondence clerk in my father's office at St. Helens, being about twenty-five at the time. During my first season he acted as manager of the chorus, later on as sub-manager of the company, and in 1913 I placed him in full charge of all my musical undertakings. His education was of the smallest, and his outward appearance had nothing whatsoever in common with that of the theatre director of convention, a suave and smiling creature in a top hat and frock coat. But he had an uncanny insight into public psychology, an industry and ingenuity that were continually arousing my astonishment and admiration, and a fanatical devotion to the house of Beecham that won and held my affection. Many were the tight corners from which he rescued one or other of my war-time ventures at the eleventh hour, and his early death in the spring of 1920 was as great a loss to me as that of my equally resourceful and adroit lawyer, who about the same time was smitten with an illness that removed him from the sphere of active work.

I notified the various concert organizations with which I had been connected since 1914 of my inability to continue my association with them, and in the case of the Hallé Society counselled the appointment of a permanent conductor who would be willing to settle in the town. During the war the orchestra had been kept together with great difficulty, losing member after member every month, and had thus taken on a shape almost as impermanent as that of Proteus himself. What it needed badly was the control of a resident musician who would give all his time to the rebuilding of its badly shattered constitution, and the committee, accepting my advice, appointed Hamilton Harty, who occupied the post until 1933. So far as these institutions were concerned, my work was done: they had weathered the storm, safely reached land again, and could pursue their old courses without further aid from me.

38

THE "WINDS OF COMPLICATION" (1919)

THE TERMINATION OF THE WAR AND THE RETURN TO PEACE CONDITIONS added considerably to the costs of running an opera company. While the struggle continued I had almost a monopoly of the services of a substantial proportion of the best artists in the country; but with the relaxation of those restrictions and regulations which had crippled their activities for over four years, hundreds of concert societies came to life and, with appetites stimulated by their long fast, took up their work again where it had been interrupted. As the members of my company had been more in the public eye than any others of the profession, they were in universal demand, and I had to choose between granting them frequent leaves of absence, which must depreciate the discipline and efficiency of the ensemble, and increasing their remuneration. As the virtue and strength of the organization lay mainly in its splendid team-work, I and my colleagues preferred to accept the latter alternative, and concurrently with this went a large rise in labour charges, chorus salaries, and everything else material to the maintenance of a big theatre.

As always happens after a great war, there was a general opinion that a new era had been inaugurated with a good time at hand for everyone. The trifling circumstances that the national machine of industry had yet to be reorganized so as to absorb five or six million Service men, that the National Debt had risen from seven hundred and fifty to six thousand million pounds, and the annual budget from two hundred millions to a thousand, were overlooked in the exhilaration of the moment. Men and women alike had but one thought: to forget about the war as soon as possible and enjoy themselves, no matter at whose expense.

This all-round augmentation of costs was alarming for the future of the enterprise, for even on the reduced war-time scale the losses had been heavy, amounting to as much as two thousand pounds in a week when air raids had been frequent. Although we no longer had this super-distraction to cope with, there was the competition of other forms of entertainment which had languished during the days of danger; and the halls, musical-comedy theatres, and pantomimes regaining their old place in the capacious heart of the public, the earlier mood of simplicity and gravity that had led so many to the solace of great art vanished in favour of one that sought a class of entertainment requiring the minimum of thought and concentration.

What I had suspected for some time had now become sufficiently clear—namely, that without assistance from the State or municipality a first-rate operatic establishment could never be maintained on a permanent basis. Individual seasons might now and then be run at a trifling loss, and third or fourth-rate companies could even make a little profit for themselves, on the condition of adhering relentlessly to a standard of performance liable at any moment to cause the outraged spirit of some dead master to walk the earth again like that of Hamlet's father. But one that employs continuously the best available singers, musicians, dancers, mechanicians, producers and scene-painters is a commercial impossibility and beyond the means of any single person, unless he be a multi-millionaire. Modern history, alas, has not yet furnished the refreshing phenomenon of a multi-millionaire who has taken a really serious interest in music, probably for the reason that his concrete soul is shocked by the intangible and unsatisfactory nature of the art itself. For where are the abiding results of so much expenditure? They cannot be stowed away in the cellars of museums, hung on the walls of picture galleries, used for the better purpose of domestic decoration or, best of all, turned into solid cash once more in the auctioneer's sales-room. During one of my trips to the United States I had a visit from a benevolent gentleman who had been contributing handsomely for years to the maintenance of a great orchestra and was desirous of comparing notes with me on how such an institution should be run. I related as many of my experiences as might enlighten without terrifying him, and his parting words as he went out of the door were: "Well, sir, I guess that every time some guy draws a bow across a fiddle, you or I sign a cheque for a thousand dollars." An admirable example of the New World's inimitable capacity to express *multum in parvo*.

But I knew that for the moment anything in the nature of State aid was out of the question, as no government that had been cheerfully spending between six and seven millions a day on the work of destruction would dream of providing a mere fifty or hundred thousand a year for the maintenance of a concern which was making a fair bid to be valued as educative as well as artistic, and which ministered to the needs of an appreciable percentage of the cultured portion of the community. In Manchester it was estimated that over seventy thousand persons had visited the opera during our two recent visits there, about one-tenth of the population of the city. Besides, there was an ominous whisper in the air—deflation; and the Bank of England was seriously disturbed by the spectre of so much general prosperity. There was far too much money in circulation; some drastic surgical operation must be performed and the nation made poorer, after the fashion of Molière's *Le Médecin malgré lui*, who cautioned a patient that his perfect condition of health was alarming and would be the better for a little loss of blood. However, most of this was as yet in the future, and the only thing to do for the moment was to go on sticking to one's task without too much thought of what tomorrow might bring forth.

At the turn of the year I revived *Falstaff* at Manchester, and to judge by the reception given to it that opening night, anyone present might have surmised that this charming work, which had never been anything but the palest of successes in England, had at last come to stay. But it was not to be, for neither the later performances there, nor those I gave shortly afterwards in London, excited more than a limited interest, in spite of a really first-class ensemble. Indeed, in point of musical accuracy, intelligent stage work and diction, the English company of that time outshone all others that I have conducted in any part of the world. No matter what might be the material resources at one's disposal, it would be impossible to reproduce it today, for the general level of singing has declined and the number of gifted stage personalities is depressingly small.

I have often been asked why I think *Falstaff* is not more of a box-office attraction, and I do not think the answer is far to seek. Let it be admitted that there are fragments of melody as exquisite and haunting as anything that Verdi has written elsewhere, such as the duet of Nanetta and Fenton in the first act and the song of Fenton at the beginning of the final scene, which have something of the lingering beauty of an Indian summer. But in comparison with every other work of the composer, it is wanting in tunes of a broad and impressive character, and one or two of the type of *"O Mia Regina"*, *"Ritorna Vincitor"*, or *"Ora per sempre addio"* might have helped the situation. Also there are too many scenes, six in all, for the thin shape and light weight of the piece, and the concerted movements, until the very close when it is too late, have not the time to gather momentum and thrill the ear with that irresistible flood of tone that we have in the great finales of *Aïda* and *Otello*. Although there may be less scope for it in a work of frail texture, the harmonic side has less variety than we find in *Otello* or the *Requiem*, and finally, the whole opera is wanting a little in the human note. The characters are delightful, but never very real; and I cannot resist the impression that Verdi, in this his swan-song, was too subservient to the influence of Boïto for the good of his own natural genius. Or was it only that the stream of autumnal invention, although clear as ever, was running more slowly and fitfully?

The major event for me of the winter Covent Garden season was the revival of *A Village Romeo and Juliet*, after a lapse of ten years. When first given the work had laboured under two disadvantages: the unfamiliarity of a style which puzzled both singers and auditors, and the crushing competition of *Elektra*, which had taken the town so violently by storm that it had no mind to think of anything else. But much had happened since then; the lightning of Strauss no longer had the power to dazzle; or the Delian idiom to bewilder. The class of opera-goer who expects every new piece to be as full of lurid incident as *Tosca* proclaimed Delius to be undramatic, thereby exposing its ignorance of the meaning of the term. Obviously no work is undramatic that can in one way or another hold the stage, as *A Village Romeo and Juliet* certainly does when sung and played sympathetically; and it is a melancholy sign of the lagging cultural condition of operatic audiences that an aesthetic quarrel settled long ago in the playhouse should still be active among them. For it is nothing more than the old antithesis between the so-called drama of bustle and movement and that of thought and feeling, of which Scribe and Sardou are protagonists on the one side and Maeterlinck and Tchekov on the other. I admit freely that it is good to be roused now and then by the cheering spectacle of a gentleman vigorously chasing a lady round the room in spite of the unoriginality of the motive, or a father towing behind him the mangled remains of his child in a sack: but such excitements are not the necessary Alpha and Omega of every stage work. Also I am at one with the illustrious author of *Jane Eyre*, who once declared of an equally famous sister novelist that while she did not want her blood curdled, she did like it stirred. But there are more methods than one of achieving this aim, and the kingdom of the drama has domains enough to accommodate all tastes and fancies.

A Village Romeo and Juliet has the remotest kinship with melodrama; it is an idyll with something of the other-world or dream quality of a pastoral or fairy play. The characters are types rather than personages and express themselves with a brevity and reticence that is almost epigrammatic. I have never counted the number of words in its text, but I have little doubt that they are fewer than those in any other work of equal length; and an added reason for this is the frequency of purely orchestral episodes which play almost as important a part in the narrative as the singing. The vocal intervals are sometimes trying but not impossible, and although angular in appearance on paper do not sound strained or unnatural in execution. The music, as befits the subject, is lyrical and consistently poetical, with a recurring strain of tenderness more fully present than in any other operatic score of the past fifty years. The orchestral texture throughout is a joy to the ear and has that subdued warm tone suggestive of dark gold or rich velvet of which this composer alone has the full secret.

This was the last of our seasons to enjoy a reasonable amount of favour, though hardly prosperity. The volatile public had already begun to avert its face from Grand Opera and difficult days were approaching. Yet the standard of performance had been rising steadily month by month and the programme drawn up for the summer of 1920 was one that the most cautious of impresarios would have passed as safe and sound. Our prime novelty was *Il Trittico* of Puccini, that interesting and varied assortment of one-act pieces of which only *Gianni Schicchi* is now seen on the stage. But the other two are also effective in their respective ways, and *Suor Angelica*, I think, stood a fair chance of finding favour had it not been for the comical obstinacy of Puccini. Having seen somewhere in Tuscany a convent which realized his conception of what such a building ought to look like, he had insisted that the facsimile of it should be transferred to the theatre. As the convent was built around a large close which occupied the whole of the centre of the stage, it followed that the bulk of the action must take place either in one of the cloisters on either side of it or away at the back almost out of sight. Puccini decided to place it in the left-hand cloister very much down stage, which meant as near the proscenium as possible. But the shape of Covent Garden successfully prevented this misguided stroke of *mise-en-scène* from being visible to a considerable part of the audience, and although we all did our best to persuade him to adopt some other scheme of setting, the unlucky scene went on the stage just as he wanted and fell hopelessly flat.

The quota of fine singers included a newcomer, who proved to be one of the most accomplished of our age, Graziella Pareto. Of slight and distinguished appearance, this remarkable artist had a voice of exquisite beauty, haunting pathos and flawless purity. Of the various roles she undertook, Leila in *Les Pêcheurs de Perles* and Violetta in *La Traviata* were the most outstanding, her representation of the latter being easily the most attractive and satisfying in my recollection. But like Claire Dux and a few others of exceptional merit, Pareto never achieved that pre-eminent position to which her gifts seemed to destine her, and although there is generally a reason for such things, in this case I am ignorant of it.

The conductor for the Italian portion of the season was the renowned veteran Mugnone, whose interpretations of Verdi I have always preferred to those of any other maestro known to me, past or present. Like some others among his contemporaries, he was a man of fiery and uncontrollable temper, and never a day passed without a stormy scene with singers, chorus and orchestra, coupled with threats to return to Italy at once. The peak point of such paroxysms was usually reached in my room after rehearsals, and upon the sixth or seventh occasion I began to find it distinctly wearing. On the next, therefore, I was fully prepared, and addressed him in some such fashion: "My dear friend, it pains me to see you so genuinely unhappy. We like you very much, but it is only too evident that you do not like us. I know you want to get away at the earliest moment, but perhaps feel in duty bound to stay here. I am quite ready, however, to release you from your contract now, and what is more, I have this morning bought tickets for yourself and family back to Milan, so that you can start tomorrow if you like." And so saying, I produced them from my pocket and offered them to him.

I have seen a good many men astonished in my time, but none quite so completely as this worthy Italian. He opened and closed his mouth, rolled his eyes, ruffled his hair and after several abortive efforts at speech finally roared out, "I will never leave you!"

"Oh yes, you will," I replied, "I know your mind better than you do yourself."

Then followed a long speech of explanation, self-justification, and protestation that he was grossly misunderstood; that he really adored London and would like to spend the rest of his days there. But he was just beginning to understand English ways, and I should in future see how well he would get on with everyone in the place. As most of his squabbles had been not with the English at all, but with his own compatriots, I was not wholly convinced; but as I saw that I had made some impression on him, I restored the tickets to my pocket and inwardly prayed for the best. Our little encounter did prove to be of some efficacy, for I heard of no further disturbances of the peace. At any rate they did not come my way.

A welcome diversion in the season was the return of Diaghileff with his company for a series of performances, which included three old Italian works arranged as opera ballets, one of them being the *Pulcinella* of Pergolesi, rewritten and orchestrated by Stravinsky. None of them was conspicuously successful and I was disappointed with the reception given to the Ballet. It is true that Diaghileff had been hard pressed to keep it alive during war time; and together they had spent most of these troubled years in Spain, wandering over the whole country and playing often for a night at a time in tiny towns on their way from one centre to another. But although some of the stars of olden days had now retired or gravitated elsewhere, it was still a splendid organization, superior to anything else of its kind in Europe. Hardly anything we gave, however, seemed to appeal to the public, and the Press too had developed a pronouncedly captious tone, considering it almost an affront that we could not repeat *in toto* the triumphs of 1914; unmindful of the fact that both Russia and Germany were for the moment as inaccessible as the planet Mercury. Lastly the slump had set in, deflation was playing havoc throughout the land, and people, bewildered by a change which was as darkness is to light, were discouraged and daunted. The financial loss on the year's work was overwhelming, and at the close of it my fellow directors declared their intention of not going on.

39

DISASTER (1920)

THE WELL-WORN ADAGE THAT IT NEVER RAINS BUT IT POURS WAS HARDLY ever better instanced than in my case during 1920. I had lost my manager and my lawyer, who were the hands of my executive machine. My opera organization, after five years of uphill work carried out under conditions of almost insuperable difficulty, was foundering through want of support just as it had reached the pinnacle of its achievement, and I was about to face the most trying and unpleasant experience of my life. I have previously referred to the failure of James White, my brother and myself either to handle the Covent Garden problem or carry out our contract to purchase the residue from the executors of my father's will, who consequently had thrown the whole estate into Chancery. The Court had made an order approving a scheme of which the materially important part was that my brother and I consented to devote the greater part of our income to the reduction of a large Bank loan, created for the purpose of placing the Covent Garden transaction on almost the same basis intended under the plan made abortive by the death of my father. We had not really much option in the matter, as until all the debts of the estate were cleared the executors would not relinquish their office, in which they were practically omnipotent. The sum of the matter was that in spite of the return of peace it had been found impossible to deal with our problems as we had all anticipated in 1917, when my brother and I had entered into the imprudent contract to buy the residuary estate for a cash sum at least twice its actual value and well exceeding half a million pounds. Had our hopes of being able to clear the Covent Garden position been gratified, it would have meant that the business would have been left free to pay both my brother and myself the very large dividends by way of profit that it was yielding annually.   Such was the undoubted intention of my father, and had these dividends been available I could not only have dealt easily with my private financial situation, but also have taken part in some new project to carry on the opera.

During the past few years, as I have related, I had expended large sums on musical ventures and incurred heavy liabilities.   When the estate went into Chancery and I agreed to accept less than one quarter of the income that would have been forthcoming to me under normal circumstances, I sold my house in the country, a quantity of valuable furniture and plate, and realized everything else of a tangible kind in an attempt to clear my obligations.   These I reduced substantially, but there was still a formidable amount outstanding.   I called my creditors together and explained how my full income was held up for a while, but that it was being preserved through the scheme under which we were working, and how it was only a matter of time before enough of it would be released to discharge my indebtedness to them.   Meanwhile they would receive a good rate of interest on their money, certainly higher than that which they could obtain elsewhere from an investment equally sound.   All agreed save one, who for some reason understood by nobody else was refractory and unfriendly.   He insisted upon being paid at an early date, otherwise he would take extreme measures.   I pointed out that in this way he could get nothing, as everything I had was so effectively tied up as to be freed only by the discretion of the Court, and this would not be exercised for some time to come.   No arguments were of avail, and the recalcitrant party presented a petition against me in bankruptcy.   As soon as this was done, all the rest followed suit, theoretically to protect their respective interests should actual bankruptcy ensue.

There was no immediate publication of this occurrence, for I took the case to the Court of Appeal, where it remained during one adjournment after another for several months.   These I obtained upon the grounds that I was not insolvent and that I had resources with which to meet all claims against me with something to spare.   I was still hoping that something might be effected in one way or another to free us from the stranglehold of the Chancery scheme, and I haunted city houses and great banks with half a dozen projects for dealing with the crisis.   But the moment was not ripe, I could not produce the rabbit out of the hat, and the day arrived when the Court of Appeal, which had been very patient, would give me no more time.   Consequently the receiving order which had followed the presentation of the petitions in bankruptcy was published to the world, which was made acquainted with the melancholy fact that I could not pay my debts.

The public of England is none too well informed on the subject of law, but there is probably no branch of it on which it is so entirely ignorant as bankruptcy.   During the past twenty years I have encountered the impression in scores of quarters both at home and abroad that at some time or other I have been a bankrupt.   This delusion to my personal knowledge has been shared by those who should know better, such as politicians and even lawyers, and I think therefore that here is a fitting place to state, and with all the clarity at my command, that never for one moment at any time have I been a bankrupt. I admit that there may have been some justification for the false impression, owing to the preposterous nature of the proceedings in which I became involved, and the Munchausen-like publicity which filled the cheaper and less responsible sort of Press.

The principal trouble lay in the obsolete condition of the law of bankruptcy. So far as I know it remains unchanged today, and is likely so to continue until another A. P. Herbert awakens to the full obsolescence of it, just as that gallant champion did in the case of our marriage statutes, until recently the most barbarous in the Protestant world, and still far from satisfying the common conception of either equity or decency. A receiving order neither implies nor involves bankruptcy. It means in the first instance that a man cannot at the time it is made meet his obligations and that his creditors must be called together by the Court to see what is to be done about it, as much in the interests of the debtor as in those of anyone else. This followed in due course, and the comedy side of the business unfolded in a blaze of farcical absurdity. In order to comply with the law, everyone to whom I owed a penny had the right to be present at the meeting and to vote for or against the adjudication of the debtor as a bankrupt. Two factors governed the operations of the ballot, the number of the creditors and the amount of the claims. The latter presented a brilliant spectacle of fictitious financial embarrassment, and included:

(a) The unpaid balance to the vendors of Covent
    Garden for which I was jointly and severally
    liable £1,500,000
(b) The residuary contract . . . £ 575,000
(c) The liability to pay up, if called upon to do so, the
    share capital in a private estate company of my
    own . . . . . . £ 500,000
(d) The bank . . . . . (circa) £350,000

and sundry other commitments in the way of family settlements and minor contracts.

The misguided creatures who had forced the order, and whose claims amounted to no more than a fraction of this mountain of apparent indebtedness, were literally overwhelmed by it and perhaps for the first time realized the fatuity of their action. For the official who presided put the vote to the meeting as to whether there should be bankruptcy or not and inevitably the majority was against. This meant in fact that I stood almost exactly where I had been before these proceedings had been initiated and that none of those who had caused them were a jot the better off. All they had accomplished was to cause an immense amount of trouble and worry to others besides myself, a large expenditure in legal fees, and a widespread publicity that no one could understand. One day an eminent banker meeting me in the street stopped and said: "Tell me, T.B., do you owe or are you owed a couple of million, I can't make out which." I replied, "Both," which in a way was partly true but left him more mystified than ever. As for the Official Receiver whose business it was to call in whatever assets the debtor might have anywhere, the income I was receiving under the scheme of the court and which had been confirmed to me under a special order was difficult if not impossible of collection; and as everything else was firmly tied up there was nothing for him to do but to sit down like the creditors and wait. As I said at the time, "For what he is about to receive, may the Lord make him truly thankful," a comment which was considered by the grave and sententious as highly frivolous and unbefitting the seriousness of the occasion.

For this solemn *divertimento* there was no other final responsibility but the imperfect machinery of the law. Under its provisions it is possible for one person, who may be irresponsible, ill-tempered or spiteful to precipitate a course of proceedings which may bring a man near to ruin. No single person should have such power or opportunity. In one European country the official in charge takes the matter into his own hands and, without the incidence of a needless publicity, investigates the whole circumstances of the case and nurses the debtor's assets until the creditors can be paid. Thus both sides are adequately protected by an impartial authority, and only when the case is hopeless and it is clear beyond doubt that the debtor can never pay is he adjudged bankrupt. But with us every solicitor in London knows that the vilest methods of extortion and blackmail are practised by a group among them who cause petitions in bankruptcy to be made solely for the purpose of creating legal charges, and then count on being bribed heavily to agree to the repeated adjournment of them in order to avoid receiving orders.* This scandalous racket is universally known in the profession and admitted to be an abuse which stands in need of drastic reform; but nothing is done about it. Truly our English law needs a Hercules to sweep clean its Augean stable.

By the close of the year the career of the opera company had run its course and for the first time for fifteen years I was without an active interest in music. I gave the whole position the fullest consideration and decided to withdraw from public life until the final determination of my complicated business tangle. There was more reason than one for this. I could not have taken a hand in any fresh enterprise, although a group of enthusiasts had come forward who would have initiated one on the condition that I gave my whole time to it. But this I would not consent to. I felt strongly that the time had come to take a much more direct share, not only in the control of my own business affairs but of those of the whole estate as well. So far I had left nearly everything in the hands of the executors and their advisers, but after all it was not their property, and it was asking too much that they should show the same zeal for and interest in it as the principals. The crux of the situation was Covent Garden, and to run it as a commercial enterprise a family company had been formed, on the board of which I was a director. I had never been satisfied even in the days of James White that the most was being made of the potentialities of the estate; they required restudying from beginning to end, and I could see no better way of passing my time than to begin the task, and without delay. I was also a little out of humour with the musical world. It had somewhat prematurely assumed that my career was at an end, that I could never rise again, and several tearful elegies appeared in the more sympathetic newspapers. Alike from the numerous societies I had worked with or assisted during a period of five and in some

---

* I am not suggesting that this occurred in my own case.—T.B.

cases six years, as well as the hundreds whom I had employed during the same period in the opera house or concert room, I failed to receive a single word of enquiry or condolence. Taking these different things into account, I decided to give the community of Art a miss for a while: doubtless some day I would return to it; not again, however, under the old conditions. But to carry out a comprehensive plan for the exploitation of the resources of the estate demanded the co-operation of another: a man of ability, technical knowledge, and personal loyalty. I had such a one in mind if he would unite his forces with mine, the Liverpool accountant, Louis Nicholas, our general secretary and adviser, the actual author of the residuary contract, the Chancery scheme, and indeed my entire temporary embarrassment.

40

RECOVERY (1923)

UNTIL THIS MOMENT I HAD KNOWN VERY LITTLE OF LOUIS NICHOLAS. Although I had met him on various occasions during the past four or five years, it was always in company with others, executors and lawyers who were, so to speak, on the other side of the table. But from the moment I made it clear that I was out for business and ready to devote all my time to it he too was seized with the urge to set about the task. Fortunately the senior executor, who was also chairman of the board, was a man of sound practical sense who gave us willing and regular support, and a little later on we had the co-operation of my brother, who until now had been giving all his time to the administration of the St. Helens business.

The plan in front of us was simple and, like the estate itself, which consisted of the market and a further half-dozen acres on which were theatres, hotels, office buildings and even churches, divided into two parts. Under it we set out to sell as much of the non-market portion as possible and to increase the revenue of the remainder. The moment was not inauspicious, for ground values were rising and the leading marketeers, having all done extremely well in the war, had money to invest.

The minutiae of commerce never fail to be tedious in narrative, and it is no part of my intention to bore the reader willingly. It is enough to say that for over three years I sat daily in the newly built offices of the company and completed satisfactorily the labour we had undertaken by selling over a million pounds of property and appreciably increasing the revenue of the balance. These transactions, aided by the accumulated profits of the business, wiped away a large slice of our load of debt and paved the way for the retirement of the executors and the termination of the Chancery proceedings. The ultimate object we had in mind was a public flotation of the sort that had been intended nearly ten years earlier; but before this could be attained it was necessary to remove from our path the receiving order, which all this while had been lying harmlessly dormant. The executors therefore applied to the Court for permission to pay on my behalf a portion of the business income that had been amassing during the past five years to the Official Receiver, who rejoiced greatly and departed from our midst. This stirring event took place in the spring of 1923, and although the Order had been next door to a dead letter, it was none the less a relief to get rid of it, as its existence served to remind me that there was an ever-present cloud in my sky.

But this period taken as a whole was without doubt the most tranquil and orderly that I had known since my first entrance into public life. The settled routine of office work furnished the most complete contrast to that of the opera house, where such things as regular hours were a frank impossibility. It had not been an uncommon experience for me to spend the entire day in the theatre, conduct a performance at night, and remain there until well into the early hours of the next morning, unravelling complications that had arisen out of the belatedness of a production or the sudden indisposition of a singer. During one particular season I did not leave the building for a moment during three days and nights, sleeping on a sofa in my room.

Looking back, then, on my business years, I cannot but believe that they were a fortunate interlude in every way beneficial for me mentally and physically. For over a decade and a half I had been working at high pressure with little opportunity for recreation, and the affairs of the musical world had become a slightly unhealthy obsession. The migration into a wholly different environment had a salutary effect upon an equilibrium slightly unsettled by the prolonged concentration on a single interest, and the contact with a class of mind which looked with another vision upon the activities which had been of paramount impoitance to me, helped to readjust it upon a steadier basis.

I was fortunate too in the character of the task I had chosen, which had none of the tedious round of ordinary office duties. For it was no average commercial concern I was assisting to direct and develop, but a highly complex organization with an individual routine of its own. The Covent Garden Market, although constituted as we know it today in 1825, is of much greater antiquity, being formerly the convent garden of an ecclesiastical establishment of the Middle Ages. Through centuries it grew from the modest state of a private possession to the proud position of the world's most famous *entrepôt* for fruit, flowers and vegetables. The produce of every quarter of the globe finds a way into its shops and stalls, and London throughout the year has a fuller and more regular supply of them than any other great centre. Working under a Royal Charter, it is a community picturesquely set apart from most others, vaunting a special police contingent and a group of public houses freed from the customary restrictions of licensing regulations. Most of the heavy work that goes on, the arrival and unloading of goods in trucks and lorries, begins about eleven at night and continues through the earlier part of the morning. By six o'clock in the evening an area that for over eight hours has been the most congested in the metropolis takes on the appearance of a deserted village, through which one may stroll without meeting any but a few officials or passers-by. But while the machine is running at top speed the scene to the casual visitor is one of bewildering confusion and creates the impression that no system of rule yet invented can ever restore it again to a condition of order and calm.

From time to time proposals have been advanced to shift the market to some outlying and less centralized locality, where it might interfere less with the transit of private motor-cars or perambulators. These have generally emanated from that type of political brain which finds its greatest happiness in uprooting ancient and useful institutions. In the present instance it was entirely overlooked that it is in the nature of a market to be a hub, and the more thronged it is the more unmistakably is it fulfilling the purpose for which it exists. But moving round historic landmarks, together with thousands of persons whose occupations are linked inseparably with them, offers no difficulty to that mechanized species of intelligence, which, in this writer's opinion, is one of the major curses of an age whose respect for the value and dignity of human life is less than has been known for a thousand years.

My freedom from the responsibilities of musical management had given me more opportunity for travel, and in 1922 I went over to Germany. My first point of call was Cologne, and I stopped at the hotel which I had known before the war. The manager related how severely they had suffered from the air raids of the Allies, not so much through actual damage as from the noise of the machines, whose constant comings and goings had robbed the inhabitants of sleep for about six weeks before the Armistice. The train which took me along the Rhine to Wiesbaden had no blinds on the windows, and as the day was very hot the journey was distinctly unpleasant. Homburg, which I remembered as a fashionable and flourishing spa, was almost empty, and an air of gloomy desolation hung over the place. One morning I drove into the pine woods to a large chalet for lunch, which formerly at this time of day was crowded with persons of every nationality. Two waiters attended to my wants, one of whom before the war had been at the Midland Hotel in Manchester, while the other had looked after the floor in the Grand Hotel, London, where Jimmy White had had his first suite of offices. They both begged that I should take them with me on my return to England, but I reminded them that the French and British armies of occupation were still in their country and that in view of past experiences it might be many years before an ex-enemy alien would be admitted again within our gates for the purpose of obtaining regular employment.

Frankfurt proved to be a little brighter, but there too the shadow of defeat darkened the atmosphere, and the cycle of the mark's dizzy flight into a financial stratosphere had already begun. It was in this district that a year later I witnessed a spectacle calculated to turn white in an hour the hair of any Victorian economist and pull down for all time from its high seat the majesty of paper money. In one portion of it, under French (or English) control, the value of a cow was in the region of fifteen of our pounds, while a few miles off, where the mark was the unit of currency, a sister of the same animal could have been bought for a penny.

From here I went through Strasbourg to Paris, which I had not seen since the spring of 1919, when it was filled with the envoys of fifty nations and their satellites, and almost in a state of carnival. This time I could not help noticing how much more slowly it was recovering than London; and how the French seemed to have been hit more severely by the war than the English. The general tone of the city was subdued, some of the old restaurants had fallen by the way, and the cuisine in many of the others was hardly an imitation of its former self. I went out to Fontainebleau to see Delius, and was worried by his appearance, which had deteriorated since his last visit to London two and a half years ago. I questioned his wife, who admitted that he was having trouble with his eyes and a general lassitude in his limbs. As I scrutinized him, I recalled the vigorous athletic figure that had climbed mountains with me only fourteen years before. He was not yet sixty, and had no business to be looking like that. I begged them to call in a specialist, as they were employing a homoeo-pathic doctor, and they promised to do so. I did not see him again for some years, when I learned that my advice had not been followed, that the malady which then had been in an incipient stage had taken a firm grip of him, and that it was almost too late to avert disaster. I made one more effort by bringing over from London an authority on such cases, who prescribed what it was ascertained afterwards was the only course of treatment likely to be effective. But once again the blind belief in homoeo-pathy prevailed and nothing came of it. The disease took precisely the course my expert had predicted, and Delius, although surviving another eight years, spent the last six of them in total blindness and paralysis.

During the summer of 1923 I spent a few pleasant weeks in the exe-cution of a long contemplated design for which I had never before found an opportunity. For several years a play-giving society, the Phoenix, had been giving special performances of old pieces, mainly of the Eliza-bethan and Restoration epochs. I cannot say that they were very well done, for the conditions of production were haphazard and the time available for necessary preparation too limited. But most of the best actors and actresses of London took part in them regularly, and I con-sidered that with adequate rehearsal and handsome mounting it should be possible to bring off a revival worthy of Fletcher's *The Faithful Shep-herdess*. Since the day I first read it in the library of Montserrat this lovely work had been a particular favourite of mine; I had never seen it on the stage, I could find no record of it having been given for years, and I thought it high time it were rescued from neglect and the public reminded of its existence.

I secured Norman Wilkinson to design the scenery and costumes, four of the most charming actresses in town, and a highly accomplished *régisseur*, Edith Craig. As the play contained several songs and choruses, and seemed to cry out for additional music here and there, I tried the experiment of having an orchestral accompaniment throughout; but so arranged as to interfere in no way with the clear enunciation of the text. I selected fragments from Handel, Mozart, and my old friends the French masters of the eighteenth century, adding a few connecting links of my own. But I could find nothing to fit Fletcher's lyrics, and happening to meet a gifted young Italian who had a pretty knack of writing in some of the old styles, I procured from him a set of songs which we ascribed to fictitious composers and which were hailed by the cognoscenti as authentic period pieces. The judgment of the audiences was that here was a de-lightful entertainment, and Havelock Ellis, as good an Elizabethan scholar as any, sacrificed a summer day by the sea to come up to town and write an appreciation of it in his *Impressions and Comments*.*

---

* "Now for the first time I clearly realize what the Arcadian Pastoral of which this is so admirable a type represents in the history of the human spirit.

"That the pastoral is the manifestation of an artificial mood of unreal playfulness in life seems usually to have been taken for granted. And it was so. But so to regard it and to leave the matter there is to overlook the motive source of its inspiration and the cause of its power. How it arose, the really essential question is left unanswered.

The admirable zeal of the Department of Inland Revenue, which a few years earlier had sought to obtain income tax returns from the authors of *The Beggars' Opera*, written over two hundred years before, was now directed to the case of Fletcher, who died in 1625. One day I received a request for his address, which they had been unable to trace, and on the principle of being helpful whenever possible, I replied that to the best of my knowledge it was the south aisle of Southwark Cathedral, that he had been there for quite a time and in all probability was not intending an early removal.

During the autumn and winter I was employed constantly over the business of achieving independence for the various interests still involved in the Chancery scheme and subject to the yoke of the executors. I had made the acquaintance of a personality of resource, Philip Hill, who talked more sense about the position of our affairs than anyone I had yet met. I invoked his aid to prepare in collaboration with Nicholas a project which would successfully accomplish my purpose, and this he agreed to give provided I also made use of the services of Sir Arthur Wheeler of Leicester, an outside broker of repute. As he might have called up the Witch of Endor for all I cared, if only she could have been of some practical assistance, I accepted the condition without demur.

The basis of the project was to unite in one company the Covent Garden Estate and the St. Helens business, the former representing solid capital value and the latter the lure of substantial income. Something like two million pounds were to be raised by a public issue of debentures and preference shares, with a much smaller denomination of ordinary shares, not at present to be marketed. The consent of all parties concerned was required, but as each one was about to receive the maximum to which he or she was entitled, there was no opposition, and the customary amount of "squeezing" and "greasing" which had been expected was forthcoming and accommodated at the eleventh hour. In most big deals there are always certain people who, without the smallest legitimate claim to a farthing, have a nuisance value through being able to pull a string or two the wrong way at a critical moment. The financial arrangements being

---

"When we consider that question we see that however artificially unreal the pastoral poem, novel, or play may seem to us it arose primarily as a reaction against an artificially unreal and dissolving culture. The pastoral never originated in an integral, simple, vigorous, straightforward stage of culture still within actual sight of true pastoral life. The pastoral belongs not to an age of strong faith and rugged action but rather to an age when faith has become uncertain and action hesitant or tortuous, an age when criticism comes to be applied to what seems a dissolute time, a time of vice and hypocrisy, a time which has lost its old ideals.

"Fletcher, following the Italians who had earlier realized the same thing in their more advanced culture, understood or else instinctively felt that the time had come in the course of the Renaissance mood, then even in England approaching its end, to find enchanting by contrast with his own age the picture of the old, strong, simple, pagan age such as tradition represented it, yet touched with a tincture of what was sweetest and purest in the Christian world. Such a form of art, a pastoral tragi-comedy Fletcher called it, has its superficial aspects and artificial unreality, but beneath that is the life blood of a genuine impulse of art exactly adapted to such a spirit as Fletcher's, so sensitively human and so finely cultured, could not fail to make it, to the situation of the immediately post-Elizabethan age of the early seventeenth century.

"For the general public, at all events that of the theatre, it appeared a little prematurely because they were not themselves yet clear where they stood. It was not till after a century later that the age having become more conscious of its own state was enabled to enjoy *The Faithful Shepherdess* and Pepys' notes that it is 'much thronged after and often shown'.

"Today after centuries of neglect, by those few people privileged to be present, it is again approved and is perhaps the most genuinely and enthusiastically applauded of the Phoenix's excellent revivals of old plays."

completed, we proceeded to the Chancery Court for its approval and blessing, and there we were met by some of our counsel (there were about a dozen altogether, representing mostly children born and unborn), who informed me that in their opinion the scheme as it stood had little chance of receiving the sanction of the Court. Would it not be better to amend it in such a way that judicial approval would be assured beyond doubt? This was really too much, and I told them that we had spent nine solid months in preparing this particular scheme, that we had not the slightest intention of altering one word of it, and that we were going before the judge there and now. And in we went. The document having been duly read, the judge asked if all the parties were in agreement, and the answer being in the affirmative, directed that the order which we were seeking should be made. The hearing was over; it had lasted less than a quarter of an hour, and the learned ornaments of the Bar could hardly believe the evidence of their ears.

Thus ended the troubled and anxious period which began with the death of my father in October of 1916 and ended that May morning of 1924 in the High Court of England. The long ordeal was a thing of the past. I could now resume my old career or take up another. Anyway, I was free once more to do as I liked.

INDEX